The Moral Foundations of Trust

The Moral Foundations of Trust seeks to explain why people place their faith in strangers and why doing so matters. Trust is a moral value that does not depend on personal experience or on interactions with people in civic groups or informal socializing. Instead, we learn to trust from our parents, and trust is stable over long periods of time. Trust depends on an optimistic worldview: the world is a good place and we can make it better. Trusting people are more likely to give through charity and volunteering and are more supportive of rights for groups that have faced discrimination. Trusting societies are more likely to redistribute resources from the rich to the poor and to have more effective governments. Trust has been on the wane in the United States for more than thirty years, the roots of which are traceable to declining optimism and increasing economic inequality, trends Uslaner documents with aggregate time series in the United States and cross-sectional data across market economies.

Eric M. Uslaner is Professor of Government and Politics at the University of Maryland, College Park, where he has taught since 1975. His many publications include *The Decline of Comity in Congress* (1993) and *The Movers and the Shirkers: Representatives and Ideologues in the Senate* (1999). Uslaner's edited books include *Social Capital and Participation in Everyday Life* and *Social Capital and the Transition to Democracy*.

"I've never trusted cows."

The Moral Foundations of Trust

ERIC M. USLANER

University of Maryland

CAMBRIDGE
UNIVERSITY PRESS

PUBLISHED BY THE PRESS SYNDICATE OF THE UNIVERSITY OF CAMBRIDGE
The Pitt Building, Trumpington Street, Cambridge, United Kingdom

CAMBRIDGE UNIVERSITY PRESS
The Edinburgh Building, Cambridge CB2 2RU, UK
40 West 20th Street, New York, NY 10011-4211, USA
477 Williamstown Road, Port Melbourne, VIC 3207, Australia
Ruiz de Alarcón 13, 28014 Madrid, Spain
Dock House, The Waterfront, Cape Town 8001, South Africa

http://www.cambridge.org

© Eric M. Uslaner   2002

First published 2002

Printed in the United Kingdom at the University Press, Cambridge

Typeface Sabon 10/13 pt.   *System* QuarkXPress [BTS]

A catalog record for this book is available from the British Library.

Library of Congress Cataloging in Publication Data

Uslaner, Eric M.
The moral foundations of trust / Eric M. Uslaner.
p. cm.
Includes bibliographical references (p.) and index.
ISBN 0-521-81213-5 – ISBN 0-521-01103-5 (pb.)
1. Trust – Social aspects.   2. Trust – Moral and ethical aspects.   3. Social
participation.   4. Trust – United States.   5. Social participation – United States.
6. Social values – United States.   I. Title.

HM1071 .U75 2002
302.5–dc21   2001052721

ISBN 0 521 81213 5   hardback
ISBN 0 521 01103 5   paperback

With love to my favorite optimists and trusters,
Debbie, Avery, and Amber

Contents

Preface

This book was a long time coming and represents both a detour in my conventional research agenda and an evolution in my own thinking. Most of my writing has been on the United States Congress. In 1993 I published a book, *The Decline of Comity in Congress*, that linked the increasing incivility in Congress to a decline of trust among the American public. For that study, trust was a surrogate for a cooperative spirit and I gave little thought to any deeper meaning – even though it played a key role in my analysis.

The next year Bob Putnam invited me to a conference on social capital in the very pleasant surroundings of Cape Cod, Massachusetts. Those invited could bring their spouses – and since this was our first trip away from home since we became parents, my wife and I were anxious to go. But I wasn't doing any work on social capital and so I had to come up with a topic rather quickly. Following the old maxim "write about what you know about," I looked to the faithful trust question in the General Social Survey and wrote a paper linking faith in others to a whole range of desirable attitudes and behavior. And this set me on a detour from my traditional research agenda of focusing on the Congress.

I still had little idea of any deeper language. I got some good reactions to this paper, so I decided to pursue the linkages further. I wrote a paper, "Faith, Hope, and Charity," that has become my most widely cited unpublished paper. It remained unpublished in part because I took a heretical position – that trust was the cause, rather than the effect, of civic engagement – and because I still did not have a clear idea as to what trust was. I believed that trust was the cure-all for our problems of civic engagement, which were indeed severe and threatening to our democratic order. For someone who had just written a book on incivility and gridlock in Congress, warning signals about our society seemed like an appealing argument.

I was making progress. Trust was important, I determined, because it was a moral value. Armed with some quotations from Glenn Loury's work, I argued that *trust* was the most important part of social capital and that civic participation was an important consequence, but participation in civic life wasn't *part* of social capital. Trust was *not* the major part of social capital, journal reviewers told me, and it was much more likely to be the effect rather than the cause of civic engagement. This manuscript kept bouncing back to me, and I soon realized that in one fundamental way I was wrong and in another I was correct. I was right to assume that trust is a value, not simply shaped by experience, and that its consequences are more profound than those of civic engagement. I was wrong to get involved in the debate over what constitutes social capital. My experience with "Faith, Hope, and Charity" convinced me that it was silly to play definitional games. Then I attended conferences on social capital in settings as diverse as the World Bank in Washington, D.C., Milan, and Cluj-Napoca, Romania, where we spent at least one full day debating what constitutes social capital.

Even the casual reader will notice that I barely mention "social capital" in the text. That was not an oversight; it reflects lessons learned the hard way. After being pummeled for redefining terms and spending too much time hearing others try to do the same thing, I decided to concentrate on what interested me: trust. Then my thinking began to get more focused and I started categorizing what it would take to argue that trust is indeed a moral value and what sorts of consequences would flow from this position. As my work developed, I realized that there were many different facets of trust and that I needed to acknowledge this. And I also began to question the linkage between trust and most forms of civic engagement. I had moved away from my initial acceptance of Putnam's argument that trust and participation formed a "virtuous circle."

I initially embraced the argument, now most strongly advocated by Dietlind Stolle, that trust came first and that civic engagement followed. Yet, the more I read and thought about different forms of participation, the more skeptical I became of the link. Then when I saw Putnam's new work extending his argument to informal socializing, my doubts multiplied. Few of us spend a lot of time in civic groups or even in socializing. But when we do, we mostly hang out with people like ourselves.

Going back to my earlier work on *The Decline of Comity in Congress*, I realized that trust helped us resolve conflicts with people with whom we disagree, and with whom we might even have little in common. The rise in incivility in both Congress and the nation stemmed from our willingness to demonize our opponents.

The sort of trust of which Russell Hardin writes – trust in people we know – seems remote from these concerns. Many of Hardin's wonderful examples are about trust in people we know well. The more I thought of his examples, the more convinced I became that there really is nothing remarkable about trusting my wife. Then I thought of some people I don't consider trustworthy and wondered whether my disdain for them would make me think twice about people in general. I asked people whether they would change their worldview if I came up to them and punched them in the face. Most looked at me rather strangely, but acknowledged that such incidents would *not* make them misanthropes.

This is a very abbreviated tale of my intellectual journey. And along the way, I have picked up many debts. Key among them are the General Research Board, University of Maryland, for a Distinguished Faculty Research Fellowship, which gave me a year off to read, write, and think about these issues in 1997–8; the Everett McKinley Dirksen Center for the Study of Congressional Leadership for a grant that helped me think about the linkages to Congress; and the American Academy of Political and Social Sciences (through Bob Putnam's generosity) for support that helped me conduct the research.

Many people and institutions provided data that made the analysis possible: the Inter-University Consortium for Political and Social Research, which provided most of the data in the book; Richard Morin, *Washington Post*; Aaron Hefron and Ari Holtz, Independent Sector; Andrew Kohut, Pew Center for The People and The Press; Robert O'Connor, United Way; Ann E. Kaplan, American Association of Fund-Raising Councils; Patrick Gilbo and Robert Thompson, American Red Cross; Michael Kagay, *New York Times*; Jingua C. Zou, CBS News; Meril James, Gallup International; Rolf Uher, International Social Survey Programme; Donald Kinder, Nancy Burns, Ashley Gross, and Pat Luevano, American National Election Studies for the 2000 Pilot Study with the "thinking aloud" questions on trust, helpfulness, and fairness; Patrick Bova, National Opinion Research Center; Rafael LaPorta; Daniel Treisman; Johannes Federke; and Robert Putnam, through the Roper Center at the University of Connecticut. None of these institutions or kind folks are responsible for any interpretations I have made.

I owe particular debts to those devoted souls who gave me their sage – and detailed – advice on the manuscript, especially Jane Mansbridge, Jeffrey Mondak, Bo Rothstein, Dietlind Stolle, and Mark Warren (listed alphabetically). A much larger group of people commented on smaller portions of the manuscript in various forms and/or gave me the benefit of their advice in conversations. Again, listed alphabetically, they are: Gar Alperowitz, Gabriel Badescu, Stephen Bennett, Valerie Braithwaite, John Brehm, Geoffrey Brennan, Mitchell Brown, Dennis Chong, Richard Conley, Eva Cox, Sue E. S. Crawford, Karen Dawisha, Paul Dekker, Keith Dougherty, John S. Dryzek, Richard Eckersley, Morris Fiorina, Francis Fukuyama, Gerald Gamm, James Gimpel, Mark Graber, Russell Hardin, Joep de Hart, Jennifer Hochschild, Virginia Hodgkinson, Mark Hooghe, Ronald Inglehart, Ted Jelen, Richard Johnston, Karen Kaufmann, Ronald King, Robert Klitgaard, Anirudh Krishna, Jan Leighley, Margaret Levi, Peter Levine, Richard Morin, John Mueller, Kenneth Newton, Jenny Onyx, Joe Oppenheimer, John Owens, Martin Paldam, Anita Plotinsky, Sanjeev Prakash, Robert Putnam, Edward Queen II, Preston Quesenberry, Wendy Rahn, Lindon Robinson, Nancy Rosenblum, Tara Santmire, Kay Lehman Schlozman, Per Selle, Marcelo Siles, Karol Soltan, Shibley Telhami, Jan van Deth, John Whaley, Paul Whiteley, Richard Wilkinson, Raymond Wolfinger, Dag Wollebaek, Robert Wuthnow, and Yael Yishai.

I have also benefited from comments made by participants at many conferences, including more meetings of the American Political Science Association and Midwest Political Science Association than I can document. Domestically, they have included audiences at the Brookings Institution; the Conference on "Civility and Deliberation in the U.S. Senate" sponsored by the Robert J. Dole Institute of the University of Kansas; the World Bank; the Conference on Democracy and Trust, Georgetown University; the Communitarian Summit organized by Amitai Etzioni in Crystal City, Virginia; the American Association of Retired Persons; the Secretary's Open Forum of the United States Department of State; the Annenberg School for Communication at the University of Pennsylvania; the Social Capital Initiative at Michigan State University; Tulane University; the Hendricks Seminar at the University of Nebraska, Lincoln; the Workshop on Social Capital and Democracy, Cape Cod, Massachusetts; and, of course, presentations at my own institution, the University of Maryland, College Park.

Internationally, I have learned much from the audiences at the European Consortium for Political Research conference in Milan and workshops in Warwick, England, and Copenhagen, Denmark. I was privileged to be able to present my findings at a conference in Solstrand, Norway, organized by the Norwegian Centre for Research in Organisation and Management and the Norwegian Power and Democracy Project; the Social and Cultural Planning Bureau, The Hague, the Netherlands; Babes-Bolyai University, Cluj-Napoca, Romania; the Romanian Cultural Foundation, Bucharest, Romania; the University of Westminster, London, England; the University of Melbourne, Melbourne, Australia; Australian National University, Canberra, Australia; the University of Technology, Sydney, Australia; and the Universidad Nacional Autonoma de Mexico, Mexico City, Mexico.

I am also indebted to the fine folks at Cambridge University Press, especially Lewis Bateman, Michael Moscati, and Lauren Levin for shepherding the manuscript through the review process and to publication. And most critically, my ever-trusting family withstood the demands of time and distractions. Avery, age 11 when the manuscript is completed, is now old enough to figure out what I do for a living, but is hardly overwhelmed. Debbie, who is a classic truster, has put up with so many of my trials and tribulations with this manuscript that she says she will wait for the movie. And our newest addition, Amber, a golden retriever we adopted from Golden Retriever Rescue, Education, and Training (GRREAT), slept through much of the recent rewriting. On other occasions, she tried to jump on the computer, but mostly landed on me. They are all joys to warm the heart of even the most diehard misanthrope.

Eric M. Uslaner

Trust and the Good Life

> Sally Forth, office worker: "I can't believe you actually took Yolanda's chair, Ralph."
>
> Ralph, office manager: "Come on Sally. She's overseas for six months. She doesn't need it. Besides, is it my fault she was so trusting as to leave her door open?"
>
> Sally: "Although I notice your door has a double bolt."
>
> Ralph: "Well, I know what kind of element I'm dealing with here."
>
> – From the comic strip *Sally Forth*[1]

Trust is the chicken soup of social life. It brings us all sorts of good things, from a willingness to get involved in our communities to higher rates of economic growth and, ultimately, to satisfaction with government performance (Putnam 1993, 1995a; Fukayama 1995; Knack and Keefer 1997), to making daily life more pleasant. Yet, like chicken soup, it appears to work somewhat mysteriously. It might seem that we can only develop trust in people we know. Yet, trust's benefits come when we put faith in strangers.

Trusting strangers means accepting them into our "moral community." Strangers may look different from us, they may have different ideologies or religions. But we believe that there is an underlying commonality of values. So it is not quite so risky to place faith in others. If we share a common fate, it is unlikely that these strangers will try to exploit our positive attitudes. The perception of common underlying values makes it easier to cooperate with strangers (cf. Putnam 1993, 171). Trust isn't the only route to cooperation (Levi 1999, 14), but

---

[1] From the comic strip *Sally Forth*, *Washington Post* (September 1, 1998), D19.

agreements based upon trust may be more lasting and don't have to be renegotiated at every step. When we trust other people, we *expect* that they will fulfill their promises, either because we know that they have usually done so in the past (Gambetta 1988, 217; Hardin 1992) or because we believe that we shall fare better if we presume that others are trustworthy (Baier 1986, 234; Pagden 1988, 130; cf. Chapter 2 in the present volume). Either way, when we trust other people, we don't have to face every opportunity to cooperate as a new decision.

When we perceive a shared fate with others, we reach out to them in other ways. We feel bad when those we trust have difficulties not of their own making. So people who trust others will seek to better the lives of those who have less, either by favoring government programs to redress grievances or, even more critically, by giving of their own time and money.

Presuming that strangers are trustworthy can't be based on evidence. So it must have a different foundation, and I maintain that it is a moral foundation (cf. Mansbridge 1999). Trust in other people is based upon a fundamental ethical assumption: that other people share your fundamental values. They don't necessarily agree with you politically or religiously. But at some fundamental level, people accept the argument that they have common bonds that make cooperation vital. And these common bonds rest upon assumptions about human nature. The world is a beneficent place composed of people who are well-intentioned (and thus trustworthy). As good as the world is, things are going to get even better and we can make it so (see Chapters 2 and 4). We have obligations to one another.

This moral foundation of trust means that we must do more than simply cooperate with others we know are trustworthy. We must have positive views of strangers, of people who are different from ourselves and *presume that they are trustworthy*. Our commitment to others means that we should be involved in good works in our communities, especially giving to charities and volunteering our time. We are all in this together, trusters say, and thus it is morally wrong if some people have advantages that others don't (see Chapter 7).

It also means that trust is not a cure-all. The moralistic foundation of trust connects us to people who are different from ourselves, not to people we already know or folks just like ourselves. So there is little reason to believe that people who join organizations made up of people with similar interests and backgrounds will be more trusting than stay-at-homes. There is even less reason to expect that trust will lead us to take part in conflictual activities such as political action. We have pictures of trusters as people who are joiners (Rosenberg 1956; Lane 1959; Putnam 2000). In a few instances this is true, but mostly it is not. Trust solves bigger problems than getting people to hang out with people like themselves. It connects us to people with whom we *don't* hang out. And that is why it helps us to solve larger problems, such as helping those who have less, both in the private and public spheres, and in getting government to work better.

If we believe that we are connected to people who are different from ourselves and have a moral responsibility for their fate, we see that trust is a fundamentally egalitarian ideal. When we take others' moral claims seriously, we are treating them as our equals. A belief in hierarchy is inimical to moralistic trust. A culture of trust depends upon the idea that things will get better for those who have less and that it is in our power to make the world better (see Chapter 2). While trust in others does not depend heavily upon our individual experiences, it does reflect our collective experiences, especially on the linkage between our sense of optimism and the distribution of wealth in a society. As countries become more equal, they become more trusting (see Chapter 8). As the income gap has increased in the United States, Americans have become less trusting (see Chapter 5).

This is a very different view of trust than the dominant one in the literature. Most discussions of trust focus on instrumental or strategic reasons why one should trust another. If you kept your promises in the past, I should trust you. If you have not, I should not trust you. Trust, on this account, is an estimation of the probability that you will keep your promises, that you are trustworthy (Gambetta 1988, 217; Hardin 1992, 163, 170; see also the discussion in Chapter 2). Yes, we talk of trusting specific people based upon our experience. But there is another side of trust as well that is not based upon experience and this is faith in strangers, the belief that "most people can be trusted" even though we can never know more than a handful of the strangers around us. And this faith in others is what I mean by the "moral foundations of trust."

CHALLENGING CONVENTIONAL WISDOM

My task in this book is to unravel the mysteries of trust – to show *how* trust matters and *where* it matters. My perspective on trust is different, though not unique (see Baier 1986; Pagden 1988; Fukayama 1995; A. Seligman 1997; and Mansbridge 1999). The moral foundations of trust

argument takes aim at some key assumptions that others have made
about trust. I begin with a survey of the arguments I shall challenge and
my responses to them.

The conventional wisdom is that we trust other people because we
know a lot about them. Instead, I argue that we can and do trust
strangers. Indeed, the "standard" trust question ("most people can be
trusted") really is about trusting people we don't know (see Chapter 3).
There are different types of trust. Putting faith in strangers is moralistic
trust. Having confidence in people you know is strategic trust. The latter
depends upon our experiences, the former does not. Trust in strangers is
largely based upon an optimistic view of the world and a sense that we
can make it better. Our personal experiences – including how well-off
we are – have minimal effects on whether we trust strangers (see
Chapters 2 and 4). Sometimes we have to discount negative information
in order to maintain trust.

The conventional wisdom argues that trust is fragile, easily broken
when people let us down. Instead, I argue that trust is an enduring
value that doesn't change much over time (see Chapter 3). Trust isn't
static. But when it does change, it reflects big events in society, "collective experiences," rather than events in our personal lives (cf. Rothstein
in press).

The war in Vietnam made people less trusting and the civil rights
movement increased interpersonal trust in the United States (see Chapter
6). Even more critically, people are more likely to trust each other when
they feel common bonds with each other. As the level of economic
inequality increases, these bonds are increasingly frayed and trust in
others declines (see Chapters 6 and 8).

Trust is a hot topic in the social sciences these days and much of the
renewed attention comes from its purported role in getting people
involved in their communities. The conventional wisdom holds that
trusting people are more likely to join civic groups and have more social
connections than people who don't trust others (Stolle 1998a, 1998b,
1999a). Even more critically, people learn to trust one another by interacting with them in civic groups (Tocqueville 1945; Putnam 1995a,
2000; Brehm and Rahn 1997). Trust, group membership, and cooperation thus form a "virtuous circle."

Once more, this view of trust is mistaken. It stems from two key mis-
takes as well as some issues of methodology. The first mistake is that
civic engagement can create trust. By the time we get involved in either
formal civic groups or even most of our adult socializing, our funda-

mental world view has been largely set. We learn about trust from our parents, early in life (see Chapter 4). Even then, we hardly spend enough time in groups to change anything as important as our moral compass (Newton 1997, 579).

Second, when we socialize with friends or attend group meetings of civic associations, *we congregate with people like ourselves*. We don't expand the scope of our moral community. We might learn to trust our fellow club members more (Stolle 1998b), but we are merely reinforcing *particularized* trust (in our own kind) rather than *generalized* trust, the idea that "most people can be trusted" (see Chapters 2, 3, and 5). There is simply no way to get from trust in people you know to trust in people you don't know. And I use more elaborate – and more complete – statistical models to make my case (see Chapter 5). Bowling leagues and choral societies are wonderful ways to have fun and socialize with friends. Having friends over for dinner is one of the best ways I know to spend an evening. Yet none of these activities creates trust with people who are different from yourself. Because most of our social connections revolve around people like ourselves, both organized and informal social life are ill-suited to generate faith in strangers (see Chapter 7). There are exceptions, among them giving to charity and volunteering time. These activities represent stronger commitments to your community's welfare than joining groups. Such good deeds generate trust, but even more they depend upon it.

We need to be clear about when trust matters and when it doesn't. Misanthropes have social lives, too. Perhaps we should not be surprised that a moral value such as trust would be important for the routines of our daily lives. And you might even insulate yourself against people who are different. Congregating with your own kind thus might destroy moralistic trust and instead build in-group, or particularized, trust (see Chapters 2, 3, and 4).

If there is no evidence that most forms of civic engagement can create trust, then the decline in group membership can neither be the cause nor the effect of the decline in trust. Falling civic engagement in either the social or the political realm does not explain falling levels of trust in the country as a whole. Declining trust is also not responsible for trends in civic involvement. The decline in trust does *not* track membership in civic groups in the United States. Some groups with diverse memberships, which are thus capable of generating trust, actually saw increases in membership. And countries that are highly participatory are not necessarily more trusting (see Chapters 6 and 8).

The conventional wisdom also holds that the sharp decline in trust from the 1960s to the 1990s stems from the passing of "civic generations" and their replacement by younger people who are successively less likely to trust other people (Putnam 1995a; 2000). Yes, there has been a sharp decline in interpersonal trust from the first national survey that asked the trust question, the 1960 *Civic Culture* study (published by Almond and Verba in 1963). In 1960, 58 percent of Americans said that "most people can be trusted." By the mid-1990s, a little more than a third did. There was a very modest recovery – to 40 percent – in 1998.[2]

The decline in trust seems to be sharp and linear.[3] I plot the decline of trust over time in Figure 1-1. The figure shows a decline of .005 in trust for each year. American society has become far more contentious in these three and a half decades. Younger people generally were less trusting than older folks. But there is one major exception: The Early Baby Boomers (born 1946–55) started out as the least trusting generation, but by the late 1980s they became the *most* trusting cohort.

The growing trust of Early Baby Boomers suggests that something other than generational replacement has been shaping the decline in trust. The Boomers' increasing trust reflects their renewed hope for the future. Other cohorts, especially the younger generations, became less trusting and less optimistic. This optimism is reflected in their growing incomes, and, especially, in how those incomes were distributed. The Early Baby Boomers had more equitable distributions of incomes than cohorts before them or after them (see Chapter 6). No wonder they were so optimistic – and trusting.

[2] The data come from a variety of surveys. Whenever possible I used data from the General Social Survey (GSS): 1972, 1973, 1975, 1975, 1976, 1978, 1980, 1983, 1984, 1986, 1987, 1988, 1989, 1990, 1991, 1993, 1994, 1996, and 1998. Other data come from the *Civic Culture* Survey (1960; see Almond and Verba 1963); American National Election Surveys (1964, 1966, 1968, 1974, and 1992); the *Washington Post* Trust in Government Survey (1995), the Quality of American Life Survey (1971); the World Values Survey (1981); the Temple University Institute for Survey Research (1979, reported in the Roper Poll data base on Lexis-Nexis), and the *New York Times* Millennium Survey (1999). See Chapter 3 for a discussion of the various surveys. The 1998 GSS and ANES became available only after I had almost completed a first draft of the manuscript; I make sparing use of these surveys. But little would change for two reasons: First, many of the standard GSS questions used (especially in Chapter 4) were not asked in 1998. Second, there was no significant shift in the magnitude of relationships for variables common to earlier surveys.
[3] The simple correlation between trust and time is −.852 (r^2 = .726).

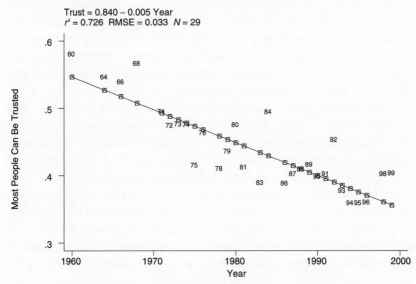

Trust = 0.840 − 0.005 Year
r^2 = 0.726 RMSE = 0.033 N = 29

FIGURE I-I. Trends in Trust over Time, 1960–99.

More generally, the decline in trust reflects a growing pessimism among Americans. In turn, this pessimism is linked to growing economic inequality. Moral values are thus not divorced from real life. Individual-level experiences may not shape interpersonal trust, but the collective well-being of a society does determine whether it is rational for people to trust each other. The wealth of a society is not as important in shaping trust as how equitably resources are distributed, both in the United States over time and across other democracies (see Chapters 6 and 8).

The conventional wisdom holds that trust is a general syndrome: People who have faith in other people are also more likely to have confidence in government. We can thus build trust through effective governmental institutions. Democracies create trust by establishing a rule of law and impartiality. Good institutions may create trust, but confidence in these institutions is even more important. The belief that the legal system is fair may be the most important guarantee that "most people can be trusted" (Rothstein 2000).

Instead I argue that trust in people and trust in government have different roots. There is no general syndrome of trust. Trusting other people makes you barely more likely to trust the government to do what is right. Trust in government reflects whether people have favorable impressions of the people in power and the institutions of government, as well as whether they agree with the policies of the incumbent regime. Confidence in government is based upon your experiences. Trust in other people is not. And this should hardly be surprising. Politics is inherently polarizing. It is about choosing sides and, ideally, also about selecting one ideology over another (Schattschneider 1960).

Interpersonal trust, volunteering, giving to charity, tolerance, and solving collective action problems is about bringing people together – and solving problems collectively – what Jewish tradition calls *tikkun olam*, or healing the world (see Chapter 5). Trust in government and faith in other people are both essential to democratic life, but their roots are very different and often hostile to one another (Warren 1996). Given this tension, it is perhaps reassuring that trends in political participation in the United States are virtually uncorrelated with trust in people (see Chapter 7) and that cross-national variations in political participation also have no relationship to faith in strangers (see Chapter 8).

Annie Oakley in *Annie, Get Your Gun* sings: "You can't get a man with a gun."[4] She was wrong: She got her man and kept her gun. But her general point was well-taken: You can't generate moral sentiments through the strong arm of the law. Countries with effective legal systems or well-functioning bureaucracies aren't more likely to have trusting citizenries. Neither civil liberties nor democratic regimes are sufficient (when appropriate controls are used) to induce trust. Democratic countries *are* more trusting, but this is largely because they depend upon cultural foundations (individualism, Protestantism, egalitarianism) that are conducive to faith in strangers.

Good government doesn't generate trust. But trust in others helps make governments work better. Congress was more productive when the American public was more trusting (Chapter 7). More trusting countries (without a legacy of Communist rule) are less corrupt, have better judicial systems, less red tape in bureaucracies, greater government spending (especially on education) as a percentage of gross domestic product, more redistribution of wealth from the rich to the poor, and more open economies (see Chapter 8). Trust is more the cause than the effect of good government, perhaps because trusting people are more likely to

---

[4] Annie Oakley was a famed sharpshooter, living in the United States in the 19th century. For a brief biography, see http://www.cowgirls.com/dream/cowgals/oakley.htm. The Broadway musical, *Annie, Get Your Gun*, is based upon Annie Oakley's life.

endorse strong standards of moral behavior (such as not purchasing stolen property). Indeed, as trust has fallen, the crime rate in the United States has increased (see Chapter 7).

THE WAYS OF TRUST

Generalized trust is a feature of modern society; in older times, we rarely ventured beyond our village and even then had a very small circle of acquaintances (Lewis and Weigert 1985, 973; Earle and Cvetkovich 1995, 10–13). Strangers in one's midst were likely to be enemies (Seligman 1997, 36–7). Societies were also highly stratified. Each economic group had its place and social relations were based on fixed role expectations. People in the lower strata did what they were told to do. There was thus no room for trust to develop across broad sectors in a society (Seligman 1997, 36–7) while trusting outsiders seemed fraught with danger. As people began to live in larger communities, they increasingly came into contact with people who were different from themselves. They established trading relationships with people from afar that enabled their economies to prosper (Ostrom 1998, 2).

As feudal relationships broke up, social relations became more egalitarian. Lord Bryce saw social equality as the key to understanding why Americans were more trusting and generous than Europeans. Bryce (1916, 873–4) observed:

People meet on a simple and natural footing, with more frankness and ease than is possible in countries where every one is either looking up or looking down. . . . This naturalness . . . enlarges the circle of possible friendships. . . . It expands the range of a man's sympathies, and makes it easier for him to enter into the sentiments of other classes than his own. It gives a sense of solidarity to the whole nation, cutting away the ground for the jealousies and grudges which distract people.

This new egalitarianism fostered social trust (Putnam 1993, 174; see Chapters 6 and 8). We know many more people: at work and in voluntary organizations, though we know few of them very well (Newton 1997, 578–9). While we may bemoan the loss of "thick" relationships, these "weaker" ties give us the opportunity to interact with people different from ourselves (Granovetter 1973; Wuthnow 1998). People willing to take the risk of dealing with a wide range of other people may reap the rewards of solving larger-scale collective action problems (including the gains from trade).

The early discussions of trust (Rosenberg 1956; Lane 1959) painted a portrait of trusters as ideal citizens – people who tolerate those who are different from themselves, who feel good about themselves, and who take an active role in their communities. These early pictures are, with a few notable exceptions (see Chapter 7), remarkably accurate. Trust doesn't cure all of the ills of society, but it can help us solve collective action problems. It leads to "better" government (LaPorta et al. 1998) and a legislature where members are willing to defer to another's expertise and where members accept the decision rules as binding (Uslaner 1993 and Chapter 5 in the present volume). It leads people to take an active role in good deeds in their communities, including giving to charity and volunteering.

Trust is in shorter supply than it used to be – by quite a bit. And the decline in trust has consequences: Charitable contributions as a percentage of gross national product and the volunteering rate for the Red Cross are both down, and these declines closely track the fall in trust. As Americans are less likely to have faith in each other, they seem to be cocooning themselves into smaller, more homogeneous communities and worrying that people who are different from themselves (minority groups, gays, immigrants) are gaining special advantages over the majority. During boom times, we believed that an expanding pie would solve the problems of poverty and discrimination. With economic inequality growing, Americans have begun to look inward, as they have done whenever people felt economically insecure. Foreigners, minorities, and immigrants are increasingly seen as outsiders and threats to the majority's well-being as both isolationism and fundamentalism take center stage. Generalized trust gives way to particularized trust, where we only have faith in our own kind (see Chapter 5).

People who trust others have an inclusive view of their society. They are tolerant and welcoming of people different from themselves and want to expand opportunities for those who are less fortunate. They also welcome involvement of the United States in the world and favor opening markets to free trade (see Chapters 6 and 8). Particularized trusters take the opposite viewpoint: Too many groups are fighting for their own advantage. There is a common identity, but it is *my identity*. It is not a melting pot. And, as the share of generalized trusters drops, the claims that others are getting unfair advantages become more shrill.

While life in a trusting society is pleasant, life in a country where a majority distrusts other people is highly contentious. Where mistrust runs rampant, daily life can be a struggle to survive (Banfield 1958; Perlez 1996). Most societies are not torn apart by mistrust. But when close to two-thirds of Americans believe that "you can't be too careful in dealing with people," it should hardly be surprising that many key issues that confront the polity are more difficult to resolve.

THE PATH AHEAD

Demonstrating these claims is the path ahead. I support most of my claims through analyzing public opinion surveys in the United States. Because my claims are so broad, there is no single survey – or even set of polls – that provides the data I need. So I shall examine a wide range of surveys (see Chapter 3 for details). I shall also examine trends over time, sometimes by aggregating survey results (as in Figure 1-1) and at other times using time-series data for the United States derived from other sources.

This is primarily (from Chapter 2 to Chapter 7) a study of trust in the United States. But the theoretical framework is rather general and there are larger issues, such as whether institutional structures can generate trust, that cannot be discussed within a single-country study. Thus, I look beyond the United States to examine trust in comparative perspective (in Chapter 8) using aggregate data from a variety of sources, including the World Values Surveys that contain information for a large number of countries on both trust and optimism (among other variables).

There are diverse audiences for this argument. Some folks want to see all of the evidence, others find statistics tedious at best. So, taking Solomon's advice a bit too seriously, I have "split the baby in half." The statistical results are in tables, figures, footnotes, and appendices. I have tried to make the text as clear and jargon-free as possible, while still describing what I have found in my data analysis. There will be too little discussion of data for some, still too much for others.

I lay out the theoretical foundation for the study, distinguishing between moral (or generalized) trust from both strategic (knowledge-based) and particularized trust in Chapter 2. Then I demonstrate that interpersonal trust really *is* faith in strangers in Chapter 3 and also show there that trust is a rather stable value. Over the course of panel surveys (where the same respondents are interviewed at different points in time), interpersonal trust is among the *most* stable questions asked: not quite as consistent as party identification, but more so than abortion attitudes.

I also take up some measurement issues in Chapter 3, including discussing the surveys I shall examine and arguing that the simple measure of trust is superior for my purposes than the more widely used "misanthropy" scale (Rosenberg 1956; Brehm and Rahn 1997).

Then I move to test the theoretical framework I set out in Chapter 2. In Chapter 4 I show that trust reflects an optimistic view of the world and the belief that you can control your own fate. And trust does *not* generally depend upon your life experiences, including your wealth, your marital status, and a variety of other factors. Only race and education are consistent demographic predictors of interpersonal trust. In Chapter 5 I show that joining civic groups or partaking in social activities does *not* generally either depend upon trust or produce trust. Volunteering and giving to charity are notable exceptions. The morally rich get morally richer. And I also show that the relationship between trust in government and trust in people is largely ephemeral.

Next I show what has shaped changes in trust, at both the individual and aggregate level in Chapter 6. Opposition to the Vietnam War made people less trusting of others in the 1970s, my analysis of panel surveys shows, while support for civil rights helped build trust in strangers. At the aggregate level, increasing economic inequality and greater pessimism led Americans to become less trusting over time. And, of course, as economic inequality grew, so did pessimism. One generation defied the general trend: Early Baby Boomers, who became more trusting and more optimistic as they fared relatively well economically, with fewer people being very rich or very poor than the cohorts before or after them. On the other hand, most Americans became less trusting, even of their own groups. Growing inequality tore apart many different social fabrics and made American political and social life more combative.

Then I turn to the consequences of trust in Chapter 7. Generalized trusters are more tolerant of people who are different from themselves. They favor government policies that redress inequalities and don't feel threatened by immigrants or free trade. They also see society as having a common culture and oppose proposals that would isolate one ethnic community from another. As trust has declined, however, American society has become more contentious, making it harder to enact major legislation, leading to less volunteering and a smaller share of our national wealth going to charities.

Finally, I look at the relationship between government and social trust (Chapter 8). As I noted above, trust in government is not strongly related to trust in people. What shapes support for one is *not* what generates backing for the other. And this is true in aggregate cross-national results, as well. In fact, there is little linkage between democratic structure and trust in multivariate tests. Rather, I find that *cross-national variations in trust (at least for countries with no legacy of Communist rule) depend heavily upon a society's distribution of income. The same factor that led to the decline in interpersonal trust in the United States – economic inequality – also explains why some nations are more trusting than others.* The distribution of income, of course, is a fundamental moral issue, and my findings lead to questions about what it is that binds societies together, which are raised in the Epilogue.

2

Strategic Trust and Moralistic Trust

It's not that I'm ignoring what's going on – well, I guess to a certain extent
I do ignore it – but it's because I want to stay focused on the positive things
I want to accomplish.

 – Carol Erhard, a volunteer living in the Washington suburbs
 and a member of the Optimist Club.[1]

The Uslaner family regularly makes trips to the Delaware beaches and
on the way from suburban Maryland there is a fruit stand that is only
rarely staffed. Yet, there is usually fruit available for purchase on the
honor system. You take what you want and put the money into a lock
box. One of the customers I met seemed very impressed. He turned to
others and said, "How trusting!" I bought my fruit, paid, and felt a bit
warmer toward society. The owner said (on one of the infrequent occur-
rences I found him there) that people rarely betray him and take fruit
without paying.

The fruit stand owner doesn't know who bought (or took) his fruit.
He has had to *presume* that most people are trustworthy. Yes, he has
some evidence. Clearly, if people routinely ripped him off he would have
to close his stand when he couldn't be there himself. Yet, at some point,
he was willing to take an initial gamble that "most people can be
trusted."

Perhaps the fruit stand owner might have relied upon personal experience rather than upon trust in strangers. Yet it would be foolish to
extrapolate his experiences with close associates to people he has never

---

[1] As quoted in Finkel (1996, 15, 27); the Optimist Club is a civic group that promotes
good works such as volunteering.

met. If you live in a rural area along the Maryland-Delaware border, you are likely to know many (maybe even most of your neighbors) and you can determine whether most of them are trustworthy. But they are not the primary patrons of a fruit stand on the road to the beach. Big-city folks – strangers – have been the customers whenever I stopped there and there is no way that the owner can have any knowledge of their characters.[2] The fruit stand owner might just as well shut down his wooden shack.

The fruit merchant demonstrated faith in others *without expecting anything specific in return.* This type of trust in strangers is an essential foundation of a civil society. I call it "moralistic trust." This is trust in people whom we don't know and who are likely to be different from ourselves. We can't base trust in strangers on their trustworthiness, because there is no way for us to know whether they *are* honorable. Instead, we must presume that other people are honorable.[3] We believe that others share our fundamental moral values. Moralistic trust provides the rationale for getting involved with other people and working toward compromises.

A week and a half after our 1996 stop at the fruit stand, I left a cooler to guard a parking space at the beach. When I arrived with the car, the space was still there, but the cooler was gone. My wife turned to me and said, "You believe too much in what you write about. You trust people too much." We don't give others the benefit of the doubt because trust "pays" better than mistrust. I saved at most a dollar or two by buying

---

[2] Jane Mansbridge (personal communication) suggests that the fruit store owner might simply be a rational actor seeking to make the best use of his time. He might have put out a basket or two of fruit initially to free him from having to tend his stand. When he found that people paid for the fruit, rather than stealing it, he would then incrementally increase the amount of fruit in the stand as his experiences proved "fruitful." This is an alternative account, but it did not square with my discussion with this particular fruit stand owner. On the relationship between trust and community size, Putnam (2000, 138) argues that data from the 1972–96 General Social Survey (GSS) and the DDB Needham Life Style surveys show that people from big cities are less trusting than are folks from small towns, but this relationship vanishes when I analyze the GSS data separately by race. Then, for whites, there are no statistically significant differences by size of community. In the 1972 American National Election Study, people born in rural areas are *substantially* (by more than 10 percent) less likely to trust others, to say that you should be cautious in dealing with strangers, and to have negative views toward out-groups (such as customers shopping at your fruit stand).

[3] Hardin (2000, 10) argues that claims about the moral foundations of trust are really misplaced claims about trustworthiness rather than about trust. But if moralistic trust is based upon *presumptions* of trustworthiness, rather than actual evidence, then either Hardin is wrong or the debate is beside the point.

fruit from the "trusting vendor" rather than under the watchful eye of a salesperson at a stand down the road. My trusting behavior in leaving the cooler on the road cost me $15. Was this a bad deal? Would I have been better off not being so trusting? In the short run, yes. But in the long run, no. I no longer leave coolers in parking places. Yet my overall faith in others remains unshaken.

Should the fruit stand owner trust people he will never meet? Should my own faith in humanity have been revised in light of this bad experience? Conventional accounts of trust would answer "no" to the first question and "yes" to the second. In this chapter I shall show why this view of trust is incomplete. I offer an alternative view of trust as a moral value that reflects an optimistic worldview and helps us explain why people reach out to others in their communities who may be different from (and less fortunate than) themselves. How others treat you is less important than your general worldview in shaping moral trust.

The "standard" account of trust, what Yamigishi and Yamigishi (1994) call "knowledge-based trust," presumes that trust depends on information and experience. Offe (1999) states that "trust in persons results from past experience with concrete persons." Hardin (2000, 10) is even more emphatic: "My trust of you must be grounded in expectations that are particular to you, not merely in generalized expectations." On this account, the question of trust is strategic and not at all moral (Hardin 2000, 76, 97).

Consider two people who will join us in this chapter: Bill and Jane. If Jane trusts Bill to keep his word and if Bill trusts Jane to keep her word, they can reach an agreement to cooperate and thus make each other better off. Even without some external enforcement mechanism (such as an arbitrator, the police, or the courts), they will keep to their agreements.

If Jane and Bill did not know each other, they would have no basis for trusting each other. Moreover, a single encounter will not suffice to develop trust. Jane and Bill have to interact over time to develop reputations for keeping their word. And, even when they get to know each other better, their mutual trust will be limited to what they know about each other. Jane and Bill may feel comfortable loaning each other $20. They know from experience that each will pay the other back. But Bill won't trust Jane to paint his house and Jane will not trust Bill to repair her roof since neither has any knowledge of the other's talents in this area (Coleman 1990, 109; Hardin 1992, 154; Misztal 1996, 121 ff.).

The decision to trust another person is essentially *strategic*. Strategic (or knowledge-based) trust presupposes risk (Misztal 1996, 18; Seligman, 1997, 63). Jane is at risk if she does not know whether Bill will pay her back. And she is at risk if she knows that Bill intends to default on the loan. As Dasgupta (1988, 53) argues: "The problem of trust would . . . not arise if we were all hopelessly moral, always doing what we said we would do in the circumstances in which we said we would do it." Trust helps us solve collective action problems by reducing transaction costs – the price of gaining the requisite information that Bill and Jane need to place confidence in each other (Putnam 1993, 172; Offe 1996, 27). It is a recipe for telling us *when* we can tell whether other people are trustworthy (Luhmann 1979, 43).[4]

This account of trust is incomplete. First, it seems a bit strange to talk of trust *as an alternative to moral reasoning*. Second, it is not at all clear why strategic trust should be of interest to anyone other than game theorists, who are interested in why people cooperate in different strategic situations, and philosophers, who make their living parsing the intricacies of daily interactions. Most critically, there is a wide range of trusting behavior that simply doesn't fall under traditional conceptions of strategic trust.

Unlike strategic trust, moralistic trust is not primarily based upon personal experiences. The fruit store owner could not have any experience with his customers, yet he put his faith in them. Even though people would occasionally take his fruit without paying, he remained a trusting person. I did not lose faith in humanity when someone took my cooler and someone else broke into my house. Both incidents were disturbing, but it would make little sense to judge *most people* on the basis of a few actions, particularly when they are of minor consequence.[5] Moralistic trust is not about having faith in particular people or even groups of people. It is a general outlook on human nature and *mostly* does not depend upon personal experiences or upon the assumption that others are trustworthy, as strategic trust does (Hardin 2000, 14, 174). Instead,

---

[4] The term "strategic trust" is mine. Most of the people I cite would like find the terminology congenial. Hardin (1992, 163) emphatically holds that "there is little sense in the claim of some that trust is a more or less consciously chosen policy." Trust based on experience can be strategic even if we do not make a deliberate choice to trust on specific occasions.

[5] Brehm and Rahn (1997, 1012–13) in the GSS find that experiencing a burglary in the past year makes people less trusting. Stolle (1998a) reports that being betrayed by someone also makes you less trusting. But my models in Chapter 4 are different and find little impact for such personal experiences.

moralistic trust is a commandment to treat people *as if* they were trustworthy. It is a paraphrasing of the Golden Rule (or Kant's "categorical
imperative"), which can easily be seen to demand trust (cf. Baron 1998,
411).[6]

Moralistic trust is the belief that others share your fundamental moral
values and therefore should be treated as you would wish to be treated
by them. The values they share may vary from person to person. What
matters is a sense of connection with others because you see them as
members of your community whose interests must be taken seriously.
Other people need not share your views on policy issues or even your
ideology. They may have different religious beliefs. Yet, despite these differences, we see deeper similarities. Fukayama (1995, 153) states the
central idea behind moralistic trust: "Trust arises when a community
shares a set of moral values in such a way as to create regular expectations of regular and honest behavior." When others share our basic
premises, we face fewer risks when we seek agreement on collective
action problems.

Placing trust in others does *not* require agreement on specific issues
or even philosophies. Instead, it is a statement of toleration of differing
ideas because each side sees something that binds it to the other. Seeing
others as part of your moral community may mean very different things
in some societies than in others. We can't say that it requires agreement
on, say, the Ten Commandments, because moralistic trust does not
logically depend upon a Judeo-Christian culture (although empirically
it seems once again to do so, as I show in Chapter 8). We can't say that
moralistic trust depends upon democracy, becauses this type of trust *does
not logically depend upon democratic governance* (although empirically
it seems once again to do so, as I show in Chapter 8).

Rather, moralistic trust is based upon "some sort of belief in the goodwill of the other" (cf. Yamigishi and Yamigishi 1994, 131; Seligman
1997, 43). We believe that others will not try to take advantage of us
(Silver 1989, 276).[7] Moralistic trust is not a prediction of how others

---

[6] Hardin (1998a, 13–14) sees strategic trust as knowledge, rather than action. Moralistic
trust, in contrast, must also take action into account. What sense would it make to say
that we need only *think about* doing unto others as they do unto us?

[7] The original trust-in-people scale designed by Rosenberg (1956; cf. Brehm and Rahn,
1997) included a question of whether people were basically fair or would try to take
advantage of them. The two ideas are related in the General Social Survey (tau-b = .421,
gamma = .763), though they are clearly not the same thing. Almost 20 percent more
people say that "most people are fair" (61.5 percent) than agree that "most people can
be trusted" (42.5 percent). People who think that others will try to take advantage of

will behave. Even if other people turn out not to be trustworthy, moral values require *you* to behave *as if they could be trusted*.

It is easier to specify what moralistic trust *is not*: the mistrust that characterizes some societies marked by strong class, ethnic, or racial divisions. Such conflicts lead to strongly polarized societies, where people do *not* see common interests with other groups. In such societies, people are likely to begin with the premise that members of out-groups are *not* trustworthy. And personal experience may be a very good guide to such expectations.

A history of poverty with little likelihood of any improvement led to social distrust in the Italian village of Montegrano that Edward Banfield (1958, 110) described in the 1950s: "Any advantage that may be given to another is necessarily at the expense of one's own family. Therefore, one cannot afford the luxury of charity, which is giving others more than their due, or even justice, which is giving them their due."

Montegrano is a mean world, where daily life is "brutal and senseless" (Banfield 1958, 109), much like Hobbes's "nasty, brutish, and short" existence. All who stand outside the immediate family are "potential enemies," battling for the meager bounty that nature has provided. People seek to protect themselves from the "threat of calamity" (Banfield 1958, 110).[8] Yet, Montegrano is the extreme case. It is hardly unique: One can think of many other cases, such as contemporary Bosnia or for minority groups in the American inner cities, who have long faced dire economic circumstances. In most cases, however, the evidence about the trustworthiness of others is not so overwhelming as to deter people from putting faith in others.

There is a lurking suspicion that trust has ethical roots, even among some who hold that trust is essentially strategic. Putnam (1993, 170)

---

them are almost certain (83.8 percent) to distrust others. But agreeing that most people are fair is no guarantee, and not the same as saying that most people can be trusted: Only 59 percent of people who say that people are fair trust others.

[8] Forty years after Banfield wrote about Montegrano, Jane Perlez (1996, A3), a *New York Times* reporter, uncovered Old Tropoje, Albania, where "[w]eapons . . . are valued as much as human life" and "unchecked violence . . . is combined with extreme poverty." Families fight blood feuds with each other, seeking revenge for age-old conflicts. People design their houses as military fortresses. Perlez adds: "The Communist-era hospital has been looted so often that robberies have subsided because there is nothing left to steal. International aid agencies are too frightened to come to help. Many families make do with one chicken a week made into broth and served with a plank of hard cornbread. There is no industry and only families who have men abroad . . . can make ends meet."

argues for the knowledge-based view when he writes that "trust entails
a prediction about the behavior of an independent actor." But he also
argues, just one page earlier (1993, 169) that trust is a "moral resource."
And he quotes with admiration (Putnam 1993, 89) Gianfranco Poggi,
who holds that "[i]nterpersonal trust is probably the moral orientation
that most needs to be diffused among the people if republican society is
to be maintained."[9]

I am hardly alone in asserting that trust has a moral foundation.
Mansbridge (1999) writes of "altruistic trust," Horsburgh (1960) of
"therapeutic trust," and Yamigishi and Yamigishi (1994) of "general
trust." Wilson (1993, 231) argues that we are "faithful both because we
wish others to accept our word and because we consider dishonesty and
infidelity to be signs of wickedness." David Hume (1960, 518) made a
similar claim in the mid-18th century: "If we thought, that promises had
no moral obligation, we never shou'd feel any inclination to observe
them" (see also Bryce 1916, 876–7; Hertzberg 1988, 315; Pagden 1988,
133–4, 139). Tocqueville (1945, 122–3) wrote of "self-interest rightly
understood," what we would now call trust, and argued that its foundations were not simply based upon experience, but upon values that
stem from religious ideals.

The moral dimension of trust answers questions that the strategic view
cannot. Bill and Jane may develop confidence in each other as they learn
more about each other. Each successive cooperative decision Bill makes
increases Jane's faith in him and vice versa. But why would Bill or Jane
decide to cooperate with each other in the first place? If Bill were a
Scrooge and Jane a Bob Cratchitt, Jane's confidence in Bill would be misplaced. And this sour experience might lead Jane not to trust other people
in the future, assuming that she accepted a maxim that appears straight
out of knowledge-based trust: "Fool me once, shame on you. Fool me
twice, shame on me." The strategic view of trust would lead us to expect
that both Bill and Jane would be far more likely to be Scrooges than
Cratchitts. In a world of Cratchitts, you wouldn't need strategic trust (cf.
Dasgupta 1988).

If trust connects us to our community and helps us solve collective
action problems, it must be moralistic trust that does the job. Strategic
trust can only lead to cooperation among people you have gotten to
know, so it can only resolve reasonably small-scale problems. Should Bill

[9] The quote comes from Poggi, *Images of Society* (Stanford: Stanford University Press,
1972), 59.

loan $20 to Jane? Should he hire her to paint his house? Moralistic trust helps get us involved with people who are different from ourselves. It connects us to a broader community and leads us to do good works and to resolve disagreements.

This chapter is about different types of trust. I briefly lay out my argument for the primacy of moralistic trust in studies of cooperation and collective action. I then move to a more elaborate discussion of types of trust, distinguishing between generalized and particularized trust. Generalized trust, the belief that "most people can be trusted," is largely (though not entirely) based upon moralistic trust; it does have some foundations in experience. A sense of optimism and control over the world is more important than experience for generalized trust. We learn (or fail to learn) generalized trust from our parents.

Much of what happens to us in adult life does not affect how much faith we place in strangers. Socializing and group membership, contrary to Putnam (2000, 93–4, Chapters 3 and 6) and others, cannot produce trust because they bring us into contact with people very much like ourselves. Particularized trust is the notion that we should only have faith in people like ourselves, and this restricts the size of our moral community. We think that we know about people like ourselves, so particularized trust is more likely to reflect our experiences. And government can't produce generalized trust. Confidence in government is strategic trust, and it does not readily translate into faith in other people.

THE VARIETIES OF TRUST

Moralistic trust differs from strategic trust in several crucial respects. Moralistic trust is not a relationship between specific persons for a particular context. Jane doesn't trust Bill to repay a $20 loan. Jane just "trusts" (other people in general, most of the time, for no specific purpose). If the grammar of strategic trust is "*A* trusts *B* to do *X*" (Hardin 1992, 154), the etymology of moralistic trust is simply "*A* trusts."[10] If you argue that trust *must be* strategic (cf. Hardin 1992, 1998a; Offe 1999; Putnam 2000, 135–6), you will find my etymology

---

[10] A more formal statement would be:

$$\forall B \text{ and } \forall X: A \text{ trusts } B \text{ to do } X.$$

As I note below, it is foolish to trust all of the people all of the time. Moralistic trust doesn't demand that. But it does presume that we trust most people under most circumstances (where "most" is widely defined).

of trust rather strange. It has neither a direct nor an indirect object. But ordinary language usage supports my distinction between the two types of trust: We *do* speak of "trusting people" generally, much as the grammar of moralistic trust would lead us to expect.

Moralistic and strategic trust play different roles in resolving collective action problems. Beyond the range of trust – whether we place confidence in selected persons for specific purposes or people in general – the two types of trust have different foundations. There is no single definition of strategic trust. Yet, there is a common thread: Strategic trust is an expectation that Bill's behavior will meet Jane's expectations at least on one specific task. Bill could let Jane down, but he won't (Dasgupta 1988, 51; Misztal 1996, 24). Strategic trust is a prediction about another person's behavior (Hardin 1992).[11] Prescriptions about how you ought to behave depend upon the fulfillment of your trust. If Bill proves trustworthy (in a particular circumstance), Jane should reciprocate. But this dictate is merely strategic: Jane will be better off if she trusts Bill in turn. The claim has no moral force (Levi 1998, 81).

Strategic trust can help overcome the temptation to simply walk away from a deal. You can't be sure that your roofing contractor is honest or competent, so you check his references as best you can and rely upon this information in your decision to let him do the job. You really don't want to – or can't – do the job yourself. When you make inquiries about a contractor, you focus on his qualifications for *this job*. You don't inquire about his personal life (would it bother you if he were divorced and didn't pay child support?) or about his expertise in other areas (would it bother you if he flunked high school algebra?).

Strategic trust is not predicated upon a negative view of the world, but rather upon uncertainty. Levi (1997, 3) argues: "The opposite of trust is not distrust; it is the lack of trust" (cf. Hardin 1992, 154; Offe 1999). Strategic trust is all about reducing transaction costs by gaining additional information, be it positive or negative. But moralistic trust must have positive feelings at one pole and negative ones at the other. It would be strange to have a moral code with good juxtaposed against undecided. So we either trust most people or we distrust them.

---

[11] Not all who discuss strategic trust agree. Luhmann (1979, 88) and Offe (1999), following him, distinguish between confidence (which they see as a prediction) and trust, which both leave undefined but imply is somewhat more ephemeral than a simple calculation. Cf. Luhmann's (1979, 32) statement that "[t]rust rests on illusion."

Strategic trust reflects our expectations about how people *will* behave. Otherwise there is no deal. Moralistic trust is a statement about how people *should* behave. *People ought to trust each other.* The Golden Rule does *not* demand that you do unto others as they do unto you. Instead, you do unto others *as you would have them* do unto you. The Eighth Commandment is *not* "Thou shalt not steal unless somebody takes something from you." Nor does it state "Thou shalt not steal from Bill."

Moral dictates are absolutes (usually with some exceptions in extreme circumstances). Adam Seligman (1997, 47) makes a telling distinction: "the unconditionality of trust is first and foremost an unconditionality in respect to alter's response. . . . Were the trusting act to be dependent (i.e., conditional) upon the play of reciprocity (or rational expectation of such), it would not be an act of trust at all but an act predicated on [one's expectations of how others will behave]" (cf. Mansbridge 1999).

Moralistic trust is predicated upon a view that the world is a benevolent place with good people (cf. Seligman 1997, 47), that things are going to get better, and that you are the master of your own fate. The earliest treatments of interpersonal trust put it at the center of an upbeat worldview (Rosenberg 1956). The moral dictate to treat people as if they were trustworthy cannot persist in a world of pessimists. Only someone with a positive view of human nature and its prospects could treat others as trustworthy on faith. Optimists not only believe that things will get better. They also maintain that *they can make the world better by their own actions* (Rosenberg 1956; Lane 1959, 163–6).

TRUST AND EXPERIENCE

Strategic trust lowers transaction costs by providing concrete information about other players in a collective action dilemma. In experimental games, Jane may worry that Bill will not cooperate with her, so she will observe his initial moves before deciding on her own strategy. In everyday life, Jane may worry that a contractor may try to take advantage of her by doing a shoddy job even though she pays him handsomely. So she seeks out additional information about him from references or consumer affairs bureaus of our local government. She might even ask to see some of his work on other houses. In each case, Jane bases her strategy – cooperate with Bill, hire the contractor, look for someone else, or do the job herself – on her experiences. Once she has gathered the data she needs, she has a shortcut to future decision making. She knows whether she can count on Bill to cooperate with her in future games. And she may now have found a reliable contractor who can do other work on her house, and whom she can refer to friends.

Let us not draw this distinction so sharply that we partition the world into strategic and moralistic trusters (but see Yamigishi and Yamigishi 1994, 139; Seligman 1997, 94). All but the most devoted altruists will recall – and employ – the Russian maxim (adopted by President Ronald Reagan in dealing with the Soviets): trust but verify. When dealing with specific people, we use strategic trust. It is hardly contradictory for someone who places great faith in *people* to check out the qualifications and honesty of *specific persons*, such as contractors, mechanics, and doctors. Moralistic trust is *not* faith in specific people; rather, it is faith in the "generalized other." On the other hand, people who are *not* generalized trusters can only rely on strategic trust. For them, "trust" means experiences with specific persons.

Strategic trust develops slowly, as people gain knowledge about how others behave. They engage in a Bayesian decision-making process: Bill continuously updates his experiences with Jane each time they meet (Rempel et al. 1985, 96–7; Dasgupta 1988, 51, 64–5; Gambetta 1988, 217). Hardin (1992, 165) argues:

Suppose ... that I started life with such a charmed existence that I am now too optimistic about trusting others, so that I often overdo it and get burned. Because I am trusting, I enter into many interactions and I collect data for updating my Bayesian estimates very quickly. My experience soon approaches the aggregate average and I reach an optimal level of trust that pays off well in most of my interactions, more than enough to make up for the occasions when I mistakenly overrate the trustworthiness of another.[12]

Strategic trust is fragile, since new experiences can change one's view of another's trustworthiness (Bok 1978, 26; Hardin 1998a, 21). Trust, Levi (1998, 81) argues, may be "hard to construct and easy to destroy" (cf. Dasgupta 1988, 50).

Moralistic trust is a moral dictate to treat others well, even in the absence of reciprocity. Values are not divorced from experience, but they

---

[12] Hardin (1992, 154) is emphatic that trust depends upon experience with a particular person in a particular context, but this quotation (see also Hardin [1992, 170]) comes perilously close to an experience-based view of moralistic trust. In Hardin (2000, 145), you must know more than how someone has acted toward you in the past to trust her. You must also know whether she is taking *your interests* into account in her behavior.

are largely resistant to the ups and downs of daily life. Moralistic trust is thus *not fragile at all, but quite stable over time* (see Chapter 3). It is more difficult to build than to destroy because trust is not so easily transferable from one person to another. Putnam (2000, 21) points to this *generalized reciprocity*, where we do things "without expecting anything specific back . . . in the confident expectation that someone else will do something for me down the road." We can express faith in others even without demanding that someone, sometime will reciprocate, even though we may expect that others will not let us down more generally (Silver 1989, 276–7).[13]

People realize that it is not wise to extrapolate from individual cases to the general. Instead, we either seek some rationalization for our disappointing experience or simply wave it away as irrelevant (cf. Baker 1987, 5; McKnight et al., in press). This reflects the optimistic worldview that underlies moralistic trust. Optimists are not worried that strangers will exploit them. If they take a chance and lose, their upbeat perspective leads them to try again. Setbacks are temporary; the next encounter will be more cooperative (M. Seligman 1991, 4–5).

Optimists are prone to discount bad news and give too much credence to good tidings. Pessimists overemphasize adversity and dismiss upbeat messages. Both groups look at evidence selectively. Their reasoning is a "cognitive 'leap' beyond the expectations that reason and experience alone would warrant" (Lewis and Weigert 1985, 970; cf. Baron 1998, 409, and Mansbridge, 1999). It may be a good thing that moralistic trusters aren't concerned with reciprocity, for they might well make erroneous decisions about who is trustworthy and who is not. Orbell and Dawes (1991, 521, 526) report results from an experimental game showing that trusters are overly optimistic about the motivations of others. They use their own good intentions (rather than life experiences) to extrapolate about whether strangers would cooperate in experimental games.

Moralistic trusters are also significantly more likely than mistrusters to say that other people trust them.[14] People who feel good about them-

---

[13] The distinction here is between expectation of help and a generalized view of others as having good will. In practice, the distinction is likely to be minimal.

[14] This finding comes from the Pew Research Center for the People and the Press's 1996 Trust and Citizen Engagement Survey in metropolitan Philadelphia. Ninety-seven percent of moralistic trusters said that other people trust them, compared to a still very high eighty-six percent of mistrusters (tau-b = .174, gamma = .627). This result may reflect either reality – perhaps we are more likely to trust people who trust us – or it may also be part of the general syndrome of overinterpretation.

selves interpret ambiguous events in a positive light, while people who have a poor self-image and who look at life pessimistically interpret the same experiences negatively (Diener, Suh, and Oishi 1997). Since moralistic trusters look at the world with (at least partial) blinders on, it should not be surprising that this type of trust is not at all fragile.

Where does moralistic trust come from? Mostly, though hardly exclusively, from our parents (see Chapters 4 and 5). Our parents are our first moral teachers. Children respect parental authority and they also follow parental guidance as a way of expressing their love (Damon 1988, 51–2). Children are likely to have positive views of themselves if their parents have a strong sense of self-esteem and if they have warm relationships with their parents (Parcel and Menaghan 1993; Smith 1999b). For both children and adults, an upbeat view of yourself is one of the strongest predictors of trust. We develop our disposition to trust or distrust early in life (Erikson 1968, 103), which explains why trust is so stable.[15]

WHOM DO YOU TRUST?

Beyond the distinction between strategic and moralistic trust is a continuum from particularized to generalized trust. Generalized trust is the perception that *most* people are part of your moral community. Its foundation lies in moralistic trust, but it is not the same thing.[16] Generalized trust is a measure of the scope of our community, and it is based upon both morals and our collective experiences. The optimism that underlies generalized trust is not a constant. Sometimes things look good and sometimes they don't. Our values (moralistic trust) don't change readily. But the way we interpret them does reflect some experiences from daily life. And this is what distinguishes generalized from moralistic trust: Generalized trust goes up and down, though it is basically stable. Moralistic trust is a more lasting value.

The difference between generalized and particularized trust is similar to the distinction Putnam (2000, 22) draws between "bonding" and "bridging" social capital. We bond with our friends and people like ourselves. We form bridges with people who are different from ourselves. *The central idea distinguishing generalized from particularized trust*

---

[15] Even Hardin (1992, 173) admits that children learn about trust early in life from their parents.
[16] I am indebted to Jane Mansbridge for emphasizing this distinction.

is how inclusive your moral community is. When you only trust your own kind, your moral community is rather restricted. And you are likely to extend trust only to people you think you know. So particularized trusters rely heavily upon their experiences (strategic trust) or stereotypes that they believe to be founded in knowledge in deciding whom to trust. But they are not agnostic about strangers. Particularized trusters assume that people unlike themselves are *not* part of their moral community, and thus may have values that are hostile to their own.

The idea of generalized trust is well captured in the "standard" survey research question that many of us have relied upon for several decades: "Generally speaking, do you believe that most people can be trusted or can't you be too careful in dealing with people?" The question asks your attitude toward "most people," recognizing that even the most warmhearted soul will recognize that *some* people rightfully should not be trusted.[17] The question makes no mention of context (cf. Hertzberg 1988, 314). It does *not* ask whether most people can be trusted to repay a $20 loan, although some basic honesty of this type *appears* to be implicit in moralistic trust.[18] It certainly doesn't ask whether most people can be trusted to paint your house, since neither this nor any other specific deed seems relevant to the a moral dimension of trust.

The foundation of generalized trust is moralistic trust. The etymology is similar: *A* trusts, rather than *A* trusts *B* to do *X*. Like moralistic trust, it does not depend upon reciprocity. But generalized trust is not as unconditional as moralistic trust. First, its scope is more limited. We realize that we cannot, and do not, trust everyone. The standard survey question about whether most people can be trusted is thus a measure of how widely people view their moral community. Second, generalized trust is stable, but hardly a constant over time (see Chapter 3). People's level of

---

[17] A skeptical Jean Cohen pressed me on this issue at a conference a few years ago. Trying to cast aspersions on the way the question was posed, she asked, "Do you believe that most rapists can be trusted?" I responded: "No they can't, but thankfully most people aren't rapists."

[18] The 1972 American National Election Study asked both the interpersonal trust question and whether people are basically honest (which I dichotomized). Just 47.5 percent of the sample said that most people can be trusted, while 86.2 percent said that most people are honest. Almost all (97.5 percent) of people who said that most people can be trusted agreed that most people are honest, but 76 percent who believe that "you can't be too careful in dealing with people" also agree that most people are honest. Only 57.3 percent who said that most people are honest agreed that most people can be trusted. Overall, the relationship is moderate according to tau-b (.311), though considerably higher for the curvilinear gamma (.847).

trust changes in response to their environment, and, to a limited degree, to their life experiences (see Chapters 4 and 5). Generalized trust is moralistic trust in the real world – not immutable, not so universal, and more tentative.

Placing faith only in our own kind is *particularized trust.*[19] Particularized trust uses group categories to classify people as members of in-groups or out-groups (do you belong, or don't you?). Particularized trusters have positive views of their own in-group and negative attitudes toward groups to which they do not belong. Their faith in others in their own group is *not* restricted to specific circumstances (as strategic trust is), but they are wary of many, if not most, other people in the society. Their moral community is rather restricted.

The grammar of this type of trust is thus: A trusts B; not simply A trusts, as in generalized trust, nor A trusts B to do X, as in strategic trust. And the class, B, is much larger than a single individual.[20] Though not based on knowledge about each person, particularized trust has an informational foundation: the reputation that people extrapolate about people like themselves from their experiences with others of their own group. Generalized trust, on the other hand, cannot be based upon such knowledge. We don't know what strangers think, and in the realm of moral absolutes, we shouldn't pay heed to small pieces of evidence that might distract us from our more general optimism.

Generalized trusters have faith in a wide range of strangers. Placing a lot of faith in your in-group does not inevitably lead to a hostile attitude toward out-groups. If you like your in-group, you may well have favorable opinions of others. If you don't, you may simply be a misanthrope. As the Jewish sage Hillel said, "If I am not for myself, who will be for me? If I am for myself alone, what am I?"

Particularized trusters only rely upon people they are sure share their own values. Generalized trusters *presume* that most people they meet share their values; particularized trusters demand evidence that people outside their own circles (or identity groups) share their beliefs. Almost everyone trusts their immediate family. We also trust our friends because

---

[19] Yamigishi and Yamigishi (1994, 145) have a similar concept that they call "trust in closely related others."

[20] Again, a more formal statement would be:

$$\forall B: A \text{ trusts } B.$$

B here represents a class of people. As in note 4, the logical notation all is too encompassing.

we know what to expect of them (Silver 1989, 275–6; Misztal 1996, 123). Our connections to family and friends are based upon "thick" trust, which "is generated by intensive, daily contact between people, often of the same tribe, class, or ethnic background. Communities of this kind are generally socially homogenous, isolated, and exclusive, and able to exercise the strict social sanctions necessary to enforce thick trust" (Newton 1997, 578).[21] Thick trust is based upon what Granovetter (1973) calls "strong ties." It is based on staying with the familiar and shunning the uncertain. We trust people we know well. Generalized (or "thin") trust is based upon "weak ties," bonds formed by occasional interactions with people who are different from ourselves.

Thick trust is ubiquitous. The 1990 World Values Survey in the United States and the 1996 Trust and Civic Engagement Survey in metropolitan Philadelphia (conducted by the Pew Center for the People and the Press) report that 97.9 percent and 96.6 percent, respectively, of respondents claim to trust their families.[22] And we are also likely to place great faith in people we interact with regularly and closely. I report the percentages of groups the two surveys examined in Table 2–1.

We place our highest levels of trust in people we interact with most closely and who are most like ourselves: our family and our friends. We also trust people whom we may not know but whom we admire. Respondents to the Pew survey trusted firefighters slightly more than they did their own families.[23] We reserve our highest levels of trust for people who share our values, especially people who go to the same churches we do. Not far behind are people we know well – who belong to the same clubs we do, who work with us, and who live in our neighborhoods. We place less faith in people whom we know only slightly – the folks who work in the stores where we shop – and only a modest amount in strangers –

---

[21] The concept of thick trust was originally formulated by Williams (1988).

[22] The World Values Study posed these specific questions as a five-category scale ranging from "strongly trust" to "strongly distrust." I collapsed the five categories into a dichotomy with the middle (neither trust nor distrust) as indicating lack of trust.

[23] If we only consider "trust a lot" rather than "trust a lot" *and* "trust some," families outpace firefighters by 86 percent to 79.5 percent. The World Values Survey shows that Americans trust Canadians, whom they are likely to perceive to be much like themselves, about as much as they do American blacks. Canadians rank higher than American Hispanics, who are slightly more trusted than Mexicans, who rank at about the same level as "most people." We are considerably less likely to trust people who either look different from ourselves or live in societies with different forms of government that have traditionally been at odds with our own, for instance the Chinese and the Russians.

TABLE 2-1. *Whom Do We Trust? Levels of Trust Americans Place in Various Groups*[a]

1990 World Values Study		1996 Trust and Civic Engagement Survey	
Family	97.9	Fire Department	97.8
Americans	73.9	Family	96.6
Canadians	61.4	People at Your Church	95.5
Blacks	60.2[b]	Your Neighbors (Suburbs)	93.1
Hispanics	55.7	People at Your Club	91.9
Mexicans	51.8	People You Work with	89.3
Chinese	44.5	Police	86.0
Russians	41.7	Your Boss	84.6
		Your Neighbors (total)	85.3
		People Who Work Where You Shop	80.8
		Public Schools	79.3
		Television News	75.8
		Your Neighbors (Center City)	73.9
		Daily Newspaper	72.9
		State Government	61.0
		People You Meet on Street	57.0
		Federal Government	54.4
Most People	51.0	Most People	44.3

[a] Percent trusting.
[b] For whites only, 59.2 percent.

people we meet on the street (just 57 percent in the Pew survey). We have considerable confidence in institutions we either admire or know well (firefighters, the police, public schools, and even television news), but less in structures that may change more frequently or seem more remote (local, state, and especially federal governments).

We are predisposed to trust our own kind more than out-groups (Brewer 1979). Messick and Brewer (1983, 27–8; italics in original) review experiments on cooperation and find that "members of an in-group tend to perceive other in-group members in generally favorable terms, particularly as being *trustworthy, honest, and cooperative*." The Maghribi of Northern Africa relied on their extended Jewish clan – and other Jews in the Mediterranean area – to establish a profitable trading network in the twelfth century. Models from evolutionary game theory suggest that favoring people like ourselves is our best strategy (Hamilton 1964, 21; Trivers 1971, 48; Masters 1989, 169).

The more dependent we are on our close associates and kin, the more we think of the world in terms of "we" and "they." We won't trust "most people," especially strangers (Pagden 1988, 139). Particularized trust, in contrast to generalized trust, may lead to situations where in-groups pursue policies that harm out-groups, perhaps even exploiting them (Baier 1986, 231–2; Levi 1996). Or it may lead to a civic dead-end, where people participate only with their own kind, neither contributing to nor taking away from trust in the larger society.

The differences between particularized and generalized trusters stem from their view of the world, and what strangers can offer them. Particularized trusters view the outside world as a threatening place, over which they have little control. They may even see conspiracies against them. They are self-centered, fear that the deck is stacked against them, and have authoritarian tendencies; they often have difficult times establishing personal relationships. Most of all, they are pessimistic about the future and their own ability to control it. They thus shy away from close contact with strangers, who may be trying to exploit them. Tocqueville (1945, 98) worried about such disengagement, which stemmed from what he called "individualism": "Individualism . . . disposes each member of the community to sever himself from the mass of his fellows and to draw apart with his family and his friends, so that after he has thus formed a little circle of his own, he willingly leaves society at large to itself."

Particularized trusters (such as "outlaw" bikers and members of hate groups) try to segregate themselves from the outside world. Rituals, symbols, and other signals help members distinguish in-group from out-group members. And these rituals (initiation rites and private parties) and symbols (clothing) separate them from the larger society. They are signals to group members about whom they can trust and whom they should avoid (Wijkstrom 1998, 35).[24]

A high school student in Littleton, Colorado justified membership in cliques after two other students went on a rampage and killed 12 other students and a teacher in 1999. This student explained: "Because the good times in my clique have convinced me that I am an O.K. person, I can take risks and get involved outside my group without worrying – very much – about failure. There will always be my closest circle of friends to fall back on." Sounds good, but the link to outsiders seems more tenuous when we realize that "[e]ach of these groups is as

---

[24] Some religious groups, such as Chasidic Jews and the "plain people" among the Amish and Mennonites, also wear distinctive clothing that sets them apart from others in society. These groups mostly reserve trust for their own kind and avoid unnecessary contact with the larger society.

autonomous as any sovereign nation" (Black 1999, A29). Some people (like this young man who wrote so well in an Op-Ed piece in the *New York Times*) might well use their inner circles as bridges to the outside, but others might not. The student himself wrote: "By excluding the outsiders, the members of a clique feel secure, even superior to those they are shutting out" (Black 1999, A29).

It would be easier to monitor trustworthiness if we could simply look at people and determine whether we should trust them. Their appearance would send us a signal that they would not betray us. In a world where knowledge is costly and sometimes scarce, we often find this tactic a useful device to reduce uncertainty.

One fail-safe solution to the problem would be for trusters all to wear outfits with a "T" and mistrusters to wear clothes marked with an "M" (cf. Frank 1988). Clearly this is infeasible. So for good or ill, we are likely to trust people who look and think most like ourselves. People who look like ourselves are most likely to share our values. So beyond people we know from our places of work and worship, we are most likely to trust people from our race, our ethnic group, or our religious denomination, or any other group with which we strongly identify.

Particularized trust offers a solution to the problem of signaling. Maghribis and other Jews did not wear clothing with a "J" (for Jew) or "T" (for trustworthy). But, as a small enough minority group, Jews could identify each other. They believed that others in their in-group were more likely to deal honestly with them, so they could minimize being exploited when trading with people they did not know (Greif 1993). As long as members of an in-group can identify each other, they can limit their interactions to people they expect to be trustworthy.

Using signals such as appearances or ethnic identification may be useful in determining trustworthiness (Bachrach and Gambetta 2000), but only for particularized trusters. Generalized trust, after all, is not based upon trusting specific people, and it does not depend on evidence.

THE WORLD VIEWS OF GENERALIZED AND PARTICULARIZED TRUST

When you feel good about yourself and others, it is easy to have an expansive moral community. *Generalized trusters have positive views toward both their own in-group and out-groups. But they rank their own groups less highly than do particularized trusters.* If you believe that things are going to get better – and that you have the capacity to control your life – trusting others isn't so risky. Generalized trusters are happier in their personal lives and believe that they are the masters of their own fate (Rosenberg 1956, 694–5; Lane 1959, 165–6; Brehm and Rahn 1997, 1015). They are tolerant of people who are different from themselves and believe that dealing with strangers opens up opportunities more than it entails risks (Rotter 1980, 6; Sullivan et al. 1981, 155).

When you are optimistic about the future, you can look at encounters with strangers as opportunities to be exploited. Optimists believe that they control their own destinies. Perhaps you can learn something new from the outsider, or maybe exchange goods so that you both become better off. Even if the encounter turns out to be unprofitable, you can minimize any damage by your own actions. For pessimists, a stranger is a competitor for what little you have. She may also represent the sinister forces that control your life (as pessimists believe). Montegranans suspect that outsiders are trying to exploit them. And, given their long-term history, they have reason for such suspicion. But they might also overestimate the likelihood of a bad experience with a stranger, depriving themselves of the opportunities of mutual exchange. Just as some bad experiences are not going to turn optimists into misanthropes, a few happy encounters with strangers will not change long-term pessimists into trusters. Change is possible, but it is likely to occur slowly.

This portrait of generalized and particularized trusters captures their traits well. The 1972 American National Election Study (ANES) contains the largest number of questions on trust, optimism, and control over one's life of any survey. I constructed a measure of particularized trust that I shall discuss in Chapter 3; I use the standard interpersonal trust question to measure generalized trust.[25] The bivariate patterns are clear, and most hold up in a multivariate analysis: Generalized trusters expect that life in the United States will get better in the next five years, find their own lives satisfying, and believe that they have had fair chances

[25] Briefly, the measure is derived from feeling thermometers for blacks, whites, Southerners, Catholics, and Jews. Each respondent is characterized as being part of the in-group or out-group for each demographic group. I then calculated in-group thermometers (adjusted for varying means) and out-group thermometers by averaging in-group and out-group ratings. The measure I employ here is the in-group score minus the out-group score.

in life.[26] They believe that most of what happens to them is their own doing, that other people are *not* primarily looking out for themselves and do care what happens to you, and that most clerks they meet are honest.

Trusters are less likely to say that they need to be cautious with strangers than mistrusters and don't go around looking for hidden meanings in people's words: 67.6 percent of people who strongly agreed that "you should be cautious with strangers" don't trust others, while 68.8 percent of respondents who strongly disagreed were trusters. And 53 percent of generalized trusters feel comfortable entertaining strangers at home, compared to 39 percent of mistrusters.[27]

Particularized trusters show the *opposite pattern on every question*. They don't think that people mean what they say. They strongly believe in being cautious with strangers. They believe that outside forces control their lives, that they don't have a fair chance, and that other people don't care about them but are looking out for themselves instead. Generalized trusters see the world as a hospitable place, particularized trusters as a hostile place. No wonder that generalized trusters are more likely to get involved in their communities than particularized trusters.

Particularized trusters are wary of strangers, but they have faith in a wider range of people than "pure" strategic trusters. They will withdraw from civic engagement with people unlike themselves. But they may be just as active as moralistic trusters in groups composed of their "own kind" (Uslaner 1999c; Wuthnow 1999). Religious and ethnic institutions provide havens for people who want to get involved, but only with people like themselves. Particularized trusters may get involved in their communities, but they will shy away from activities that bring them into contact with people unlike themselves. They will concentrate their efforts among people they know to be like-minded. Outlaw bikers may perform acts of beneficence for other bikers. But they will shy away from helping people outside of their own groups.

---

[26] Because not all questions were asked of all respondents, I could not test a single multi-variate model that included every question. Instead, I estimated separate multivariate models that also included family income, education, age, and race. For generalized trust, seeing life as good and clerks as honest were not significant in multivariate estimations. For particularized trust, seeing life as good, having a fair chance, whether people looked out for themselves, and whether clerks are honest dropped out. In each case, the insignif-icant coefficients reflect collinearity with other predictors. The question on entertaining strangers at home comes from the 1993 GSS.

[27] The correlations between trust and being cautious with strangers are: tau-c = .262, gamma = .457. For entertaining strangers at home, gamma = .218.

Generalized trust, since it is based on moralistic trust, is mostly shaped by feelings of optimism and control. Because particularized trusters only place confidence in people like themselves, they do draw upon their personal experiences. And I shall show that life experiences matter more for particularized trusters than for generalized trusters (see Chapter 4).

Yet, generalized trust can hardly be divorced from experience, just as any other value reflects not just your worldview but your world (Toulmin 1950). Across a wide range of surveys, more highly educated people are more trusting, while African-Americans have less faith in others (see Chapter 4). In the 1990 World Values Study, American blacks are more likely to trust other African-Americans than they are to trust "most people" (most of whom are whites): 70.2 percent of African-Americans say that blacks can be trusted compared to 23.2 percent of "most people." And blacks are more likely to trust their own race than whites are to trust African-Americans (58.9 percent).[28]

Yet, both of these predictors show the limits of personal histories. Education may represent more than experience. Education, Smith (1997, 191) argues, "may cultivate a more benign view of the world and of humanity." Students in integrated grade schools are more trusting of out-groups (Rotenberg and Cerda 1994). A college education broadens our horizons by teaching us about people different from ourselves and bringing us into contact with them (Sniderman and Piazza 1993). If experience were the key determinant of trust, we would expect *income* to have at least an equal effect on trust – it does not. Most of the time, it is not even significant at all (see Chapter 4). Education increases trust among people with both high and low incomes.

Race is the only other "personal experience" variable that is a consistently significant predictor of trust. A lifetime of disappointments and broken promises leads to distrust of others, as Banfield's Montegranans showed. They thus put their faith only in their immediate families. Life for many contemporary African-Americans is hardly as desperate as it was for Montegranans. Yet, "[t]he history of the black experience in America is not one which would naturally inspire confidence in the benign intentions of one's fellow man" (Campbell, Converse, and Rodgers 1976, 456). Losing a cooler will not change your view of human

[28] There is obviously some positivity bias in the figures for trusting specific groups, as whites are slightly more likely to trust blacks than they are "most people" (58.9 to 54.5 percent).

nature. Two years later someone broke into our house when we were in
Australia. Yet neither I nor my wife became ill-disposed toward others.
Even betrayal by a close friend or a spouse should not change your fundamental worldview. But consistent bad experiences, rarely punctuated
by expressions of good will, can readily lead people to mistrust most
people. Even then, there must be a presumption of others' ill will and a
deeper-seated sense of pessimism. Many poor people don't see the deck
stacked against them (see Chapter 4).[29]

Indeed, among African-Americans objective measures of life experience including income and education have rather modest effects on interpersonal trust for blacks.[30] Blacks with high incomes and at least a high
school education are about as trusting as lower-income whites who only
completed eight years of school. Lower trust among African-Americans
reflects years of discrimination and dashed hopes, not individual setbacks. Moralistic trust is not immune from personal experience. They
are just not the most important factors shaping our values. I cannot rule
out indirect effects of personal experiences on trust, since I have not
investigated all of the roots of optimism. While the evidence in Chapter
4 suggests that optimism does not strongly depend upon personal circumstances, it is likely that some of the measures of optimism and
control that shape interpersonal trust do depend more heavily on life
circumstances.

[29] The simple correlation between the best measure of optimism in the General Social
Survey, whether the "lot of the average person is getting worse," and family income is
only .129. For African-Americans, the correlation is only .061. The wealthiest group of
African-Americans (on the 13-point GSS scale) is *more* pessimistic than the poorest group
of whites.

[30] In the 1972–96 General Social Survey, the correlations for income and education with
interpersonal trust are higher for whites (.228 and .123) than for blacks (.128 and .117).
Forty-one percent of whites who attended high school trust others compared to 28
percent who only went to grade school. For African-Americans, the comparable figures
are 13 percent versus 12 percent. Fifty-five percent of whites who attended or gradu-
ated from college, but only 22 percent of blacks with the same education, are generalized trusters. Sixty-seven percent of whites who attended graduate school are trusters,
compared to 36 percent of African-Americans. While blacks who attended graduate
school are three times as trusting as those who only went to high school, just 2 percent
of African-Americans in the 1972–96 GSS sample continued their education beyond
college. Indeed, even for two measures of optimism that are strong predictors of social
trust (see Chapter 4) – whether it is fair to bring a child into the world and whether the
lot of the average person is getting better or worse – the correlations are considerably
higher for whites than blacks (.254 versus .179 for fair to bring a child into the world,
and .215 versus .094 for lot of average person).

Yet there are some types of experiences that matter mightily for generalized trust: *collective experiences*. At the individual level, trust is rather stable over time. In the aggregate, there is considerably less trust in the United States now than 40 years ago. Much of this change is generational: Young people are less trusting than their elders (see Chapter 6 and Putnam 2000, 140–1). But simply noting demographic changes doesn't explain why young people have become less trusting or why Early Baby Boomers have become *the most trusting cohort*.

Collective social experiences, such as the civil rights movement and the war in Vietnam in the United States (see Chapter 7) and the history of labor strife in Sweden (Rothstein, in press), lead us to become more or less trusting. Not just any "collective" experience will change trust. Only major events that lead to ruptures (the Vietnam War) or repairs (the civil rights movement and the labor peace in Sweden) in the social fabric will reshape trust. So experience may matter mightily.

These collective events shape the ways we interact with one another, and how we view others as part of our moral community. The civil rights movement initially made American political and social life highly contentious, but eventually it created much more goodwill, especially among the cohort that came of age during the years of protest. The civil rights movement was *all about* accepting *all* Americans as part of our moral community. Vietnam, on the other hand, split the country apart and led people to distrust each other. Increasing economic inequality has similarly fostered distrust, not only in the United States, but also cross-nationally (see Chapter 8).

Collective events have the potential to redefine our sense of community in the way that individual experiences don't. Bill may treat Jane badly, even deceive her. But there would be little reason for Jane to change her worldview based upon a single bad experience, or many bad experiences. Even the most committed generalized trusters must know many people they consider untrustworthy. Unless you live in a truly mean world such as Montegrano, your daily experiences will not make you more or less of a generalized truster. Your own experiences are simply too limited to generalize to the larger society. But collective events speak precisely to the inclusiveness of others in our moral community. It is easy to see the effects of "big events" such as the civil rights movement or the Vietnam War in the United States, as well as the destructive consequences of ethnic conflict in Bosnia and Rwanda. But these are not the only types of collective experiences that may matter.

The distribution of resources in society also shapes generalized trust, for two reasons. First, optimism for the future makes less sense when there is more economic inequality. People at the bottom of the income distribution will be less sanguine that they too share in society's bounty. There are fewer trusters in American society today because there are fewer optimists. We have less faith in the future because economic inequality has grown dramatically over the past four decades (see Chapter 6). How well the country is doing collectively, rather than how well any of us is doing individually, leads to changes in interpersonal trust (cf. Kinder and Kiewiet 1979).

Second, the distribution of resources plays a key role in establishing the belief that people share a common destiny and have similar fundamental values. When resources are distributed more equally, people are more likely to perceive a common stake with others. If there is a strong skew in wealth, people at each end may feel that they have little in common with others. In highly unequal societies, people will stick with their own kind. Perceptions of injustice will reinforce negative stereotypes of other groups, making trust and accommodation more difficult (Boix and Posner 1998, 693).

Putnam (1993, 88, 174) argues that trust will not develop in a highly stratified society. And Adam Seligman (1997, 36-7, 41) goes further. Trust *cannot* take root in a hierarchal culture. Such societies have rigid social orders marked by strong class divisions that persist across generations. Feudal systems and societies based on castes dictate what people can and cannot do based upon the circumstances of their birth. Social relations are based on expectations of what people must do, not on their talents or personalities. Trust is not the lubricant of cooperation in such traditional societies. The assumption that others share your beliefs is counterintuitive, since strict class divisions make it unlikely that others actually have the same values as people in other classes.

TRUST AND CIVIC ENGAGEMENT

In between the arguments that strategic trust is tough to create and that moralistic trust is difficult to destroy there is a third thesis: Trust can be built up and destroyed fairly easily. When we interact with other people, we become more trusting.

This approach is rooted in strategic trust, but it tries to establish a linkage between trusting people we know and people we don't know. Our experiences with people we know give us the confidence to have faith in others. As Putnam (2000, 288–9) argues (cf. Hardin 2000, 187):

People who have active and trusting connections to others – whether family members, friends, or fellow bowlers – develop or maintain character traits that are good for the rest of society. Joiners become more tolerant, less cynical, and more empathetic to the misfortunes of others. When people lack connections to others, they are unable to test the veracity of their own views, whether in the give-and-take of casual conversation or in more formal deliberation. Without such an opportunity, people are more likely to be swayed by their worst impulses.

Putnam sees the relationship between both formal and informal social ties, on the one hand, and trust, on the other hand, as "mutually reinforcing": "The more we connect with other people, the more we trust them, and vice versa" (1993, 180; 1995b, 665).[31]

Tocqueville (1945, 108–9) offers the most famous statement on how socializing builds trust:[32]

Feelings and opinions are recruited, the heart is enlarged, and the human mind is developed only by the reciprocal influence of men upon one another. . . . These influences are almost null in democratic countries; they must therefore be artificially created, and this can only be accomplished by associations.

Putnam (1993, 90) writes: "Participation in civic organizations inculcates skills of cooperation as well as a sense of shared responsibility for collective endeavors." And Stolle (1998b, 500) elaborates: "Membership in voluntary associations should increase face-to-face interactions between people and create a setting for the development of trust. . . . The development of interpersonal trust and cooperative experiences between members tends to be generalized to the society as a whole" (cf. Levi 1998).

In other words, our direct experience (strategic trust) with people like ourselves (particularized trust) leads us to have faith in people we don't

---

[31] Later, Putnam (2000, 137) argued: "The causal arrows among civic involvement, reciprocity, honesty, and social trust are as tangled as well-tossed spaghetti."

[32] Tocqueville himself offers contradictory explanations. Only a few pages after arguing that reciprocity can only be developed through group membership, Tocqueville (1945, 121, emphasis added) reverses the causal ordering, from trust to civic engagement: "I have already shown . . . by what means the inhabitants of the United States almost always manage to combine their own advantage with that of their fellow citizens; my present purpose is to point out *the general rule that enables them to do so*." Tocqueville's "present purpose" was to describe "self-interest rightly understood," or the generalized trust that leads us to recognize that "man serves himself in serving his fellow creatures."

know (generalized trust). As Dasgupta (1988, 64–5) argues (cf. Luhmann 1979, 74):

Society is not composed of culturally alienated beings. In dealing with someone you learn something not only about him, but also about others in his society. You learn something about population statistics. Therefore, if you meet several honest persons and no dishonest ones you might want to revise your prior opinion of the society at large.

The link between particularized and generalized trust sounds nice. But a little reflection reveals two fundamental difficulties. First, if generalized trust only weakly depends upon life experiences, it is unclear why socializing or group membership should lead people to have greater faith in others. Most people spend minuscule amounts of time in voluntary organizations and even the most committed activists rarely devote more than a few hours a week to group life – hardly enough time to shape, or reshape, an adult's values (Newton 1997, 579). People join groups too late in life to shape their fundamental disposition. Even joiners aren't more likely to discuss civic affairs (Mondak and Mutz 1997), so they may not forge enough common ground with others to generate trust at all. And when people do discuss civic affairs, they talk to people who already agree with them, mostly family members (Bennett, Flickinger, and Rhine 2000).

Second, and more critically, there is little evidence that people extrapolate good feelings from groups or informal circles they join to the larger society. Stolle (1998b, 500) argues that the extension of trust from your own group to the larger society occurs through "mechanisms not yet clearly understood." An even more skeptical Rosenblum (1998, 45, 48) calls the purported link "an airy 'liberal expectancy' " that remains "unexplained."

Most of the time, membership in voluntary organizations and informal socializing does not require faith in people who are different from ourselves. We socialize with people we already know. We join bowling leagues with friends or at least people with similar interests, and, most likely, worldviews as well. You don't have to be a truster, or an especially nice person, to join a bowling league. There is little evidence and a shaky theoretical foundation for assuming that either formal or informal social connections can produce trust in people we don't know, especially when they are likely to be different from ourselves (and our friends).

Putnam assumes that hanging out with people like yourself will make you more likely to trust people who are different from yourself. Why are members of bowling leagues more likely to trust members of choral societies than people who stay at home? Why should my socializing with other academics make me more trusting of auto mechanics? There is some reason to believe, as in the children's song, "The more we get together, the happier we'll be." But there are few grounds for expecting that "good luck will rub off when I shakes (sic) hands with you," as in the chimney sweep's ode in *Mary Poppins*.

Some associations may be populated by people who don't trust outsiders (such as "outlaw bikers" and, in the extreme, racists, but also including religious fundamentalists). Ethnic associations may not provide the bridges across different types of people necessary to build more widespread civic cooperation (Putnam 1993, 90; Uslaner and Conley 1998). Organizations composed of particularized trusters will not generate moralistic trust. They may even reinforce in-group ties (Stolle 1998b). No wonder that Stolle (1998a, 1998b) found only small – and fleeting – increases in generalized trust when people joined voluntary organizations and a negative correlation between trust in other members of your group and trust in people more generally. A strong sense of group identity can lead to more collective action within a group, but less cooperation with outsiders, as Dawes et al. (1990) report in experimental results of collective action games.

Many of Putnam's (1993, 2000) groups connecting people to one another – choral societies, bird-watching groups, bowling leagues, card-playing clubs – may bring together people with similar passions who quickly develop strong ties to each other. Now, choral societies and bird-watching groups (among others) will hardly *destroy* trust. Birders aren't outlaw bikers. And there is nothing wrong with such narrow groups. They bring lots of joy to their members and don't harm anybody. But they are poor candidates for creating social trust (cf. Etzioni 1996, 96; Levi 1996; Rosenblum 1998). If our social and organizational lives revolve around people just like ourselves, it would hardly be reasonable to make inferences about the larger society (Silver, 1989, 276–7; Offe 1999).

It is ironic that neither birders with sweet dispositions nor rough-and-ready outlaw bikers will create trust by joining groups or even socializing with each other informally (see Chapter 5 for the evidence). Birders may be generalized trusters to begin with, but it is far from clear that you can create more trust in other people by socializing with your own kind. Outlaw bikers may, in contrast, reinforce particularized trust by creating their own community.

You can't get from particularized to generalized trust. We are asked to make inferences about people we don't know with evidence about people we do know, without any expectation that the two groups will be like each other. Indeed, it is likely that they *won't be like each other*. If we had reason to believe that other people would be very much like our own group, the problem of generalized trust might never arise. We could get by with particularized trust quite well.

We *can* produce trust by interacting with people who are different from ourselves. The civil rights movement seems to have had this effect by bringing blacks and whites together for collective action. In more routine examples, volunteering time and giving to charity tie us to people in our community who may well be different from ourselves. People who give to charity or volunteer often feel a "warm glow," an extra boost in their view of themselves and others (Andreoni 1989).

Yet, the people who take part in these activities are already likely to be generalized trusters. The motivations for giving time and money are largely altruistic: People want to help others and they trace this impulse to give of themselves to their religious faith (Wuthnow 1991, 51; Hodgkinson et al. 1992, 203, 218; Wilson and Musick 1997, 708–9). Volunteers reject materialistic values in favor of ideals such as a world at peace, inner harmony, and true friendship (Mahoney and Pechura 1980, 1010; Williams 1986, 167). They don't expect anyone to repay their kindness (Gerard 1985, 237). People who give money to charities have motivations similar to those of volunteers.[33] Such activities can and do increase generalized trust (see Chapter 5). Yet, they also *depend upon generalized trust*. If you see people in need as part of your moral community, you will take part in activities that make you even more trusting.

In a similar way, trust depends primarily upon optimism, but optimism also depends upon generalized faith in others. As with volunteering and giving time, the relationship is reciprocal. It is plausible that trusters become more optimistic through their good deeds (though there is no direct evidence for this). Yet, the impact of optimism on trust is *substantially greater* than that of trust on optimism (see Chapter 5). So

[33] According to the 1992 ANES and the 1996 Giving and Volunteering Surveys, almost 90 percent of people who volunteered also made charitable contributions.

optimism is the beginning of the causal chain – leading to trust and then to good deeds – and then back to more optimism. Thus, the morally rich get morally richer.

Particularized trusters may help their friends, their family, and people like themselves. But generalized trusters will reach out to others. They are more tolerant of people unlike themselves. The view that people who are different are part of your moral community leads generalized trusters to feel guilty when others face discrimination or cannot get by. This leads them to take action, both in the private sector (volunteering and giving to charity) and through government programs (civil rights and other antidiscrimination laws). This breadth of view also allows generalized trusters to solve collective action problems such as enacting legislation in Congress and having more efficient and less corrupt government across nations. It will also produce more open markets, greater economic growth, and more redistribution from the rich to the poor (see Chapters 7 and 8). Particularized trust may make life better for your own kind, but it will not make a society prosper. Only generalized trust can do that (Woolcock 1998).

TRUST AND THE STATE

Levi (1998), Offe (1999), and others (Pagden 1988, 139; Misztal, 1996, 198; Cohen, 1997, 19–20) argue that a state, and particularly a democratic state, can produce trust in people. Levi (1999, 82) maintains that states build trust through "the use of coercion" and that "democratic states may be even better at producing generalized trust than are non-democratic institutions ... because they are better at restricting the use of coercion to tasks that enhance rather than undermine trust." Rothstein (in press) elaborates on the link between trust and coercion: "If people believe that the institutions that are responsible for handling 'treacherous' behavior act in fair, just and effective manner, and if they also believe that other people think the same of these institutions, then they will also trust other people." Levi (1998, 87) holds that "[t]he trustworthiness of the state influences its capacity to generate interpersonal trust." Rothstein (in press) elaborates on this linkage:

If you think ... that these ... institutions [of law and order] do what they are supposed to do in a fair and effective manner, then you also have reason to believe that the chance of people getting away with such treacherous behavior is small. If so, you will believe that people will have very good reason to refrain from acting in a treacherous manner, and you will therefore believe that "most people can be trusted."

A strong legal system will reduce transaction costs, making trust less risky. The more experience people have with compliance, the more likely they are to have confidence in others' good will (Brehm and Rahn 1997, 1008; Levi 1998; Offe 1999).

So Bill knows that if he hires Jane to paint his house and she accepts his payment and does a poor job, he can take her to court for redress. Thus, he won't worry so much if he has to look for a new painter. My own family benefited from this very type of protection: We hired a contractor to repave our driveway and he used an inferior grade of concrete. After a year or more, the Maryland Home Improvement Commission ruled in our favor and we recovered our initial investment. Cohen (1997, 19) argues that "legal norms of procedural fairness, impartiality, and justice that give structure to state and some civil institutions, limit favoritism and arbitrariness, and protect merit are the *sine qua non* for society-wide 'general trust,' at least in a modern social structure."

There is plenty of evidence that people are more likely to obey laws and pay taxes if they believe that laws are enforced fairly and if people trust government (Tyler, 1990; Scholz and Pinney 1995). But the link between government and trust in people is tenuous. Across 42 nations, there is but a modest correlation ($r = .154$) between trust in people and confidence in the legislative branch of government.[34] If trust in people is a long-standing value that changes but slowly *and* if trust in people is not largely based upon our experiences, then it is hard to see how government can generate faith in strangers. If trust in people were simply a form of strategic trust – where it is reasonable to withhold confidence until you have evidence that others are trustworthy – then government could generate faith in others. For Levi and others are certainly right when they argue that trust in government is contingent.[35] And they are just as assuredly wrong when they argue that generalized trust in people rests primarily upon demonstrations of trustworthiness (see Chapter 5).

[34] See Chapter 8 for a description of the data base. I focus on the legislative rather than the executive branch since most democratic governments are parliamentary systems. The correlation is not much different for nations with and without a legacy of Communist rule ($r = .143$ and $.189$, respectively).

[35] Fenno (1978) and Bianco (1994) provide compelling arguments that members of Congress must expend much effort to develop trust among their constituents.

Government, taken generally, can't lead people to trust each other. But the situation may be different for the branch that is responsible for adjudicating disputes between strangers, the legal system. Rothstein (in press, 19, 21–2) argues (Misztal, 1996, 251; Offe, 1996, 27; Seligman, 1997, 37; Levi 1998):

> Political and legal institutions that are perceived as fair, just and (reasonably) efficient, increase the likelihood that citizens will overcome social dilemmas. . . . In a civilized society, institutions of law and order have one particularly important task: to detect and punish people who are "traitors," that is, those who break contracts, steal, murder, and do other such non-cooperative things and therefore should not be trusted. Thus, if you think that particular institutions do what they are supposed to do in a fair and efficient manner, then you also have reason to believe . . . that people will refrain from acting in a treacherous manner and you will therefore believe that "most people can be trusted."

Rothstein (2000, 21) argues in favor of the linkage between trust in the legal system and faith in people by citing correlations between the trust in different governmental institutions and generalized trust in Swedish surveys conducted from 1996 through 2000. Of 13 governmental institutions, the correlations with trust in people are highest (though barely) for the police and the courts.

There is little reason to presume that government enforcement of laws will build trust. Yes, coercion can increase *compliance* with the law. Obeying the law because you fear the wrath of government will not make you more trusting, no matter how equally the heavy hand of the state is applied. Generalized trusters are, in fact, less likely than mistrusters to endorse unconditional compliance. In the General Social Survey, just 35 percent of trusters say that you should *always* obey the law, even if it is unjust, compared to 48 percent of mistrusters.[36] Simply getting people to obey laws will not produce trust. Perhaps this is a caricature of the argument on building trust, but it is easy to confuse compliance with voluntary acceptance, to confuse the law-abiding people of Singapore with those of Sweden (cf. Rothstein, in press). Even in countries with comparatively high levels of trust, such as Sweden, the linkage between confidence in the legal system and the police and trust in people is not very strong (Rothstein, in press).[37]

---

[36] Phi = −.128, Yule's Q = −.269. The question was asked in 1985, 1990, and 1996.

[37] The correlation between trust in people and confidence in the legal system in the World Value Survey is modest (tau-c = .069, gamma = .122). And the country by country correlations tend to be higher where trust in people is higher.

Courts can save us from rascals only if there are few rascals (cf. Sitkin and Roth 1993). Law abiding citizens, not rogue outlaws, create constitutions that work. You may write any type of constitution that you wish, but statutes alone won't create generalized trust. Macaulay (1963, 58, 61–3) argues that business executives and lawyers prefer transactions based upon trust – where a handshake seals the deal – to those based upon contracts and threats of legal sanctions. Most executives and even lawyers have faith that other people will keep their end of a bargain. Resorting to formal documents might undo the goodwill that undergirds business relationships (Macaulay 1963, 63; Mueller 1999, 96). Coercion, Gambetta (1988, 220) argues, "falls short of being an adequate alternative to trust. . . . It introduces an asymmetry which disposes of *mutual* trust and promotes instead power and resentment" (cf. Baier 1986, 234; Knight 2000, 365). Generalized trust does *not* depend upon contracts. Indeed, trusting others is sometimes said to be a happy substitute for monitoring their standing (Offe 1997, 12; Putnam 2000, 135).[38]

There is a linkage between confidence in the legal system and trust in people; the direction of causality goes from trust to confidence in the legal system. Trusting societies have strong legal systems, able to punish the small number of scofflaws. Rothstein (in press) argues that Russians have low levels of trust in each other because they don't have faith in the law. It seems more likely that this direction of causality runs the other way: Russians have a weak legal system because not enough people have faith in each other. Seeking to instill generalized trust from the top down (by reforming the legal system) misses the mark in most cases.

Yet, there are likely to be key exceptions. Long-standing poverty and discrimination can lead people to withdraw trust in strangers. Groups that have faced such discrimination will also experience unequal treatment before the law. Minority groups that have faced discriminatory treatment by the police and the courts may well come to believe that the majority population cannot be trusted to ensure justice. People who have long-standing beliefs that the legal system is unfair may generalize their experiences with the law to the larger population. This clearly would hold in many low-trust societies where the law – and the entire social system – is not neutral, including Montegrano, Albania (see

---

[38] Others who see trust as knowledge-based – notably Dasgupta (1988, 53), Hardin (1995, 8–9), and Misztal (1996, 121–3) – argue that it is *based upon* reputation.

note 7), Bosnia – and minority groups in the United States, notably African-Americans and Hispanics.[39] Most people don't have frequent interactions with the police or the courts, certainly not as defendants.[40] More routine encounters with the legal system – small-claims court, traffic tickets, divorce proceedings, arbitration, and the like – should not shape a person's overall worldview. When my wife and I finally got redress for our cracked driveway – after several hearings, countless lost documents, and some clerks who regularly forgot who we were; and this was a case *where the system worked* – our sole emotion was relief. Perhaps it was fortunate that our experiences with the law did not affect our trust in others.

If courts, or government more generally, can build up any type of trust at all, it is strategic trust. Bill may trust Jane to paint his house if he knows that she is bonded against poor performance. Strategic trust depends more on compliance than on motivations. Why should Bill care whether Jane might really rather cheat him? Here the long arm of the law may work almost as efficiently as good relations between buyer and seller, even though most of us would really rather deal with contractors we know and trust. And this suggests that the role of courts, and government more generally, is to guarantee fair treatment and to redress grievances (Levi 1998).

Our trust in government depends upon how well it functions and whether we like its policies and the people in power. Trust in government is much more like strategic trust: For this reason, it cannot produce trust in people and is very different from it (see Chapter 5). For similar reasons, you can't produce trust in people through institutional reforms. Trust is about, in Putnam's (1993) terminology, "making democracy work," not simply "making democracy." Indeed, as countries democratize, they may become (at least in the short run) *less* trusting. Democratic reforms shake things up – and the move from a controlled economy to free markets may increase economic inequality – and distrust (see Chapter 8). People don't become trusting because they live in democracies. Rather, trusting people help democracies function better, with more efficient bureaucracies and judicial systems and less corruption (cf. Putnam 1993, 115). People in trusting nations have more faith in the legal system, though countries with more faith in the law are *not* more

---

[39] The logic may be compelling, but there are no data sets that can adequately test it.

[40] In the General Social Survey, 11 percent of whites and 16 percent of blacks say that they have been arrested.

likely to have large numbers of trusters. So we trust the law because *we don't believe that we will need its strong enforcement powers to get our fellow citizens to behave themselves.*

Trust in people may not lead to trust in government, but it seems to lead to *better* government (Putnam 1993, 101, 113, 115). In the United States (the only country where there is good information), trust leads to a greater willingness to compromise and enact major legislation. Nations with high trust also have strong commitments to people who are less fortunate (cf. Rothstein 2000). They are more likely to redistribute resources from the rich to the poor. A more equitable division of resources leads to greater trust in other people, which in turn produces more redistribution. Cross-nationally, more trust also leads to both more open markets and greater wealth. At both the individual level and in the aggregate, trust brings us many good things. Yet, while trust does not generally depend upon governmental institutions, it is not an alternative to strong government. A trusting society is not at all conducive to anarchy. Indeed, it provides the moral foundation for an activist state.

Government is not irrelevant to trust. It cannot produce trust, but it can destroy it. The cross-national patterns I discuss in Chapter 8 hold largely for countries without a legacy of communism. In the formerly Communist countries, most of the links don't hold. Years of repression under rigid political regimes destroyed trust. The linkage between economic inequality and trust is actually *reversed* in formerly communist regimes: the least egalitarian countries have the *most* trust. Too strong a state can break down the ties between people that are essential for the development of trust.

REPRISE

Different types of trust work help to resolve collective action problems differently. Knowledge-based trust is useful for small-scale problems. It can help you decide how much you should contribute to a collection to help a neighbor in need. You can observe collections from your neighbors. You may well know enough about them from the start that you can guess whether each contributes much (if anything). You might even know – if you've been very attentive – how much (if anything, once more) you should contribute at your house of worship. But there is no way you can know whether you need to contribute to the American Cancer

Society or your local public television station, lest either fall into fiscal straits.[41]

Knowledge-based trust can help you determine which roofing contractor to hire. It can help researchers design collective action experiments, since they can control the amount of information people have about the preferences of others – and can even manipulate whether a person will be a truster or a mistruster (Deutsch 1958, 1960). One survey of experimental results even *defined* trust as "reliance upon the communication behavior of another person in order to achieve a desired but uncertain objective in a risky situation" (Giffin 1967, 105).

If we are looking to solve larger-scale collective action problems, ranging from civic engagement (Putnam 1993, 1995a) to reaching compromises in national legislatures (Uslaner 1993), we must rely upon generalized trust rather than knowledge-based faith in others. There is presumably some moral good in solving collective action problems (Putnam 1993, 88, 180). And the way we get there is also moral (Putnam 1993, 169). But knowledge-based trust, Levi (1998, 81) argues, "is neither normatively good nor bad; it is neither a virtue nor a vice."

If this argument is correct, one might wonder why people have expended so much effort understanding how to go about hiring a roofing contractor. Well, yes, such knowledge would be useful within the context of a manual on how to be a more informed consumer. Knowledge-based trust also has given us some fascinating experimental results in game theory. We know that in many ways communication among players can help build knowledge-based trust, which in turn helps us solve collective action problems, such as how much people are willing to contribute to a public good. Yet, virtually no one seems to take the trouble to make the leap from experimental studies to solving collective action problems in real life. How can knowledge-based trust solve larger-scale collective action problems when communication problems can be so difficult to overcome?

---

[41] It doesn't help to follow trend totals. My local paper, the *Washington Post*, noted that a local campaign for public television station WETA began very weakly. Other reports were sporadic and not very informative until the campaign ended, when we learned that WETA had a record fund-raising drive. Will this lead to a drop-off in contributions in future campaigns from people who might have been concerned that WETA was in trouble?

Maybe we've been concentrating on the wrong type of trust in our search for how faith in other people helps solve collective action problems. Moralistic trust is, I suggest, the key to a wide range of collective action problems, and to creating a climate in which people reason well together. Even in experimental situations, the impacts for measures of trust are often – dare I say usually – stronger for moralistic trust compared to knowledge-based faith in others (see Rotter 1971, 1980; Yamigishi 1986, 1988; Wrightsman 1991; Yamigishi and Yamigishi 1994). Moralistic trust is a message of shared values and shared concerns for others. It unlocks lots of doors, even though its gratifications may not be as immediate as those of chicken soup.

3

Counting (on) Trust

Lucy: "I'm getting so I don't trust anybody."
Linus: "Don't you even trust *me?*"
Lucy: "I trust you as far as I can throw that blanket."
Linus tosses the security blanket he always holds tight.
Linus (talking to Charlie Brown): "My sister trusts me eight feet."
– From the comic strip *Peanuts*[1]

If there are multiple dimensions of trust, then particularized and generalized trust ought to be distinct from each other empirically as well as analytically. If generalized trust is a value, it ought to be stable. In this chapter, I make no bold theoretical claims. Instead, I take on some methodological issues. First, I discuss the measurement of generalized and particularized trust. Then I consider methodological issues in establishing that trust is indeed a value. If trust does indeed reflect moral concerns, it should be stable over time. After all, people don't change their minds on their core values. And people should think about trust as something that is general, not simply reflecting their day-to-day experiences. I find support for both claims: Trust *is* stable, or at least as stable as most predispositions in political and social attitudes. And when people "think aloud" about trust, they discuss it in general terms. I also consider some reservations expressed about the standard trust question. There are methodological problems that won't go away, but they are not severe.

---

[1] From the comic strip *Peanuts*, about the daily life of children. Linus is Lucy's brother, Charlie Brown the main character in the strip.

Rarely is there a survey that asks a wide range of trusting questions, such as the Pew Center survey discussed in Chapter 2. Such a data source permits a test of my argument that generalized and particularized trust are distinct components of faith in others. Usually, a survey that contains *any* social trust question will only use the format for generalized trust.[2] The Pew Center data support my contention that this item taps (very well) generalized trust. I suggest an alternative way of measuring particularized trust using questions that are available in some national surveys (those conducted, at least prior to 1996, by the American National Election Studies).

As elsewhere, I have tried to restrict as much of the technical discussion as possible to tables and footnotes. But this *is* a chapter about measurement issues, and so, perhaps inevitably, I may not be as successful as some might like. The faint of heart or those who trust me (strategically) may safely move to Chapter 4.

GENERALIZED AND PARTICULARIZED TRUST

Morris Rosenberg (1956) developed what has become the standard interpersonal trust question asked in a plethora of surveys: "Generally speaking, do you believe most people can be trusted or can't you be too careful in dealing with people?" As I indicated in Chapter 2, trusting "most people" means that we trust strangers. If we only put our faith in people we know or we place our confidence in people we think we know well (folks like ourselves), we are particularized trusters.

If we think of trust as a single concept, we may use the standard question to make arguments about how we place confidence in others based upon our experiences (Offe 1997, 17). This doesn't make sense either analytically or empirically. Often there seems little we can do. Few surveys ask about trusting specific groups. One that does is the Pew Research Center metropolitan Philadelphia survey of 1996. As I showed in Chapter 2, this survey asks a wide range of trust questions, providing 16 indicators of trust in other people generally (the standard question), strangers (including people you meet on the street), family members, friends and coworkers, members of churches and other groups people join, and various levels of government, as well as specific agencies thereof.

---

[2] Questions on trust in government, however, are considerably easier to find.

If generalized and particularized trust are separate empirically as well as analytically, they should form separate spheres. The data reduction technique of factor analysis lets us determine the underlying structure of the 16 trust questions. More specifically, I expect this diverse set of questions to reflect three dimensions of trust: a generalized trust factor that includes the standard question as well as faith in strangers, a particularized trust dimension emphasizing one's family and people you know well, and a trust in government factor. Confidence in our leaders is different from faith in other people, whether we know them well or not (see Chapter 5).

And this is what I find (see Table 3-1). The factor analysis shows three distinct dimensions, just as predicted.[3] And the three factors reflect trust in strangers, friends and family, and government. The variable with the highest loading (correlation) on the strangers dimension is people you meet on the street. Not far behind is the standard interpersonal trust question, followed by the people where you shop. *The highest loadings on this dimension reflect people we don't know at all – as does the standard question, which clearly is linked to trusting strangers.* The friends and family dimension is marked by high loadings (in order) for people at work, your boss, people at your church and club, your family, and the fire department. There is also a strong loading for your neighbors, but neighbors also fit on the strangers dimension. And this makes sense. Some neighbors we know well, others we don't.[4] So trusting neighbors is a mixture of faith in both friends (slightly higher loading) and strangers (slightly lower).

The highest correlations with this factor are for people we know well: our coworkers, people at our places of worship and in our club. The correlation for our family is somewhat lower, and this should not be surprising, since the family is special for everyone.[5] The loading for the fire department is somewhat surprising insofar as we might expect it to load on the government factor. Many fire departments, however, are made up of volunteers, not government employees. People may regard firefighters, especially volunteers, as something other than service providers. They show up, rather peculiarly, on the friends and family

---

[3] The dimensions were rotated using the Varimax criterion, an orthogonal rotation that makes the factors as independent as the data structure permits.

[4] Or it may be that this question is too specific to respondents (as Jeffrey Mondak has suggested to me), making it less than ideal as a measure of either generalized or particularized trust.

[5] With less variation, the correlation will be smaller.

TABLE 3-1. *Factor Analysis of Trust Measures in 1996 Pew Philadelphia Study*

Trust Measure	Trust Strangers	Trust Friends/Family	Trust Government
Trust People Meet on Street	.484	−.245	−.309
Most People Can Be Trusted	.446	−.224	−.134
Trust People Where You Shop	.430	−.391	−.231
Trust Neighbors	.414	−.481	.195
Trust People at Work	.157	−.619	−.203
Trust Your Boss	.071	−.589	−.236
Trust People at Church	.159	−.576	−.157
Trust People at Your Club	.328	−.534	−.104
Trust Your Family	.129	−.391	.011
Trust Fire Department	.117	−.318	.142
Trust Schools	.148	−.306	−.339
Trust City Government	.215	−.208	−.631
Trust State Government	.065	−.147	−.706
Trust Federal Government	.061	−.077	−.741
Others Trust You	.137	−.240	−.122
Trust People Your Own Age[a]	.029	−.035	.025

Entries are rotated (Varimax) factor loadings.
[a] Question is whether it is easier or more difficult to trust people one's own age.

dimension rather than the stranger factor. Overall, the friends and family dimension appears to represent particularized trust.

The negative loadings on the friends and family factor, compared to the positive ones for the strangers dimension, are of no particular import. They do *not* indicate that people who trust strangers don't have faith in their friends and family, or vice versa. Just the opposite is true. People who believe that "most people can be trusted" place greater faith in friends and family, strangers, and government for *every* specific trust question. The correlation between the factor scores for generalized and particularized trust is positive, even moderate (.386).[6]

The differences between the two dimensions is that the gaps are much greater between trusters and mistrusters for strangers than for friends and family. Generalized trusters place confidence in everyone, particularized trusters only in people they know well. I shall show in Chapter 4 that the pattern I have uncovered in the data reflects the theoretical argument I made in the previous chapter: Trust in strangers reflects an

[6] Factor scores are composite variables weighted by the factor loadings.

optimistic worldview rather than one's life circumstances. Trust in friends and family depends on experiences to a far greater extent.

There is a third dimension, as I hypothesized. This factor represents trust in government, with the highest loading for the federal government and slightly lower correlations with the state and city governments. The schools have a much lower loading, perhaps reflecting the distinctive status of our educational system.[7] The government dimension is distinct from the other two factors: It has weak correlations with both the stranger and friends and family factors.[8] Finally, two trust items – whether it is easier or more difficult to trust people your own age and whether others trust you – don't load on any factor.[9]

We can distinguish, empirically as well as analytically, between generalized and particularized trust. The standard interpersonal trust question serves as a good measure of generalized trust, or faith in strangers. It has a simple correlation of .69 with the stranger factor scores. It is more difficult, however, to get a measure of particularized trust. Surveys don't regularly ask about trust in friends and family.

I thus suggest an alternative strategy. It does not measure trust per se. But it is based on the logic of particularized trust and exploits data that are available at least in most ANES surveys. Particularized trusters have faith only in their own kind. So black particularized trusters would feel most comfortable with blacks and less positive toward whites. A similar dynamic works in reverse: White particularized trusters are more positively disposed to other whites than toward blacks. ANES surveys generally ask people to place groups on "feeling thermometers" ranging from zero (very negative) to 98 (very positive). While such measures do not measure trust, they provide good indicators of people's

---

[7] Parents with children are somewhat more supportive of the school system than are people without children ($p < .005$). And schools are obviously more salient to parents. The levels of government in the survey do not have the specialized clientele groups that schools do – or perhaps the overall level of goodwill. Schools are considerably more popular than any level of government in the survey.

[8] The correlations are .167 and .164, respectively.

[9] People may not worry about trusting people who are older or younger, at least not now. In the late 1960s and early 1970s, young people warned each other not to trust anyone over 30. Young people are still more likely to place greater faith in people their own age ($r = -.261$ with age). But people don't link trusting people of different ages with trusting strangers. The correlation between trusting people of different ages and the standard question is $-.003$; the correlation with trusting people you meet on the street is .004. And there is little indication that reciprocity matters. Believing that others trust you does not make you more likely to place greater confidence in either strangers or friends and family.

predispositions to people like themselves and people who are different from themselves.

Using the 1992 ANES I constructed measures of in-group and out-group particularized trust. I selected thermometer scores based upon the availability of demographic information. The groups I employed are Asian-Americans, blacks, whites, Hispanics, Southerners, Catholics, and Jews.[10] I classified each respondent as either belonging or not belonging to each group. Each person has two scores: one for how they rate in-groups and the other for how highly they judge out-groups. The particularized trust score is the average adjusted thermometer rating for each bloc of in- or out-group.[11] Particularized trusters will have strongly positive evaluations of their own group and negative appraisals for others. Thus, positive scores for in-groups and negative ones for out-groups reflect particularized trust, faith in people like yourself rather than "most people."

Thermometers are not available in all years. Even when they are, not all groups are included each year. So I developed measures that employ only those groups that are common to a large number of surveys: blacks, whites, Southerners, Catholics, and Jews. The reduced and more expansive lists are almost perfectly correlated. The 1992 in-group measure using seven groups has a correlation of .999 (because there are few Asian-Americans or Hispanics in the sample) with the reduced list, while the out-group indices correlate at .966.

As with the Pew measures, people with positive views of their own groups also tend to like out-groups.[12] But the two measures have very different consequences for civic engagement, as I shall show in Chapter 7. People who like their own groups tend to withdraw from the forms of civic participation that stem from trust (volunteering, giving to charity, willingness to serve on a jury). People with positive evaluations of people different from themselves tend to get involved in their communities.[13]

---

[10] There are also thermometers on gays, legal immigrants, and illegal immigrants, but there is no way to determine whether a respondent fits any of these categories. I also constructed measures of particularized trust for political in-groups and out-groups (the poor, liberals, conservatives, union members, feminists, and fundamentalists); see Uslaner (1998a).

[11] I adjusted the score by subtracting the mean for each group from each individual's score, so as not to weight favored (or disliked) groups too much.

[12] The correlation is .522.

[13] The two measures do not correlate very highly with interpersonal trust. People with high scores on in-group trust are somewhat less trusting ($r = -.134$), but there is little

THE STABILITY OF TRUST

If trust is a value, then it should be stable over time. Values should be enduring. "Mere" preferences may not be. At the extreme, I may prefer strawberry ice cream one day and coffee ice cream the next. I may have confidence in government when the Democrats are in power but not when the Republicans hold office. I may favor a particular policy alternative until someone gives me good reasons to change my mind.

On core values, however, I am not likely to change my mind readily. It is hard to imagine how someone might believe in God on weekends but not on weekdays (even if they act as if they do and don't in this manner). Nor are we likely to be tolerant toward people different from ourselves some days but not on others. In part what sets a value apart from a preference is how deeply rooted (and thus how enduring) the latter is. Most political and social attitudes are notoriously unstable, largely because people don't pay a lot of attention to issues (Converse 1964). But people hold values dear. Values *do* change, but far less frequently than do preferences for one policy outcome over another. How stable, then, is trust? If trust does not persist over time, we ought not to call it a value.

To investigate stability, we need panel data: repeated measurements on the same people over time. There are two data sources that permit comparisons over several years.[14] First is the (aforementioned) American National Election Study (ANES) panel in 1972, 1974, and 1976. Second is the Niemi-Jennings socialization study of high school students and their parents in 1965, 1973, and 1982. Both sets of surveys tap

correlation between trust and out-group evaluations ($r = .004$). For other years, out-group evaluations have higher correlations with generalized trust. The patterns are (all entries are Pearson correlation coefficients; the 1972 and 1976 scores use the shorter list):

Year	In-group trust	Out-group trust
1964	−.005	.155
1972	−.084	.061
1976	−.071	.141

[14] The 1996 American National Election Study asked the trust question in both the pre- and postelection surveys. The interval between the two surveys, however, was quite short (only a few months). And the second wave appears "contaminated" by question order effects (see below). The trusting share jumps from 38.7 percent to 50.8 percent. The preelection question is preceded by a battery of questions on spending priorities, while the postelection question follows a question on volunteering.

attitudes on trust and many other questions over a fairly lengthy period
of time. The ANES panel permits me to compare attitudes over a four-
year period. The Niemi-Jennings survey covers a 17-year period and
has data on both youth and their parents. This will also allow me
to examine the effects of parental values on their children's ideals (see
Chapters 4 and 5).

Both sets of surveys share a common drawback, however. They overestimate, sometimes substantially, the share of trusters in the population.
There are more consecutive (or nearly consecutive) measures of trust in
the General Social Survey (GSS) than in virtually any other survey.[15] The
GSS trend shows a steep decline in interpersonal trust in the 1970s from
the higher figures measured by the Civic Culture Survey in 1960 and the
ANES surveys in the 1960s (see Chapter 1 and Putnam 1995a).

The Niemi-Jennings surveys show higher levels of trust than other
surveys, with gaps of between 17.5 percent and 30 percent.[16] The ANES
1976 survey also shows a considerably higher level of trust than the GSS
in any surrounding year, or even in the 1972 or 1974 ANES. These differences suggest mild caution in interpreting the ANES panel and greater
care in making inferences from the Niemi-Jennings panels. But they are

---

[15] For 1972 and 1974, the ANES panel data are reasonably close to the GSS trend (off by
2.5 percent in 1972 and 4.6 percent in 1974). The 1976 ANES sample from the panel,
however, indicates that 59 percent of Americans believe that "most people can be
trusted," the highest figure since the *Civic Culture* Survey in 1960. The 1976 panel
sample is almost 13 percent more trusting than are the GSS respondents. Looking at the
full 1976 ANES – not just the panel respondents – the gap falls sharply. In the 1976 ANES,
52.8 percent said that most people can be trusted – a difference of 6.7 percent with the
GSS. In all of the tables, I use figures from the panel rather than from individual surveys.
In contrast, for the Niemi-Jennings survey, the data in this chapter come from the parent
and child surveys separately in order to maximize the number of cases.

[16] In 1965, trust was still relatively high in the United States: 54.1 percent from the means
of the 1964 and 1966 ANES. But the Niemi-Jennings parent sample found 72.6 percent
trusting: a gap of almost 20 percent. Almost 65 percent of high school students said
most people can be trusted, a figure reasonably close to an ANES estimate. The 1968
ANES was the first survey to have sufficient responses to calculate a cohort mean for the
1965 high school students ($N = 62$). It showed that 67.2 percent of young people were
trusting. So the gap is only 2.5 percent. The gaps don't close over time. In 1973, 68.1
percent of adults in the Niemi-Jennings data are trusters, compared to 47.4 percent for
the GSS. For the children, the gap grows to 17.5 percent: 59.5 percent in Niemi-Jennings
and 42 percent in the GSS are trusters. By the 1980s, the difference is almost 30 percent.
The children appear to have a slight increase in trust in the Niemi-Jennings data. In
contrast, the GSS sample for this cohort in the early 1980s shows only 33.7 percent
trusting, an 8.3 percent drop from 1973. There is also a 22 percent gap for the parents,
who do show a substantial fall-off in trust levels.

the only panels we have and they can be instructive about what shapes change, even if they don't tell us much that is useful about the *direction* of change.

There is no simple criterion for determining stability. I use three straightforward measures. The first is the percentage of people who give the same response from one time period to the next. What share of the population is consistent – either as trusters or mistrusters – over time? Second, what is the linear relationship over time periods? I employ tau-b, a linear correlation for ordinal data, and its nominal counterpart, phi. Tau-b is particularly useful since it measures the difference between "concordant" and "discordant" observations; or, more straightforwardly, between people who are consistent and those who are not.

Absolute consistency may be too much to expect in the face of value change (even if measured in the wrong direction!). So I also employ a third measure: the curvilinear correlation coefficient gamma, used for ordinal data, and its nominal counterpart, Yule's Q.[17] Tau-b can only equal 1.0 if everyone is consistent: Trusters must remain trusters and mistrusters must stay misanthropes. Gamma, on the other hand, can attain a value of 1.0 if most people are consistent and all changers move *in the same direction*. I present each of these three measures – the percentage consistent, tau-b, and gamma – in Tables 3-2 and 3-3. These are all simple indicators of stability. I could employ more sophisticated measures, such as test-retest reliability correlations, but their interpretation is not so obvious and they would not change the conclusions I present below.[18]

For both the ANES and Niemi-Jennings panels, I selected variables that tap political or social dispositions and that were asked in all three waves of each survey. In a few cases I selected questions that were only asked twice but that are particularly relevant to studying attitude stability. I sought – and found – a wide range of issues and values in each survey, encompassing attitudes that ought to be very stable and those where one might expect greater fluctuation.

The attitudes that ought to be most strongly anchored are attitudes that we are most likely to learn from our parents: deeply held moral

---

[17] For dichotomies such as trust, tau-b reduces to phi and gamma to Yule's Q. To avoid confusion, I refer to all correlations as either tau-b or gamma.

[18] The test-retest correlations I calculated are uniformly higher than tau-b and lower than gamma, but usually closer to gamma.

tenets and identifications such as partisanship. It takes a lot to shake people from their core values, often based on religious principles. Until recently, partisan identification was almost as enduring and "inheritable" as were ideals based upon faith (Campbell et al. 1960). There is a vigorous debate over whether partisanship is still so stable as it was in the 1950s and 1960s (see Niemi 1980; and Miller and Shanks 1996, among many others). Whatever the answer, party identification should still display more consistency over time than many other social and political attitudes. Beyond core values and identification are what Carmines and Stimson (1989) call "easy" issues. These are public policy positions that depend on these deeply held ideals. Examples include attitudes on race, abortion, and morality in daily life. *If trust in other people is a value, then it should show a high level of consistency –* perhaps not quite as high as religious values, but comparable to other easy issues.

Trust should also be more consistent than affect toward the political system, personal efficacy, or mere policy preferences, all of which are likely to change over time or simply be unstable (Converse 1964). In the ANES panel, 24 percent did not pick an ideological identification at all in 1972, and 63 percent of those who did changed their position (on a three-point scale) by 1974. In contrast, only 2 percent of 1972 respondents did not have a party identification and just 19 percent had changed (again on a three-point scale) by two years later.

Second, some questions may be salient, but not rooted in core beliefs. In the 1972 postelection survey, only 2 percent of panel respondents had no opinion on whether they trust the government to do the right thing. But trust in government is often not very stable: From 1972 to 1974, 43 percent of people changed their minds (on a three-point scale). Trust in government is not a deeply held value as much as it is a reflection of the current conditions in the nation and the popularity of the incumbent administration (see Chapter 4). So we would expect considerable fluctuation in how much people trust the government even though they may care very much about national performance.

I present the results of for the ANES panel in Table 3-2 and those for the Niemi-Jennings panel in Table 3-3. (In the latter table, the results for parents are in regular type and those for children are in *italics*.) In both tables, the survey questions are listed in order of the value of gamma over the full course of the panel (from 1972 to 1976). As mentioned above, I collapsed multicategory data to either dichotomies or at most three-point scales. Recall that all statistics are based only on people with complete data on each question for each comparison.[19]

For the ANES panel, there is strong support for trust in people as a stable predisposition. Of 17 questions considered, social trust ranks fourth in overall stability. Across the three waves of the panel, about 75 percent of the respondents take the same position. Only party identification, when abortion should be allowed, and whether one can run one's life as one wishes have generally higher percentage agreements across time. Trust seems at least as stable as the optimistic worldview about running one's own life. It ranks considerably higher than whether one thinks one's plans are usually realized. And trust in others outperforms attitudes on civil rights and women's rights (both of which were in flux during the 1970s), as well as both internal efficacy and evaluations of government performance. It ranks far above trust in government, ideology, and more specific issues, such as a federal job guarantee and rights of the accused.

To be sure, the tau-b values for trust are only moderately high (ranging from .462 to .521) – about the same as we find for ideology and equal rights for women. But the gammas are very strong. In the 1974–6 wave, the curvilinear correlation was .826, about the same as running one's life as one wishes and within striking distance of the most stable question in the panel: party identification. In the ANES panel, movements over time are hardly random. Even using the more conservative measures, such as percent stable and tau-b, interpersonal trust fares better than all but a handful of survey questions. It clusters with traditional patterns of party identification, with an optimistic worldview, and with deeply held moral views (marijuana legalization and when to permit abortions).

There is initially strong support for the notion that generalized trust is a deeply held and stable value. Additional evidence comes from Elizabeth Smith's (1999a, 20) survey of 389 tenth-grade students in the fall and spring of 1996 and an ANES panel from the 1998 election survey and a 2000 pilot survey on trust. Smith reports a "stability coefficient" of .82 for trust, higher than that for "locus of control," "self-concept," political efficacy, political knowledge, political discussion, civic duty, and political trust. In the 1998–2000 ANES panel, 79.2 percent gave consistent answers on trust (tau-b = .590, gamma = .882, N = 260).

---

[19] So a person who is a truster in 1972, who did not answer the question in 1974, and who is a mistruster in 1976, would be included in the percentages (and correlations) for the 1972-74-76 comparison, but not for the 1972-74 or 1974-76 computations.

TABLE 3-2. *Stability of Attitudes on ANES Questions over the 1972–74–76 Panel*

	Percent Stable			tau			gamma		
	72–74	74–76	72–76	72–74	74–76	72–76	72–74	74–76	72–76
Party Identification[a]	81.4	81.5	79.9	.747	.747	.725	.918	.914	.902
Favor Marijuana Legalization[a]			71.0			.569			.795
Can Run Life as One Wishes	81.7	82.3	81.1	.461	.462	.416	.824	.830	.790
Trust in People	**73.1**	**76.1**	**73.4**	**.462**	**.521**	**.473**	**.762**	**.826**	**.784**
When Allow Abortion[b]			80.1			.558			.738
Civil Rights too Fast		63.0			.469			.707	
People Like Me Have No Say		72.0			.400			.706	
Public Officials Don't Care	70.5	70.9	69.5	.415	.413	.393	.710	.707	.685
Voting Only Way to Have Impact	70.3	73.1	69.8	.453	.401	.390	.757	.695	.679
Politics Too Complicated	76.2	75.0	72.9	.408	.456	.356	.735	.780	.671
Favor Equal Rights for Women[a]	63.3	68.6	61.5	.482	.531	.437	.686	.741	.633
Members of Congress Lose Touch	71.2	74.1	69.8	.371	.408	.322	.673	.734	.621
Plans Usually Realized	71.4	69.9	67.3	.398	.427	.346	.688	.723	.619
Trust Government[a]	57.5	70.2	56.9	.353	.406	.334	.624	.697	.602
Ideology[a]	63.1	62.4	62.0	.515	.553	.463	.632	.661	.596
Federal Government Guarantee Job[a]	57.6	56.6	56.1	.366	.384	.385	.535	.569	.568
Rights of the Accused[a]	55.8	56.7	56.1	.331	.368	.370	.557	.548	.552

Note: **Bold** represents values for trust in people, which is the subject of the study – bolded to make it easier to find.
[a] Recoded to three-point scale.
[b] Percent stable based upon collapsed categories.

The support appears somewhat more equivocal for the Niemi-Jennings data set, as I expected it might be (given the much higher level of trust in these surveys). For parents, trust ranks sixth of 13 questions based on the 1965–82 gamma. For the children sample, the 1965–82 gamma is among the lowest of all questions (only four items rank below trust). But this is hardly evidence that trust is unstable. The correlations (both tau-b and gamma) for trust for 1965–82 are distinctly lower than those for either 1965–73 or 1973–82. Both of these correlations (especially the gammas) compare favorably with other questions. And note that the Niemi-Jennings questions contain far more "easy" issues than the ANES battery.

Three of the five items above trust in the ranking for parents deal with religious values (whether one is a member of a fundamentalist denomination, interpretation of the Bible as the literal word of God, and how often one attends religious services). A fourth is whether a Communist should be allowed to hold office. And the fifth is party identification. All tap either fundamental values or a deep sense of personal identification (party attachment).

In the Niemi-Jennings surveys, trust in other people has considerably stronger correlations and at least equal stable percentages as evaluations of one's life circumstances (plans usually realized and can one run one's life as one wishes); one's sense of self-control (mind is hard to change); evaluations of government (general trust and the belief that most officials are crooked); and policy issues (rights of the accused and equal rights for women). Overall, the pattern is quite similar to that for the ANES panel. Trust is not the most stable value, but it does rank higher than most other questions.

The children are much less stable than their parents, especially when comparing trust in 1965 to trust in 1982. Is this just a function of young people "growing up" and developing their own values? Not necessarily, for the share of children expressing the same attitude on trust as their parents barely budges over time: It was 60.9 percent in 1965, 60.8 percent in 1973, and 60.1 percent in 1982. The high school students of the 1960s displayed considerably less stability in trust as adults in 1982 than their parents did when they were relatively young (in 1965). This suggests that young people did not become more consistent as they grew older.

Instead of a life cycle explanation, the best explanation may be generational. I cannot completely rule out life cycle effects, but I believe that the case for a generational account is powerful. The high school students

TABLE 3-3. Stability of Attitudes on Niemi-Jennings Questions for Youth and Parent Panels[a]

	Percent Stable			tau			gamma		
	65–73	73–82	65–82	65–73	73–82	65–82	65–73	73–82	65–82
Religious Fundamentalist Denomination	91.0	90.3	90.3	.819	.806	.809	.981	.979	.982
	85.8	86.3	82.0	.714	.712	.636	.953	.948	.914
Party Identification[b]	81.2	83.6	80.2	.717	.772	.700	.902	.938	.902
	61.3	69.3	60.2	.421	.558	.381	.626	.766	.589
Interpretation of Bible[c]	93.2	93.4	92.6	.576	.576	.529	.826	.822	.776
	89.5	89.3	89.5	.453	.587	.410	.728	.841	.672
How Often Attend Religious Services	62.3	63.4	60.1	.592	.633	.557	.775	.811	.743
	37.7	53.8	42.2	.301	.527	.285	.489	.691	.446
Let Communist Hold Office	69.5	76.8	71.8	.366	.523	.391	.680	.829	.711
	63.6	77.8	64.6	.335	.536	.333	.651	.847	.635
Trust in People	73.8	74.1	71.7	.403	.449	.388	.725	.763	.708
	66.6	71.8	63.9	.308	.419	.228	.580	.722	.453
Ideology[a]		64.7			.483			.693	
		51.6			.320			.472	
People Like Me Have No Say	72.2	70.6	69.6	.243	.327	.271	.551	.631	.596
		73.1				.270		.578	

	(1)	(2)	(3)	(4)	(5)	(6)	(7)	(8)	(9)
Voting Only Way to Have Impact	67.7	67.0	63.1	.359	.340	.289	.640	.683	.554
	66.2	*70.4*	*68.5*	*.251*	*.365*	*.310*	*.501*	*.660*	*.593*
Plans Usually Realized	69.7	75.8	67.9	.316	.371	.261	.615	.712	.544
	67.5	*74.7*	*67.7*	*.237*	*.371*	*.215*	*.489*	*.707*	*.466*
Can Run Life as One Wishes	64.5	68.5	64.7	.290	.370	.286	.540	.653	.532
	59.0	*65.6*	*59.6*	*.164*	*.306*	*.180*	*.326*	*.561*	*.354*
Mind Is Hard to Change	75.8	73.4	69.8	.374	.328	.214	.712	.648	.473
	72.2	*76.8*	*74.0*	*.178*	*.322*	*.193*	*.439*	*.673*	*.480*
Government Officials Mostly Crooked	46.8	48.4	47.0	.238	.273	.239	.364	.419	.435
	44.2	*52.9*	*43.9*	*.169*	*.244*	*.139*	*.280*	*.399*	*.233*
Government Should Help Minorities[c]		47.4			.272			.413	
		28.7			*.287*			*.435*	
Trust Government[b]	47.3	60.0	44.8	.192	.334	.196	.331	.558	.356
	40.0	*54.7*	*29.9*	*.137*	*.276*	*.141*	*.239*	*.481*	*.257*
Rights of the Accused[b]		50.1			.183			.305	
		42.9			*.243*			*.397*	
Favor Equal Rights for Women[b]		32.2			.094			.163	
		63.7			*.333*			*.599*	

Note: **Bold** represents values for trust in people, which is the subject of the study – bolded to make them easier to find.

[a] Parents in regular type; youth in italics.

[b] Recoded to three-point scale.

[c] Percent stable based upon collapsed categories.

of the 1960s became the (Early) Baby Boomers. As I shall show in Chapter 6, other age cohorts became less trusting throughout the 1970s and remained so in the 1980s. The Boomers had very sharp declines in trust in the early 1970s, but by the late 1980s had become *the most trusting age cohort.* The Boomers were mightily affected by the social forces that marked the years when they came of age: the civil rights movement and the Vietnam war (see Chapter 6).[20]

The 1960s, 1970s, and early 1980s were periods of value change for Baby Boomers. Between 1972 and 1974, 33 percent of Boomers, compared to 25.5 percent of non-Boomers changed their positions on trust; between 1974 and 1976, the percentages were 30.6 percent and 22.2 percent. Looking at the ANES panel for Boomers and their elders, we see the same pattern as in the Niemi-Jennings data, though in not such great relief (see Table 3-4). Boomers are consistently less stable in their responses to the trust question than are non-Boomers.[21]

The Niemi-Jennings data and the ANES panel for Boomers constitute a severe test. The Boomer generation rebelled against their parents on a wide range of values and issues, as Table 3-4 shows. Even party identification is marked by a sharp drop in stability from 1965 to 1982. The percentage of consistent trusters is even slightly greater (63.9) than unwavering party identifiers (60.2) among the children sampled in 1982. And the seemingly low share of children giving the same answer on trust as their parents – around 60 percent – is not that much lower than the share of Boomers who take the same party identification as their parents (cf. Carmines, McIver, and Stimson 1987).[22]

Interpersonal trust is enduring for most people, as a deeply held value should be. Most people don't shift from being a misanthrope to a truster

---

[20] In Chapter 6, I show that attitudes toward civil rights and Vietnam played a key role in shaping *changes* in trust across the 1972-74-76 ANES panel. The relationship was stronger for Baby Boomers than for non-Boomers. The simple correlations between change in trust from 1972 to 1976 and attitudes toward Vietnam were −.158 for Baby Boomers and .011 for non-Boomers. Changes in trust show correlations with changes in feeling thermometers toward blacks of .103 for Boomers and .011 for non-Boomers.

[21] The 1972-74 change difference is significant at $p < .01$, the 1974-76 at $p < .005$. Over the ANES panel, the average gamma for Boomers is .678 compared to .812 for non-Boomers; 68.8 of Boomers were consistent, compared to 76.5 percent of their elders.

[22] In 1965, 68.5 percent of parents and children shared party identification. In 1982, 63.8 percent did. But in 1973, only 58.5 percent had a common partisanship – lower than any figure for interpersonal trust. Only on core religious values is there strong continuity for the Boomers. The Boomers were not torn over trust. They displayed less consistency than their elders on all sorts of issues. Overall, then, the Boomers' consistency on trust does not seem quite so low when placed in perspective.

TABLE 3-4. *Stability of Interpersonal Trust by Cohort in the 1972–4–6 ANES Panel*

	Percent Stable	tau-b	gamma
1972–74 Pre-Boomers	74.6	.490	.791
Early Baby Boomers	66.9	.347	.626
1974–76 Pre-Boomers	77.8	.554	.855
Early Baby Boomers	69.4	.383	.676
1972–74–76 Pre-Boomers	74.1	.483	.792
Early Baby Boomers	70.0	.417	.732

over short periods of time – indeed, most people don't change much over longer periods either. If generalized trust were encapsulated experience, then we would expect larger shifts in trust across panels *unless* people met predominantly others who are trusting or mistrusting. In recent years the public has been split, sometimes rather evenly, between trusters and mistrusters. The likelihood that most people would interact largely with people like themselves (trusters with trusters and mistrusters with mistrusters) is small.

The impressive stability we have seen for most instances of trust (especially for the 1972-74-76 ANES panel and the parent sample for the Niemi-Jennings study) suggests that trust is an enduring value. Particularly in contrast to trust in government, which clearly reflects experience with the rulers of the day, trust in other people seems resistant to change for most people. And when we do see large shifts – for the Early Baby Boomers especially, in the Niemi-Jennings data – the causes of the disruption are rooted in social conflicts such as Vietnam and civil rights (see Chapter 6), rather than the happenstance of daily life.

Particularized trust is not quite as stable as generalized trust. Across the ANES panel, in-group trust is correlated at .449 from 1972 to 1976 (the requisite thermometers are not available in the 1974 wave). Out-group trust is more variable, with a correlation of .383. This may reflect imperfect measurement, changes in attitudes toward out-groups over time (whites rated blacks 11 percent less favorably in 1976 than in 1972), or both. Overall, the public became more sympathetic to their own groups and *less* favorably disposed to out-groups.[23] The intense social

[23] The mean in-group trust increased from –.513 to –.153. The mean out-group trust fell from –.036 to –.254.

conflict during the 1970s suggests that these (linear) correlations are reasonably high. The correlations are not quite as strong as one finds for interpersonal trust, which is what I would expect for a type of trust that depends more on personal experience.

TRUSTING THE QUESTION

We can measure both generalized and particularized trust. They are *not* the same thing. And generalized trust is quite stable, more so than particularized faith. There are two problems with particularized trust measures: They often do not use the word trust at all and they are not always available in surveys. There are problems with the generalized trust question, as well. It may have been asked too often, or at least too often in the wrong context.

Smith (1997) argues that responses to the trust question in the GSS series depend on where in the survey the question is asked. In most years the GSS survey has at least two forms. In one version the trust question follows some queries on whether life is exciting, work values, how one gets ahead in life, and two sexual morality items. In the second version, trust follows items on political ideology, reducing gaps in income between the rich and the poor, divorce laws, legalization of marijuana some of the time, and attitudes on crime in other years. Not surprisingly, the second trust series shows less trust than the first. Smith reports a 7.7 percent overestimate of trust in the first series compared to the second. He argues that the trust question calls "for global assessments of people in general based presumably on one's entire life experience. Making judgments based on such massive, cognitive retrievals are difficult and open to variability" (Smith 1997, 174).

Is the trust question reliable? Or should we heed Smith's implicit warning that we ought not place great confidence in measures "open to variability"? Smith's observations are clearly correct, but they seem to overstate the dangers in utilizing the trust question. We should be wary of using survey results that appear to overestimate the level of trust in American society. When there is no alternative, however, the evidence does not suggest that we are likely to make substantial errors of interpretation. Both of Smith's time series trend downward. By 1996, the two series come close to converging (Smith 1997, 177). The "overestimated" series declines from 1973 to 1996 by 28 percent, the "underestimated" series by 24 percent from 1975 to 1996. The 1972 and 1976 ANES measures seem to be overestimates based upon the order in which the survey questions were asked (see Schuman and Presser 1978).[24]

Despite the four-year time lag during a period of political and social turbulence and the different contexts presented by the order of questions, the 1972 and 1976 trust items were strongly correlated.[25] In 1996, there was a much shorter time lag between the pre- and postelection ANES samples – just a few months. The preelection question yielded 39 percent trusters, not appreciably different from three other surveys conducted in 1995 and 1996. The postelection question indicated that 51 percent of the population believed that "most people can be trusted." The preelection question followed items on spending priorities and confidence in the federal government; the postelection item came after some queries on political efficacy and whether one volunteered. This suggests a halo effect in the postelection survey, but not in the preelection poll. Yet, again, there is strong stability.[26] I only need one trust question from the 1996 ANES, so it makes sense to use the preelection item. But were I forced to use two, I doubt whether I would make too many erroneous inferences. Such problems call for recognition and even some caution. But they are hardly reasons for panic. The presence of other studies showing similar trends to the GSS is reassuring (see note 15).

These caveats point to another cause for concern in studies of trust. Following Rosenberg (1956), most people who study trust really use his misanthropy scale or some variant on it (see Brehm and Rahn 1997; Smith 1997; Stolle 1998b). This scale includes the standard trust question, as well as queries about whether most people would be fair or take advantage of one and whether most people would be helpful or are just looking out for themselves. The rationale for constructing such a scale is that multiple indicators of the same concept improve statistical reliability.

Even though the three items consistently form a unidimensional scale with reasonable properties, there are six fundamental problems with this

[24] We know from other surveys discussed above (the 1976 and 1996 ANES and the Niemi-Jennings samples for both children and parents) that trust will appear too high when it is preceded in a survey by questions on optimism and self-control. If people give positive responses to questions of optimism and/or self-control, they may be more likely to say that they trust other people. The optimism questions may have set the stage for "false positive" responses. The 1972 ANES trust question followed a battery on economics, as well as trust in government and a question on morality – so it should not be contaminated by any "feel good" effects of optimism. In the 1976 ANES trust was preceded by batteries on optimism and political efficacy.
[25] Tau-b = .473, gamma = .784.   [26] Tau-b = .588, gamma = .895.

measurement strategy.[27] First, saying that people might be helpful isn't the same thing as saying that you trust strangers. Bill might think that Jane would be helpful – giving him directions on how to get from one place to another – even though he might not trust others. You can be a misanthrope and still think that people will help you. Thirty-seven percent of the 1972–98 GSS sample who don't trust other people nevertheless still believe that folks would help them. More people think that others would be helpful across the GSS time series (54.2 percent) than trust others (41.6 percent).

Fairness may be too ambiguous. Fewer people think that others would be fair, but 43.5 percent of *mistrusters* still believe that most people would be fair (rather than try to take advantage of them). There may be strong gammas among the three questions, but they do *not* measure the same thing.[28] And this is the core of my second concern: You don't need to say that someone shares your values just to say that they might help you out. But you may need to know much more about others – more details about their values – to say that they are fair. If we are concerned with trust, we should stick with an "unadulterated" measure of trust.

Third, the three questions don't display the same time trend. So a concern for waning trust doesn't translate into a worry about a decline in helpfulness. The correlation of trust with time from 1960 onward is −.862. Fairness has also decreased, although less sharply ($r = -.534$). But helpfulness has barely fallen ($r = -.221$).[29] And the over-time trend shows a good correlation between trust and fairness ($r = .652$), but weak relationships between helpfulness and both trust ($r = .146$) and fairness ($r = .132$). Fourth, there is some evidence that both

---

[27] The correlations between trust and helpfulness in the 1972–98 GSS are .377 (tau-b) and .673 (gamma). The correlations between trust and fairness are .424 (tau-b) and .766 (gamma). For fairness and helpfulness, tau-b = .445 and gamma = .757. The ANES asked the trust questions in 1964, 1966, 1968, 1972, 1974, 1976, 1992, 1996, and 1998. But it only asked the fairness question in 1972 and 1996 and it only posed the helpfulness query in 1964, 1968, 1972, and 1992. Nevertheless, the ANES correlations are uniformly higher (gammas ranging from .808 to .875); and the correlations from the 1971 and 1978 Quality of Life Survey are also higher (ranging from .772 to .855). Even so, in the 1972 ANES, 23.4 percent of respondents who mistrusted other people nevertheless felt people would mostly be helpful. And 37.4 percent of mistrusters nevertheless felt that most people would be fair.

[28] See also the generally strong patterns of linkage among the three questions in Chapter 5.

[29] The b in a regression of helpfulness and time is insignificant, with $t = -1.068$.

TABLE 3-5. *Stability of Misanthropy Measures in the Niemi-Jennings Child-Parent Samples*

		Trust	Fairness	Helpfulness
Children 1965–73	tau-b	.308	.266	.223
	gamma	.580	.562	.437
Children 1973–82	tau-b	.419	.302	.264
	gamma	.722	.600	.505
Children 1965–82	tau-b	.228	.174	.181
	gamma	.453	.399	.367
Parent 1965–73	tau-b	.403	.411	.373
	gamma	.725	.818	.707
Parent 1973–82	tau-b	.449		.456
	gamma	.763		.757
Parent 1965–82	tau-b	.388		.340
	gamma	.708		.665

fairness and helpfulness may be less stable than trust in people (see Table 3-5).[30]

Fifth, trust should matter more for reaching out to people who are different from yourself than either helpfulness or even fairness. And it does. The 1996 GSS asks people if and where they volunteered. Across 15 types of organizations and four summary measures, trust had higher correlations with volunteering than fairness for seven groups and all four summary indicators.[31] The two measures had similar correlations for two organizations, neither had much effect for five groups, and fairness had a higher correlation for just one (religious volunteering). For five of the 15 types of volunteering, people who thought others would be helpful are *less* likely to get involved in their communities. For only two groups – religion and education – is there any relationship between helpfulness

[30] The 1972-74-76 ANES doesn't have multiple measures on either helpfulness or fairness. But the Niemi-Jennings socialization study has data for both children and parents across three waves for helpfulness and measures of fairness for all three waves for children and for two waves for parents. But there is a big caveat here: These surveys show that more people believe that others would be fair than helpful – in sharp contrast to all other studies. And parental stability on fairness may be high simply because the vast majority of these samples (86 percent in 1965 and 81 percent in 1973) agree that most people are fair. Nevertheless, both the tau-b's and the gammas are higher, often considerably, for trust than for either fairness or especially for helpfulness (see Table 3-5).

[31] The summary measures are two dummy variables and two totals. I constructed dummies for whether one volunteered at all and whether one volunteered for secular organizations. The totals are also for all volunteering and for secular organizations.

and civic engagement. So trust predicts civic engagement far better than either fairness or helpfulness.

Using a scale may thus obscure some of the associations between trust and participation. I constructed a misanthropy scale (through factor analysis). But trust had higher correlations with volunteering than the composite scale in nine of the 19 comparisons. The overall message is straightforward: Since the standard trust question really seems to measure generalized trust, why bother to make it more complicated than it needs – and ought – to be?

The same caveat applies to Putnam's surrogate measure of trust in the DDB Needham Life Style Surveys, "Most people are honest." The honesty measure might work if, as Putnam (2000, 135–6) argues, we were really interested in perceptions of trustworthiness. But this is not my central concern and it is far from clear that honesty and trust are the same thing, even if they are related. The 1972 ANES asked people if they agreed that "most people are basically honest": 86.4 percent agreed, compared to just 46.7 percent who said that "most people can be trusted." The two measures are correlated, to be sure, but the relationship is moderate.[32] Almost all people who believe most people are dishonest say that "you can't be too careful in dealing with people." Yet barely more than half of people who say that most people are honest are ready to trust strangers. Trust is trust. It isn't helpfulness, fairness, or even honesty.

Finally, and most critically, we now have evidence that people mean different things when asked open-ended questions about trust, fairness, and helpfulness. The 2000 ANES Pilot Survey asked subsamples of respondents to "think aloud" about what they meant by each of the questions in the misanthropy scale. I then coded the responses for each question according to whether the respondent referred to personal experience, a general worldview, or no content at all.[33] For

[32] Tau-c = .345 and gamma =.617. The honesty measure is a five-point Likert measure, but I dichotomized it and recoded the small share of people in the middle (7.4 percent) as missing values. The correlations are based upon the full five-point scale for honesty. For the dichotomous measure, phi = .311 and Yule's Q = .847. Putnam has made the DDB Needham data from 1975 to 1998 available on his web site, http://www.bowlingalone.com. I downloaded the data and calculated means for each year. The over-time correlation between trust and perceptions of honesty is just .453.

[33] I am grateful to Donald Kinder, Nancy Burns, Pat Luevano, and especially Ashley Gross of the American National Election Studies for making the data available to me. The ANES sent me transcripts of the "think aloud" statements with (mis)identifying respondent numbers. I coded the statements and the ANES staff integrated my codes into

the generalized trust question, some responses based upon personal experience were:

I basically think people can't be trusted, the people that work for me. You have people you have to tell them on a day-to-day basis simple things, following rules.

and:

I would say that on the whole most people can be trusted. Trying to think of with whom I have entrusted duties. And how many times that has been broken, and how many times the promises have been kept. Ninety-five percent have kept their promises.

Comments that reflect general worldviews include:

Still an optimist about people and you try to trust people first.

and:

Well, you can't be too careful in dealing with people. The fact is that a lot of them are thinking of themselves and they are after one thing and one thing only and that's what is going to benefit themselves.

Others gave no meaningful response at all, mostly simply repeating the question.

Overall, 147 respondents "thought aloud" about trust, 117 about fairness, and 138 about helpfulness. Here we see big differences among the three misanthropy measures (see Table 3-6). Fifty-eight percent of respondents gave "general" responses to the trust question; only 22.5 percent referred to their experiences. In contrast, 29 percent gave general responses to helpfulness, while 45 percent mentioned specific examples where others helped them. The question on trust brings up general evaluations of society to many people, while issues of helpfulness bring up specific incidents such as:

[For the] most part people try to be helpful, thinking of people in general, thinking of people opening doors for you if your hands are full and at the grocery store, people will reach something for you if you can't reach it and just in general.

The fairness question is right in the middle, with 43.6 percent referring to general ideas, 34.2 percent to experience, and 22.2 percent to nothing

the regular ANES pilot data set, so that it is impossible to trace comments to specific individuals.

TABLE 3-6. *"Thinking Aloud" about Trust, Fairness, and Helpfulness*

Misanthropy Measure	% Response	% Response (Adjusted)
Trust	General: 57.8	General: 72.0
	No Content: 19.7	Experience: 28.0
	Experience: 22.5	
Fairness	General: 43.6	General: 56.0
	No Content: 22.2	Experience: 44.0
	Experience: 34.2	
Helpfulness	General: 29.0	General: 39.2
	No Content: 26.0	Experience: 60.8
	Experience: 44.9	

at all. When I exclude the middle category, the results are more powerful: 72 percent of people who could give a distinct reply to the trust question "thought aloud" in general terms, compared to 56 percent for fairness, and just 39 percent for helpfulness. People think about trust, helpfulness, and fairness in distinct ways. *They also think about trust largely in general, or moral, terms – and not primarily based upon their personal experiences.* And this pattern is ubiquitous. Mistrusters are only very slightly more likely to rely upon personal experiences (by 30 percent to 26 percent for trusters) – this difference is not statistically significant.[34]

THE ROAD AHEAD

I have a simple solution to the problem of question order on trust questions: Use multiple surveys to mitigate the risk of unwarranted inferences. Even if there were no questions about the GSS surveys (or any others), I would adopt this strategy. Different surveys tap different aspects of trust as well as its roots and consequences. A more common strategy is to develop a theme and test it on a single data base. But no single survey – or even a group of surveys – can help me answer the many questions I want to pose about trust.

[34] The ANES did not ask the generalized trust question to the same sample as it asked the "thinking aloud" question. Almost all of the "thinking aloud" sample answered the question in 1998, however. Given the stability across the panel (79 percent, see above), it seems reasonable to make this comparison. The correlations between the type of argument used and trust in 1998 are phi = −.047 and Yule's Q = −.106, eliminating the "no responses" (the tau-c and gamma with the "no responses" are −.055 and −.111).

So I make a virtue out of necessity. Each survey I examine tells a slightly different variant of the larger story I shall tell. But together they add up to a portrait of the trusting person as an optimist who believes that she can control her own fate, who lives in a benign world, who bases her trust on this worldview more than on life experiences, who values diversity and civil rights yet sees a country with a common culture, and who is willing to participate in civic life with people different from herself. I turn now to the roots of trust. Even values have their roots in people's predispositions and I set out to show in Chapter 4 what moves moralistic (generalized) and knowledge-based (particularized) trusters, armed with the measures developed in this chapter and the reassurance that the trust data are, indeed, trustworthy.

4

The Roots of Trust

Maybe [her optimism] came from "Pollyanna." Or maybe it came from having a mother who always seemed to have the time to sing for her. Or a father who always seemed to be singing.
– On the optimism of Carol Erhard of suburban Washington[1]

A television commercial for the brokerage house Smith Barney warns that "[w]e are not born with an instinct to trust. Trust must be earned." Performance may be the key to trusting a stockbroker, but it is *not* the answer to why we trust strangers more generally. We may not be born trusting, but our inclinations to place faith in others start very early in life. Erik Erikson (1963, 249) held that "the amount of trust derived from earliest infantile experience [depends] on the quality of the maternal relationship. Mothers create a sense of trust in their children."

Smith Barney and Erikson are not at odds. They are talking about different types of trust. Confidence in your stockbroker is strategic trust, which is based on experience. New evidence may lead to different conclusions on who is trustworthy and who is not, including which brokerage firm ranks highest. Erikson's faith in others is generalized trust, which does not change readily. We develop trusting instincts early in life. Generalized trust stems from an optimistic view of the world that

---

[1] As quoted in Finkel (1996, 27); see the more extended discussion of Carol Erhard below. *Pollyanna* was a novel written by Eleanor Hodgman Porter and published in 1913. Pollyanna was a young girl whose "glad game" of unbridled optimism always converted her mean adversaries into trusting characters, and thus she set right whatever was wrong with the world.

we initially learn from our parents. We are not likely to shift from trust to mistrust if we discover new information about any particular person, group, or even "most people." Our life histories do shape our generalized trust, but are *not* the central determinants of it. *Trust must be learned, not earned.* Generalized trust reflects our outlook on the world and is stable over time. Across two very turbulent decades (the 1960s and the 1970s), almost two-thirds of young people and more than 70 percent of their parents were consistent trusters or mistrusters (see Chapter 3). If Erikson is correct and we learn to trust early in life, then such stability is hardly surprising.

In this chapter, I shall present evidence that generalized trust *is* largely based on an optimistic view of the world, *rather than* objective life circumstances, and also that optimism and trust are *not* simply two names for the same idea. I shall also show that your trust depends upon how much your parents trusted others and, more generally, how nurturing your home environment was (cf. Renshon 1975). Attitudes toward your own group and toward outsiders are the core of particularized trust and they also shape generalized trust.

People who believe that *they* possess the truth and that other ideals are not only wrong, but dangerous, even heathen, will not trust strangers. So religious fundamentalists are likely to trust only their own kind. There is also some evidence that generalized trust is related to the breadth of one's social network. Yet we cannot simply engineer a more trusting universe by getting people involved in civic organizations. There is little evidence that group membership builds trust, though there is some support for the opposite linkage: Trusting people get involved in their communities (see also Chapter 5).

The roots of faith in others are set early in life. Yet parental influence is hardly the entire story. It is difficult to say how much of someone's trusting nature develops early in life, for the data are not good enough to make such claims. And trust *does* change over time. So the strongest claim that I can make is that adult faith in others is a mixture of values people learned as children and ideals they took up later in life.

The data analysis follows the theoretical underpinnings of trust. Alas, there is no single survey that will allow me to test my argument and to reject other theses as well. So I shall examine a variety of surveys and estimate five equations for generalized trust and two for particularized trust. The surveys I employ are the General Social Survey (and especially the 1987 sample); the 1972 and 1992 American National Election Studies (ANES); the 1996 Trust and Civic Participation Survey in metro-

politan Philadelphia by the Pew Center for the People and the Press; the
Niemi-Jennings socialization study of values held by high school students
and their parents in 1965 (with further waves in 1973 and 1982); the
1978 Quality of Life Survey from the Survey Research Center; and the
1971 Economic Incentives, Values, and Subjective Well-Being Pilot Study
conducted by the Survey Research Center in Baltimore and Detroit.

Each survey I shall analyze has its particular strengths – and weak-
nesses. The GSS Cumulative File from 1972 to 1998 provides the longest
continuous time series on generalized trust. But the GSS does not have
the best question on optimism – except in 1987, when there are also
good questions on other values I posit to affect trust (especially anti-
authoritarianism and personal efficacy). The 1992 ANES, the 1996 Pew
survey, and the Niemi-Jennings socialization study permit me to explore
the relationship between generalized and particularized trust. The 1992
ANES also permits me to explore antiauthoritarian and egalitarian values,
as well as social connections.

The Pew survey is weak on measures of optimism, but it provides
perhaps the best test of whether social networks and psychological con-
structs such as efficacy are connected to trust. It also has questions on
parents' experiences, but, alas, these are indirect measures dependent on
people's recall of their youth. The Niemi-Jennings socialization study is
the only one that lets us link young people's values with those of their
parents. Finally, the Well-Being Pilot Study is a hidden jewel that few
have exploited. Besides the generalized trust question, it has multiple
measures of optimism and a raft of indicators of economic well-being.
It provides an excellent test of my thesis that overall optimism shapes
trust far more than objective measures of economic success. And,
together with the 1972 ANES and the 1978 Quality of Life Survey,
it provides data to test the claim that trust and optimism are really the
same thing.

The data analysis to come is reminiscent of Ravel's *Bolero*. It is a constant drumbeat that may seem annoyingly repetitive. Yet the points get
clearer (if not louder) as I progress from one analysis to the next. Some
initial conclusions – that trust in government shapes trust in people and
that at least one type of organizational membership has significant effects
on generalized trust – look murkier as I progress. And others – the importance of optimism, the role of parental socialization, and the sharp
contrasts between generalized and particularized trust – come into sharp
relief as the data analysis reaches a climax.

Redundancy has its advantages: It helps us to see what is really important and what may just seem to be based upon a particular sample or
model specification (cf. Landau 1965, 44–5). But repetition can also be
maddening. So instead of concentrating on individual surveys, I focus on
groups of variables. The story of the chapter is *not* what drives trust in
any individual survey. To a considerable extent, this depends upon what
each survey organization asks. Rather, my focus is on the bigger picture:
which variables are consistently strong predictors of trust and which are
not. Three surveys do require some discussion in themselves: The 1971
Well-Being Pilot offers a clear test of whether objective or subjective
forces are most important for trust; the 1965 Niemi-Jennings high school
student sample provides insights into how trust is transmitted from
parent to children; and the 1996 Pew Philadelphia survey provides
a clear-cut comparison of generalized and particularized trust. Yet,
overall, there is no ideal poll that takes my fundamental ideas into
consideration. So I focus on the bigger picture – what matters *most* most
of the time.

My concern is the differences between generalized trusters, on the one
hand, and mistrusters and particularized trusters on the other. Each contrast is based on how people see the world, not on what their experiences have been. The Smith Barney commercial is all about strategic trust
and not at all about the other varieties of trust. Which stockbroker (or
house painter) is more trustworthy is an empirical question with no
moral content. There is likely to be some spillover from one type of trust
to the other: Cockeyed optimists may put too much faith in their stockbroker and strong pessimists may believe that the market and its agents
are all rigged against them. The converse is not likely to hold: A bad
experience with a single broker should not lead someone to believe that
all people, or even all stockbrokers, are malevolent. Someone who is
repeatedly cheated might become more pessimistic, but we don't know
how many setbacks are necessary to change a person's worldview. And
we are unlikely to find out, since no survey of which I am aware asks
people about repeated breaches of strategic trust.

TRUST AND OPTIMISM

Generalized trusters see the world as a benign place with limitless opportunities. They believe that most people share the same fundamental
values, though not necessarily the same ideology (Rosenberg 1956, 694),

and that people are not predisposed to take advantage of others. So it
makes sense to them that one give others the benefit of the doubt, and
trust people they don't know. Trusters believe that they can right wrongs
and leave the world a better place than they found it. And this "effective citizen" is an active participant in civic life.

Consider the prototypical truster Carol Erhard, who lives in a suburb
of Washington:

One of her favorite movies of all time is "Oklahoma!" – "because [she says] the
very first song he comes out singing is 'Oh, What a Beautiful Morning.'" . . . She
volunteers. She votes. She's a Cub Scout leader. She's a soccer coach. She has a
part-time job teaching tumbling to preschoolers. . . . She is aware of the evil that
people are capable of, and she knows the pettiness . . . but . . . her interpretation
tends to put everything in the best possible light.

And, of course, she is a member of the Optimist Club (Finkel 1996,
10–11).

Mistrusters, such as Banfield's (1958) Montegranans, have a diamet-
rically opposite view of the world. They see it as a mean and threatening place. For Montegranans, "the threat of calamity hangs over all" and
the only way people believe that they can preserve their family's security
is to pursue their "material, short-run advantage," rather than put any
faith in strangers (Banfield 1958, 110): "All those who stand outside of
the small circle of the family are at least potential competitors and therefore also potential enemies" (Banfield 1958, 110–11).

Mistrusters fear that others try to exploit them, to take away what
little they have. Their interests and values are at odds with those of
people outside their small circle. It is dangerous to cooperate with outsiders, who might take advantage of you the moment you let your guard
down. They are uncomfortable with strangers. Rosenberg (1956), who
was the pioneer in studying interpersonal trust, referred to mistrusters
as "misanthropes."

Optimists such as Carol Erhard feel compelled to get involved in their
communities and treat opportunities to get involved with strangers
as ways to expand their horizons. Pessimists withdraw into their own
communities. They see outsiders as malevolent. People who presume
that others are threatening may develop authoritarian attitudes (Adorno
et al. 1964). The only way to combat a corrupt society that puts
them on the bottom is an equally authoritarian world with them at
the top. Democratic and egalitarian values won't work, since they
cannot redress the imbalance between the powerful and the powerless.

Instead, we need a well-ordered society that promotes *our* values ahead of others' ideals.

Optimism is a multifaceted phenomenon. An upbeat outlook has four components. The first two are central: a view that the future will be better than the past and the belief that we can control our environment so as to *make it better*. The other elements of optimism are a sense of personal well-being and a supportive community.

Optimism leading to trust does not depend upon expectations for the short term. Optimists don't just expect tomorrow to be better than today. Each passing day should be better than the last. This may be bit a unrealistic, for things don't always go our way. Yet bad days should be exceptions. Similarly, when we shift our view to how well the society is doing, expecting an upturn in next year's economy is not sufficient to make people trusting. For there is an inevitable business cycle and what goes up will come down, and our trust may well prove to be unwarranted. If trust varies with perceptions of the near-term economy, then it will not be a stable value. Instead, it will fluctuate – perhaps sharply – over a short period of time. Optimism that undergirds generalized trust reflects a deeper sense that things are on the right track, and will continue to get better (cf. Rahn and Transue 1998).

Pessimists discount temporary upticks in the economy (and in other measures of the quality of life).[2] The optimist, Martin Seligman argues (1991, 4–5), "sees defeat [as] just a temporary setback, that its causes are confined to this one case." Carol Erhard the optimist always thinks that the glass is half-full and that a driving rain nevertheless provides nourishment for the soil (Finkel 1996, 10). Pessimists, according to Seligman (1991, 4, 44), "tend to believe bad events will last a long time [and] will undermine everything they do. . . . The bad events will persist, will always be there to affect their lives." A classic pessimist is the donkey Eeyore in the Pooh stories, who looks at the gloomy side of everything. Even a sunny day for pessimists is little more than the calm before the storm. When the ever cheerful Piglet wishes Eeyore "good morning," the donkey replies, "If it *is* a good morning . . . which I doubt. . . . Not that it matters" (Milne 1954, 84).

As important as expectations for the future are, a sense of control is no less critical. Optimists believe that tomorrow will be better than today because *they can make it better*. Optimists are masters of their own fate.

---

[2] These include issues such as war and peace, as well as other measures, such as a cleaner environment.

As Martin Seligman (1991, 5) notes: "Confronted by a bad situation, [optimists] perceive it as a challenge and try harder." Pessimists don't believe that they can control the world. They expect the worst and believe that it will last indefinitely. Banfield's Montegranans and some rural Albanians (Perlez 1998) share this fatalism.[3] Just as optimists believe that they have the power to change the world, pessimists see a dark future beyond their control. They may be tempted to blame sinister forces – the strangers in their midst – as the reason why their fate is so dire (Rosenberg 1956, 694; Banfield 1958, 111; Brehm and Rahn 1997, 1010). Pessimists who see no way out of their fate will be especially likely to see others through negative stereotypes and to believe conspiracy theories about others who might fare better than they do.[4] Though the odds of changing their fortune may be long, pessimists may still wish to strike out against the groups they see as "oppressors."

As we saw in Montegrano, pessimists are fearful of strangers and look inward to their own families. They long for an apocryphal time when things were better and people had more respect for folks like them. As they look inward, they express authoritarian views, refusing to believe that people may do good deeds without an ulterior motive. They seek to protect what little they have left – their families and especially their children – from the heathen ideas that dominate the larger society. Children need respect for parental authority and traditional values, lest they, too, get caught up in the same web of evil forces that have kept their families poor and with no hope for the future (Rosenberg 1956, 695; Adorno et al. 1964, 255). It is their only defense in a world that seems both hostile and beyond control.

Optimists, on the other hand, believe they *can* make a difference in the lives of other people. Others, even strangers, are well motivated and are willing to join in collective efforts. Such motivations are essential for social and political activists – people who want to elect candidates to office, and people who volunteer at homeless shelters (among others). The conviction that you can make a difference is inextricably linked to the idea that the world can be – and will be – a better place. Simply having the opportunity to change course appears to boost generalized

---

[3] On Albanians, see note 10 in Chapter 2.
[4] Martin Seligman (1991, 4, 49) offers a different account of pessimists. He sees them as lacking in self-esteem (see below) and thus blaming *themselves* when things go wrong.

trust. Trust in other people increases in most recent presidential election years, since elections present the possibility of a new direction for the country (see Chapter 6 and Rahn, Brehm, and Carlson 1997).

Pessimists become preoccupied with making do. They worry a lot about their financial security, even when they are doing well. So they place an extraordinary emphasis on material success (Rahn and Transue 1998). Optimists have less reason to think a lot about the way things can go wrong or to dispute the motives of others. They don't believe that people can succeed only by getting special favors.

AMERICAN OPTIMISM

While my theoretical claims are general, the two key components of optimism are particularly important parts of American culture. This is fitting since trust has also figured prominently in American culture. The United States is a nation of individualists without strong class divisions (Sombart 1976). Its immigrants represented many ethnic groups and religions. With such diversity, no group could establish hegemony. American society was thus marked by individualism, and remains so: Each person is of equal worth to every other, no group is to be favored over any other, and all are masters of their own fates (Hartz 1955). Individualism unchecked may lead people to look out for themselves and to abjure cooperation with others. But Americans temper their individualism by self-interest rightly understood, which Tocqueville argued, is a distinctly American ideal. Perhaps not, but it has been very important in American politics and society and it sounds very much like moralistic trust.[5]

As a nation, Americans have historically been optimists. Herbert Croly (1965, 3), the Progressive theorist, expressed the "American Dream" well:

Our country is . . . figured in the imagination of its citizens as the Land of Promise. [Americans] believe that somehow and sometime something better will happen to good Americans than has happened to men in any other country. . . . The future will have something better in store for them individually and collectively than has the past or the present.

[5] Note the origins of the type of self-interest rightly understood called "logrolling" (Safire 1993, 419) and the great body of work on universalism in legislatures summarized in Collie (1988). Riker and Brams (1973, 1235, note 1) note that "logrolling" was also employed in England, though most of their citations are American, as well.

Henry Steele Commager (1950, 5) argued, "Nothing in all history had succeeded like America, and every American knew it."

For most of our history the belief that tomorrow would be better than today has been paramount. In public opinion polls from the late 1930s to the 1960s, Americans believed that their children would have a better life than they did (Uslaner 1993, 76). This creed is essential to American culture; it was the promise that guided immigrants to come to a land where streets were paved with gold. David Potter (1954) called Americans a "people of plenty."

Control over our environment is also central to American values. The *Economist* (1987, 12) expressed this ideal well, and linked it to the more general belief that tomorrow will be better than today: "Optimism, not necessity, has always been the mother of invention in America. To every problem – whether racial bigotry or putting a man on the moon – there has always been a solution, if only ingenuity and money were committed to it." As the *Economist* argued, these two values are strongly linked. People are optimistic *in part* because they believe that they *can* make things better (Seligman 1991, 4–5). Pessimists see their lot as a sad one and don't believe that things will get better. They believe that the deck is stacked against them and that there is little they can do about it.

PERSONAL HAPPINESS AND A SUPPORTIVE ENVIRONMENT

The first two components of optimism are largely based upon our evaluation of life for the larger society, what Kinder and Kiewiet (1979) call "sociotropic" expectations. These perceptions are not strongly colored by how well we are doing personally.[6] Yet, we cannot divorce how people feel about themselves from how they relate to others. People who are happy in their personal lives are more likely to have a positive attitude toward strangers. Your personal mood will translate into a more generalized sense of optimism.

There is no consensus on why people translate positive attitudes about themselves to benevolent assumptions about the larger society. "Bottom-up" accounts make the linkage between objective factors in your personal life – satisfaction with your marriage, your job, your income, your health, and the like – to a positive view of the world.

---

[6] I am grateful to Richard Eckersley of the Australian National University for emphasizing this point.

"Top-down" theories maintain that people who are predisposed to think positively will say that their daily lives are going well (Feist et al. 1995, 139–41).

The bottom-up approach emphasizes objective factors – "encapsulated experiences" – in one's life. Hart (1988, 187), Silver (1989, 275), and Adam Seligman (1997, 52) argue that the close ties we develop in friendship relations serve as models for reaching out to trust strangers. People who have prospered in their personal lives – financially, in their personal relationships, and in their social circles – will feel better about themselves and will have a more positive outlook on life (Rosenberg 1956, 694; Bradburn with Noll 1969, 130, 144, 174–7; Campbell 1981, 217–18; Diener 1984; Feist et al. 1985, 146).

Clearly in some circumstances personal experiences can have a big effect on generalized trust. People who worry about crime in their neighborhoods, and especially those who worry about their personal safety, are less likely to trust strangers (Brehm and Rahn 1997, 1009, 1016). And groups that have long faced discrimination, such as blacks in the United States, are less trusting than people who have better objective reasons to be optimistic about the future (see below). But the bottom-up approach is the basis of strategic trust, not moralistic trust.

More important for moralistic and generalized trust is the top-down approach, in which personal life histories are not as important as early socialization (Diener 1984, 556; Feist et al. 1995, 139; Brehm and Rahn 1997, 1009–10). People who feel good about themselves should feel good about others.

Finally, optimism and trust are contagious. Just as having to cope with daily struggles in Banfield's Montegrano or today's Bosnia or Albania can destroy optimism and trust, so living in a more friendly environment can build optimism and trust. The environment can shape trust in four ways. First, living in a trusting area makes you more likely to trust as well. Second, trusting government may lead to faith in other people.

If most people who live around you trust others, you are likely to be trusting, as well. This is the "Lake Wobegon" effect – where all of the people in a trusting community are above (the national) average (in trust).[7] Putnam (1993, 111; 2000) argues that this contagion

---

[7] Lake Wobegon is the fictional home-town of host Garrison Keillor in the American radio program, "A Prairie Home Companion." In Lake Wobegon, "all of the children are above average."

effect reflects your life experiences: We decide whether to trust others by determining whether the people we come into contact with are *trustworthy*.

Do we base our decisions to trust on personal knowledge? Offe (1997, 22) argues: "Chances are that exclusive reliance on the old-fashioned mechanism of generating trust on the basis of personal familiarity is hopelessly insufficient, as it makes us forgo, in the absence of alternative trust-generating mechanisms, many opportunities for mutual cooperation." Granovetter (1973, 1374) argues that our "strong" (or "thick") ties with our families and close friends can't build generalized trust; only "weak" ties with strangers can accomplish that.

A top-down approach to contextual effects holds that trusting others is not simply a strategic response to others' dispositions. Instead, the upbeat message that one hears in a trusting community crowds out the cries of pessimists. An Ebenezer Scrooge will find it difficult to remain a misanthrope in a world of Bob Cratchitts; all but Mother Teresa may lose their trusting instinct if they move to Montegrano (Stolle 1999b). Models from evolutionary game theory (see especially Bendor and Swistak 1997) demonstrate that when a majority of people in society trust others, they will eventually crowd out all but a handful of mistrusters (and vice versa). And this is not simply a strategic response by mistrusters, who might, after all, fare better trying to exploit the "gullible" trusters. Instead, the minority, through persuasion or social pressures, adopts the values of the majority.

THE OTHER FOUNDATIONS OF TRUST

Two other values play a central role in shaping trust: egalitarianism and religious beliefs. Egalitarianism has multiple meanings. Two of the more important are social and economic egalitarianism. Social egalitarianism stresses equal treatment of all people. Everyone is entitled to the same basic respect. When people see each other as social equals, they feel at ease with each other and are more likely to trust strangers and to form the social bonds that promote cooperative endeavors (Bryce 1916, 813, 875–6). Economic egalitarianism is an equally important value: If you believe that you are superior to others, you will feel no need to trust them (see Chapter 2). If you believe that economic stratification is justifiable, then you have no need to trust those below you on the economic ladder. Later I shall provide strong support for the argument that trust has fallen in the United States as economic inequality has increased (see

Chapter 6) and that trust is higher in egalitarian societies (see Chapter 8). Here I focus on egalitarian values.

Religion is the other value that shapes interpersonal trust. Religion has an uneasy relationship to trust. On the one hand, faith in people and faith in a supreme being both promote civic engagement. People with faith participate more in civic affairs, especially in the more demanding activities such as volunteering their time (Hodgkinson, Weitzman, and Kirsch 1990, 203; Wuthnow 1991; Verba, Schlozman, and Brady 1995; Uslaner 1998b). Faith leads people to put less emphasis on materialistic values and more on how to help others (Rokeach 1973, 128; Harris 1994). Religious traditions exhort followers to give of themselves, especially to the needy (Cnaan, Kasternakis, and Wineburg 1993, 37): Jesus fed the poor and hungry, priests and nuns take vows of poverty and work in missions in poor countries, and much of organized Jewish life revolves around raising funds to aid those who have less. Almost half of volunteering in the United States occurs through religious organizations. And Americans join more voluntary organizations than people in other Western countries because they are more active in *religious* groups (Greeley 1997, 590).

Tocqueville (1945, 126) sees religious faith as the foundation for "self-interest rightly understood," his version of what I call generalized trust. The twelfth-century Jewish sage Moses ben Maimonides (1979, 89–93) established a hierarchy of charitable acts that links trust in strangers with religious values. Near the top is giving anonymously to someone who is nameless to you, and who thus may not be like you.[8] And churches and synagogues played important roles in the civil rights movements of the 1950s and 1960s that built bridges across the races. People of faith also tend to be optimists (Sheehan and Kroll 1990; Larson, Milano, and Barry 1996), and optimism should (and does) lead to increased generalized trust.

Yet religious values may lead people to insulate themselves from strangers – and disbelievers. Putnam (1993, 107) sees religion as an alternative to social trust, rather than as part of its foundation. People may identify so strongly with their faith that they become suspicious of others. Religious fundamentalists will regard people outside of their own circle as heathens. Fundamentalists believe that the Bible is the literal word of God and hold that a key tenet of the Scriptures is that humans are born

---

[8] At the very top is providing work for a poor person – perhaps going into business with this person. I am indebted to Richard F. Winters for the quote and for the source.

with original sin. This view of human nature stands at odds with the optimism that underlies trust in others (Schoenfeld 1978, 61; cf. Smith 1997, 189). Fundamentalists may withdraw from contact with unredeemed "sinners" and retreat into their own communities. Throughout American history, they have been active in "nativist" organizations that sought to restrict immigration and immigrants' rights. More recently, they have led the fight to bring religious practices and instruction back to public schools and to fight the teaching of evolution in the science curriculum. They fear that people who don't believe as they do are trying to deny them their fundamental rights. When they participate in civic life, they restrict their activities to their own faith's organizations (Uslaner 1999c; Wuthnow 1999).

Members of liberal – or mainline – Protestant denominations are more likely to be generalized trusters than are fundamentalists (Schoenfeld 1978, 64).[9] Membership in mainline denominations has declined over the past several decades and there has been a big surge in the number of fundamentalists (Mayer 1992, 34–5). Religiosity may have promoted trust in strangers in the past, but now it may be linked to a darker view of people of different faiths.

Some faiths – notably the Catholic Church – are marked by hierarchical authority structures. This is the principal reason why Putnam (1993, 107) sees religion (at least in Italy) as an alternative to social trust. Hierarchy is incompatible with trust, and especially with each person's sense of control of her environment. Thus Putnam's argument suggests that Catholics, as well as fundamentalist Protestants, should display less generalized trust – and more particularized trust – than mainline Protestants.

Trust may also depend upon both personal experiences with others – group membership and informal socializing – and confidence in government (see the discussion in Chapter 2). I include measures of group membership, informal socializing, and trust in government in the models examined in this chapter whenever they are available; however, the issues involved in both experience with other people (formally and informally) and trust in government are too important to discuss so briefly. So I shall postpone fuller discussions of these issues until the next chapter.

[9] Schoenfeld's fundamentalist group is Baptists, his mainline denominations are Episcopalians, Presbyterians, Congregationalists, and Unitarians.

THE DEMOGRAPHY OF TRUST

Demographic variables have been strong predictors of trust in previous research, though the comparisons are not always straightforward since many studies don't focus directly on trust. Instead, the dependent variable is often Rosenberg's "misanthropy" scale that includes the questions of people's fairness and helpfulness (see Chapter 3). Nevertheless, the logic (and results) for these variables ought to be similar.

If trust reflects life experience, then we might expect that traumatic events would make people less trusting. Yet there is scant evidence that this is the case. Unhappiness at home does not make you less trusting. People who have been divorced, are currently divorced, or whose parents were divorced are no less likely to be trusting than people who are married or whose parents stayed together (Brehm and Rahn 1997, 1012–13; Smith 1997, 189; Stolle 1998b). And this does not hide a reluctance of unhappy couples to get divorced. While there is, in the full GSS time series, a moderate correlation between satisfaction with family life and trust (gamma = .168), this relationship vanishes in multivariate analyses. And people with happy marriages are only slightly more likely to trust others (gamma = .111) – a relationship that also vanishes in more complex analyses. Brehm and Rahn (1997, 1016) report that being burglarized makes people less trusting (cf. Smith 1997, 189). But personal victimization also dropped out of my multivariate analyses. Perceptions of personal safety in your home and neighborhood do, however, remain significant predictors of trust in strangers.

Putnam (2000, 140–1) argues that trust is greater in small towns than in big cities and that's because we can get to know people better in smaller towns than in the metropolis, where everyone is anonymous and people don't know each other's names. But Putnam's claim overstates the sociability of city life. Yes, residents of big cities are less trusting than folks from small towns: In the 1972–96 GSS sample, 43 percent of people living in towns under 10,000 trust others, compared to just 37 percent living in cities with a million or more people ($p < .0001$). But this simply reflects the different composition of cities and smaller towns. More African-Americans live in cities and they are far less trusting than whites. When we look at only whites, there is a slight advantage to big cities: 45.2 percent compared to 44.7 percent for the smallest towns. And there is very little difference for size categories in between. The correlation between trust and city size is –.026 for whites and –.051 for all respondents.

Perhaps your immediate experiences are less important in this regard than are earlier ones. Your values may not reflect where you live, but *where you grew up*. Well, yes – but not as we might expect. If you want to breed a trusting generation, move to suburbs of the biggest cities (according to the 1992 ANES): In these highly educated boroughs, 54 percent of the people are trusters, compared to 44 percent who were brought up elsewhere. The least trusting souls come from our heralded small towns (39 percent) and farms (41 percent).[10]

We picture small towns as Mayberry, from the television series "The Andy Griffith Show," which played in the United States in the 1960s and 1970s. In Mayberry, the sheriff is everyone's friend and Aunt Bea looks after the whole town. Instead, they are pockets of particularized trust where people look askance at strangers. People who grew up in the country and on the farm are significantly more likely to be particularized trusters, in direct contrast to folks who grew up in the big city, who are more tolerant of people unlike themselves. Mayberry often *seemed* more trusting than it actually was: In one episode, a city slicker looking for a more friendly environment moved to Mayberry and nobody trusted him.[11] Life in the big city doesn't make you wary of other people, perhaps because there are so many strangers around. The weak bivariate relationships are no more powerful in multivariate tests, so I don't include these measures in the estimations to come.

Putnam (1995a) argues that interpersonal trust is strongly stratified by socioeconomic status (cf. Patterson 1999). Higher-status people, who have higher incomes and more education, can afford to be more trusting (cf. Smith 1997, 189). If they "bet" that others are trustworthy and they are proven wrong, they can absorb the losses better than people with fewer resources. Education is a strong predictor – in many cases, the *most important* determinant – of interpersonal trust. And the effects of education are not simply linear. College education brings a whole lot more trust than high school education, which in turn is much

---

[10] Putnam (2000, 138) disagrees, as I note in Chapter 2 (note 1). Perhaps some of the root of disagreement stems from his reliance on the DDB Needham Life Style surveys, which do not have a question on trust, but instead have a question on honesty, which is not the same as trust (see Chapter 3).

[11] I owe this example (and others, including an episode where a man came to town to record local folk music, but Sheriff Andy Griffith thought he was a con man) to Jeffrey Mondak.

more important than elementary school (Putnam 1995a). But income is not significant in *any* of the estimations for either generalized or particularized trust I report below. This suggests that education is more than a simple measure of class or status.

There is one clear instance where status matters. As noted in Chapter 2, blacks are far less trusting than whites. Race is consistently one of the most powerful determinants of both generalized and particularized trust. Black mistrust does not decline sharply with individual success. Income is no more critical for black trust than white trust. And education boosts trust primarily for whites. Race is *the* life experience that has the biggest impact on trust. And, as we shall see, not only blacks, but also Asians (at least in some surveys), are less trusting than whites.

The other major demographic variable affecting trust is age. Putnam (1995a; 1996; 2000, 140–1) argues that the generations of the 1920s and 1930s trusted others and succeeding generations have had increasingly less faith in strangers. The generations that came of age watching television – the Early and Late Baby Boomers – were less trusting than their elders, but more trusting than people born in the 1960s and the 1970s (see also Brehm and Rahn 1997; Smith 1997, 189). Since the late 1980s, trust has not declined quite so sharply with age. The Early Baby Boomers rose from being the least trusting to the most trusting. Even though trust does not decline linearly with age, a simple monotonic specification performs quite well because the drop is sharpest for the youngest cohorts.

While young people trust others less than the elderly (and a lot less than the middle aged Early Boomers), television is *not* the culprit in their misanthropy. I have exonerated television elsewhere (Uslaner 1998b). And the argument is too lengthy to lay out here in any depth. The brief story is that watching television doesn't make you think that the world is mean and violent. Instead, people seem to be able to distinguish between the "television world" and the "real world" (cf. Gerbner et al. 1980). Once I bring optimism for the future into the statistical models, the effects of watching television on trust (as well as on civic engagement) vanish, regardless of what you watch (cf. Uslaner 1998b).

Having fought the battle of television before, I have no desire to reenact it here. And television questions are asked only sporadically and sometimes of only partial samples, so that I lose a lot of leverage when television effects come into play. So I declare victory and withdraw (as Senator George Aiken suggested the United States do in Vietnam some three decades ago). There is another relevant media variable that I shall

include in some models: newspaper readership. Putnam (1996) finds a
strong *positive* relationship between trust and newspaper readership.
I don't think that reading newspapers can *build* trust in strangers (but
see Brehm and Rahn 1997, 1009). It may well be a vital sign of people
interested in their community and their world. If you want just a quick
summary of your world, you can find it on television news. If you want
to learn more about things going on not only in your own community,
but also in the wider world – in short, about strangers – you need to
read newspapers.

TRUST, SOCIAL NETWORKS, AND PARENTING

When and how do we learn to trust? The strategic view of trust would
say that we continue to make decisions about whom to trust – indeed,
whether to trust – throughout our lives. Trust reflects our experiences.
To be sure, our experiences reflect a life history, not just what happened
yesterday. So we develop predispositions based on our experiences
(Hardin 1992, 155). But they *can* change and we *can* learn to trust. For
Tocqueville and his followers, including Putnam, trust develops through
social interaction. Strategic trust *must be learned*. Without information
about others, we have no basis for trusting them. I shall elaborate on the
linkage between trust and social networks in Chapter 5 and offer a
detailed critique. I shall also consider in great detail the causal linkage
between trust and civic engagement: Does either cause the other or is
there a reciprocal relationship? And I shall also examine whether there
is any relationship between social networks and trust. But, for now, it is
sufficient to determine whether indicators of civic engagement and social
networks can predict interpersonal trust.

The roots of generalized trust may set in well before people join voluntary organizations. Values, including trust, are largely learned from
our families early in life (Erikson 1963, 249; cf. Newton 1997, 579).
Wuthnow (1997, 16) reports that few of the people with whom he conducted in-depth interviews reported that "trust had been influenced by
participating in civic groups as an adult. Instead, they described their
attitude as something they had always had, as a character trait they had
learned as a child."

Nurturing parents make children feel good about themselves and this
"minimize(s) self-concern about interaction with other people" (Staub
1979, 111). The children of stern or inattentive parents are wary of
strangers. Not only do parents teach their children values. Children also

learn by example: Parents who are trusting, tolerant, and involved in their communities are role models leading children to trust.

There is sparse evidence linking trust across generations. Aside from the Niemi-Jennings panel, the only other investigation is Renshon's (1975) small sample of college students and their parents in the early 1970s. Renshon (1975, 76) found that parental trust was the strongest determinant of their children's faith in others. This is reassuring: Martin Seligman (1991, 127) argues that "explanatory style" – whether you are an optimist or a pessimist – "sets in early. We see it in quite crystallized form in children as young as eight." Happy adults usually had affectionate parents (Koestner, Franz, and Weinberger 1990, 713; Popenoe 1994, 99). Parenting style early in life – even for five-year-olds – translates into adult attitudes through at least early middle age. Warm and affectionate parenting styles lead to children who feel good about themselves and who are more sympathetic to others, generous, and kind (Koestner et al. 1990, 711–12; Parcel and Menaghan 1993; Smith 1999b). And children whose parents spent a lot of time with them, encouraged them to think for themselves, and generally created a nurturing environment were more likely to take active roles in their communities, while young and later as adults. They would volunteer their time to help the poor and they took leadership roles in the civil rights movement. Others see them as friendly and cooperative (Rosenhan 1969; Hoffman 1975, 608; Staub 1979, 101–9).

In the analyses to come, I test these alternative accounts. I shall show that the linkages between civic engagement and trust are weak and that parental influences are important determinants of generalized trust. Unfortunately, there are not many measures of parental influence: hardly enough to establish that trust is largely learned at home. And the only good data source on parental values comes from the problematic Niemi-Jennings child-parent panel, with its exceptionally high levels of interpersonal trust for both cohorts across all three waves. Nevertheless, I shall find more support for an account based on socialization than on contemporaneous experience.

The models I shall estimate, for both generalized and particularized trust, will thus focus on how your worldview shapes your values. I expect to find the strongest effects for measures of optimism – expectations for the future, a sense of control, antiauthoritarianism, personal happiness, and the level of trust in a person's environment. Egalitarian and religious values should also be important in shaping trust, as should some demographics (especially age, education, and race). I also expect to find powerful effects for parental socialization, when they are available. I *do not* expect strong findings for most variables that tap experiences – income, wealth, and other measures of objective well-being. Your personal life history – a happy or unhappy marriage, a divorce, and the like – should have no effect on either type of trust. Diener, Suh, and Oishi (1997) also report that their general measure of social well-being, which is a composite index of optimism and self-esteem, is not shaped either by one's income or changes in income. Nor does trust depend upon membership in voluntary associations, or even more demanding forms of civic engagement, such as volunteering time or giving to charity. Instead, the causal arrow goes from trust to civic participation, as I shall show when I estimate simultaneous equation models in Chapter 5.

I expect that the factors that promote generalized trust will lead to less *particularized* trust. Particularized trusters will be pessimists who believe that the deck is stacked against them, that they have no control over their environment, and may be unhappy in their personal lives – may even express authoritarian and antiegalitarian values. They may also feel socially isolated: not talking to their neighbors and not having social support networks. Particularized trusters are especially likely to be religious fundamentalists and say that religion is an important component of their lives. And they are likely to say that their parents warned them not to trust strangers (cf. Stolle 1998a, 1998b). Particularized trusters are likely to have less education and be younger as well as members of minority groups, who may have good reasons for trusting only their own kind.

Finally, there should be a linkage between generalized and particularized trust. Generalized trusters should be more supportive of outgroups and less biased toward their own in-group. Where this is possible, I shall test the relationship between these two components of particularized trust and the standard generalized trust question.

IS TRUST SIMPLY OPTIMISM?

Using optimism to predict trust may be, some critics have suggested, like using Fahrenheit temperature readings to predict how warm it is in Celsius. Optimism and trust are simply two terms for the same phenomenon. So, if I find (and I do) that optimism is the strongest determinant of generalized trust, I haven't really discovered anything interesting. So before I can begin estimating models of generalized and particularized trust, I must tackle the question of disentangling trust and optimism.

Optimism and trust are strongly related, but they are not the same thing. It makes little sense to trust others if you are a pessimist (though there are always some people who fit this category). But you *may* be an optimistic mistruster, believing that tomorrow might be better than today for *you* because you control your own fate. Even though you may not trust others to engage in cooperative behavior, you still may be an optimist. And, across several surveys, there is evidence that: (1) there are considerable numbers of optimistic mistrusters (but relatively few pessimistic trusters); and (2) optimistic mistrusters believe, as do optimistic trusters, that they control their own fate. If the two concepts were simply measuring the same underlying concept, we shouldn't see mistrusters who believe that they are masters of their own future. While optimism and trust are not the same thing, a positive worldview lays the foundation for trust.

I found support for this perspective in three separate surveys: the 1978 Quality of Life Survey, the 1972 ANES, and the 1971 Well-Being Pilot Study. In each study I created a combined measure of optimism and trust by cross-tabulating interpersonal trust with a dichotomous measure of expectations for the longer-term future (at least five years in the future). For each survey pessimistic trusters were by far the smallest category among the four-fold classification. For most measures, optimistic trusters ranked highest in both efficacy and the belief that they could control their own destiny. Pessimistic mistrusters ranked lowest. In between, pessimistic trusters are generally more self-confident than optimistic mistrusters. If trust and optimism were the same thing, we should not see such a clear, and generally monotonic, relationship. If there were but a single middle category – not quite so optimistic, not quite so trusting – then pessimistic trusters and optimistic mistrusters should respond similarly.

I present the results of this experiment in Table 4-1. In each survey, there were fewer – generally far fewer – pessimistic trusters than any other type. In the 1978 Quality of Life Survey, there were more than 2.5 times as many optimistic as pessimistic trusters. In the 1972 ANES, there were more than twice as many; only in the 1971 Well-Being Pilot Study were the differences not quite so stark.[12] In all three studies, across many

[12] The ratio for this study is 1.3 to 1.

TABLE 4-1. *Trust and Optimism*

	Optimistic Trusters	Pessimistic Trusters	Optimistic Mistrusters	Pessimistic Mistrusters
1978 Quality of Life Survey				
Percent of Respondents	34.6	13.2	29.7	22.5
Plans Work Out as Expected	62.1	58.7	51.6	41.4
Can Run Life as Wished	92.2	88.3	83.2	74.6
Felt on Top of World	52.7	40.0	40.5	31.7
Felt Proud of Doing Something	84.4	74.9	79.6	69.6
1972 American National Election Study				
Percent of Respondents	33.6	15.2	28.5	22.8
Plans Usually Realized	64.7	53.2	46.2	34.4
Can Run Own Life	89.7	83.9	66.8	56.9
Felt on Top of World	40.8	38.1	29.1	19.8
Proud of Recent Accomplishment	79.7	69.4	69.2	60.4
Fate Determines Outcomes	24.0	36.1	42.4	47.7
Hard Work Key to Success	71.8	71.5	64.0	55.2
Average Citizen Runs Govt.	67.8	45.8	43.5	30.7
Mean: Demographic In-group	1.843	−.787	5.355	6.451
Mean: Demographic Out-group	−.420	−3.290	−3.490	−5.443
1971 Well-Being Pilot Study				
Percent of Respondents	26.6	20.1	28.0	25.2
Family Has Enough for Comfort	55.0	49.1	38.2	27.8
Can Control Own Fate	85.4	74.6	74.4	70.8
Parents Poor[a]	2.974	2.867	2.774	2.705
Must Have Right Connections[a]	3.331	3.017	3.051	2.886

[a] Based on five-point scale with lower scores indicating agreement with statement.

measures of efficacy and control, optimists showed more self-confidence than pessimists, regardless of whether people trust others or not.

Across all three surveys, optimistic trusters are the most likely to believe that their plans will work out as expected; that they can run their lives as they wish; that they are on top of the world; are proud of doing something; that their family is comfortable; that they can control their own fate; that hard work is the key to success; that they can accomplish what they want without needing the "right" connections; and that the average citizen rather than elites runs the government. In each case, pessimistic mistrusters rank lowest. For most measures, pessimistic trusters fall behind optimistic trusters, but ahead of optimistic mistrusters. Optimistic trusters also rate (in the 1972 ANES) out-groups more positively than anyone else; pessimistic mistrusters are the most negative toward out-groups, with the two other groups in the middle. In-group ratings don't fit the pattern so nicely: Optimistic trusters are actually more biased toward their own kind than pessimistic trusters, though not as much as either type of mistruster.

This quasi-experiment demonstrates that trust and optimism are not simply different names for the same phenomenon. In every case, optimistic mistrusters believe that they have more control over their environment than pessimistic mistrusters, but less than optimistic trusters. So there is no redundancy in including measures of optimism in the models of trust. Yet this does not resolve the question of *how* optimism is related to trust. Other critics suggest that trust and optimism may not be the same thing – that I have the causal ordering wrong.[13] Optimism doesn't lead to trust; trust produces optimism. This is also a point worth considering. I shall estimate a simultaneous equation model of trust, optimism, and civic engagement. I allow optimism to shape trust and trust to determine optimism. Both affect the other, but, reassuringly, the impact of optimism on trust is almost twice as great as that of trust on optimism.

Where, then, does optimism come from? This is largely beyond the scope of the present study, although I do estimate a simultaneous equation model including the best measure of optimism in the GSS in Chapter 5: whether the lot of the average person is getting worse. This model (using the 1972–96 GSS) suggests that satisfaction with your personal life translates into a more general sense of optimism. People who find their personal life exciting, who say that their financial situation is better than that of other people, and who are satisfied with their work are much more likely to *disagree* that "the lot of the average person is getting worse." Fundamentalists are more pessimistic, as are younger people.

People who trust others *are* more optimistic. Does trust shape optimism more than optimism shapes trust? The effect of optimism on trust is *twice as large* as the effect of trust on optimism (see Table 5-2 in Chapter 5). It is also likely that other measures of optimism and control might reflect personal experiences, so there might be an indirect route from life histories to generalized trust. In Chapter 6 I show that aggregate levels of trust in the United States have declined as Americans have

---

[13] The first group of critics include my colleague Karol Soltan, as well as Dennis Chong and Robert Putnam. Putnam is the only, but very important, member of the second group.

become more pessimistic about the future, and that both lower trust and increased pessimism stem from rising income inequality in the United States.

WHAT SHAPES GENERALIZED TRUST?

I estimate a series of models for generalized trust to show how different measures of optimism lead people to trust strangers and to demonstrate that life histories play a minor role in determining faith in people. I present four models using the standard trust questions from different surveys, selecting each poll because of the range of predictors it includes. Then I estimate a model for the stranger factor from the 1996 Pew Philadelphia survey to show once more that trust in strangers *is* trust in people, and to set the stage for models of particularized trust from the ANES and the Niemi-Jennings socialization study.

I estimate the models in this chapter by two techniques: probit analysis for the standard dichotomous measure of generalized trust and ordinary least squares regression analysis for the factor scores from the Pew Philadelphia survey and for the interval measure of particularized trust from the 1992 ANES.[14] Unlike regression coefficients, probit coefficients have no ready interpretation. So instead, I employ what Rosenstone and Hansen (1993) call the "effect" of an independent variable, the difference in estimated probabilities from the predictor's highest and lowest values, letting the other independent variables take their "natural" values.

In many of the models, what you don't see may be as telling as what you do. I mostly want to concentrate on different measures of optimism and belief in control. For each model, I tested for the effects of various measures of life experience, including income, marital status, home ownership, gender, whether the respondent was a victim of a crime, and how often people socialize with friends. Most of the time these life experiences were not significant. Sometimes they had confounding effects on other variables and sometimes there were a lot of missing values on these variables. So I made a decision to delete these variables from the models unless they had confounding effects, so that I could show that they were insignificant. The models I estimate are already complex enough, with more than enough variables to capture our attention. Often trust in

---

[14] Where there was evidence of heteroskedasticity, I employed White-corrected (robust) standard errors for both the probits and the regressions.

TABLE 4-2. *Probit Analysis of Trust in People from 1987 General Social Survey*

Independent Variable	Coefficient	Standard Error	MLE/SE	Effect[a]
Contextual Trust	1.242**	.507	2.452	.189
Life Better for Next Generation	.138***	.050	2.757	.175
Officials Don't Care for Average Person	−.352****	.098	−3.580	.225
Confidence in Science	.203***	.077	2.650	.131
Satisfied with Friendships	.086**	.037	2.321	.163
Must Know Right People/Success	−.150***	.054	2.796	−.194
Pay Differences Needed for Incentive	−.097**	.055	1.764	−.072
People Earn Degrees for More Pay	−.074**	.041	1.831	−.094
Fundamentalist (Active in Church)	−.081***	.031	−2.656	−.159
Active in Professional Societies	.142**	.072	1.962	.092
Afraid to Walk at Night in Neighborhood	−.216**	.091	−2.380	−.069
Mother's Education	.027**	.015	1.806	.103
College Education	.012**	.006	1.834	.023
Age	.017****	.003	5.410	.309
Black	−.583****	.115	−5.086	−.191
Constant	−2.398****	.436	−5.495	

Estimated $R^2 = .351$ −2*Log Likelihood Ratio = 1132.704 $N = 1006$.
Percent Predicted Correctly: Probit: 70.5 Null: 54.1.
**** $p < .0001$ *** $p < .01$ ** $p < .05$.
[a] Effect calculated at maximum value of 75 for age and at minimum value of eight years for mother's education.

government also proved insignificant, and I dropped it as well. Other demographic variables were usually significant – race, education, and age are particularly important. They stayed in. In the model using the 1971 Well-Being Pilot, I include lots of insignificant variables, precisely to show how measures of optimism shape trust and more objective measures don't. I present the results of the probits from the 1987 GSS, the 1972 ANES, the Well-Being Pilot, and the 1965 high school sample of the Niemi-Jennings panel in Tables 4-2, 4-3, 4-4, and 4-5. The estimations for generalized and particularized trust from the Pew Philadelphia survey are in Table 4-6 and those for particularized trust from the 1992 ANES are in Table 4-7. The model for particularized trust from the 1965 Niemi-Jennings youth sample is presented in Table 4-8.

TABLE 4-3. *Probit Analysis of Trust from 1992 American National Election Study*[a]

Independent Variable	Coefficient	Standard Error	MLE/SE	Effect
In-group Trust	−.007***	.002	−3.286	−.273
Out-group Trust	.001	.003	.260	.025
Trust in Government	.110****	.030	3.644	.218
Standard Living Better in 20 Years	.077****	.019	4.170	.104
Prefer Kids Be Curious/Manners	.087****	.020	4.400	.118
Prefer Kids Considerate/Behaved	.082****	.020	4.046	.110
Better Worry Less about Equality	−.038*	.025	−1.519	−.051
No Say in Politics	−.055**	.025	−2.228	−.074
Number of Neighbors X Talks to	.065***	.019	3.379	.110
How Often Read Newspaper	.030**	.012	2.607	.072
Own Home	.169**	.077	2.180	.056
Age	.008****	.002	3.527	.144
High School Education	.053****	.014	3.776	.191
College Education	.062****	.011	5.585	.354
Black	−.554****	.118	−4.695	−.182
Constant	−.583*	.280	−2.085	

Estimated $R^2 = .305$ −2*Log Likelihood Ratio = 2019.082 N = 1728.
Percent Predicted Correctly: Probit: 70.0 Null: 54.5.
**** $p < .0001$ *** $p < .01$ ** $p < .05$ * $p < .10$.
[a] Effect calculated at maximum value of 75 for age.

There are powerful effects for measures of optimism, control, and antiauthoritarianism. First, on optimism: If you believe that life will be better for the next generation than for your own, you are 18 percent more likely to trust other people (1987 GSS). The effect for expecting the standard of living to be better in 20 years in the 1992 ANES is slightly less (.104). And people who think about the future (as opposed to worrying about the present) are 9 percent more trusting (1971 Well-Being). High school students who believe that their lives will be as they wish are 13 percent more likely to be generalized trusters and much less likely to be particularized trusters (Niemi-Jennings). *Overall, optimists are about 12 percent more likely to trust others than are pessimists.*

There are more measures of control than generalized measures of optimism; hence, their effects are more varied. One of the strongest is confidence in science, asked in the GSS. This is not a simple measure of expectations for the future. But it reflects an American ideal that is strongly connected to our national sense of optimism. Americans have long worshiped practical science. American ingenuity will help solve our

TABLE 4-4. *Probit Analysis of Trust from 1971 Well-Being Pilot Study*[a]

Independent Variable	Coefficient	Standard Error	MLE/SE	Effect
Think about Future	.069**	.038	1.821	.090
Wants Fulfilling Job	.141***	.049	2.878	.233
Luck Works against You	−.170***	.064	−2.653	−.211
Must Have Right Connections	−.060*	.039	−1.551	−.077
Poor Have Less Chance to Get Ahead	−.059*	.038	−1.521	−.076
Family Has Enough For Comfort	.060*	.039	1.534	.079
Satisfied with Financial Status	−.005	.047	−.111	−.010
Spend Now vs. Save for Future	−.099***	.037	−2.629	−.128
Ever Worry about Losing Job	−.003	.047	−.068	−.004
Family Income	−.000	.000	−.235	−.024
Own vs. Rent Home	−.095	.174	−.544	−.031
Have Savings or Reserves/Stocks	.105**	.060	1.753	.134
Have Pension Plan	.005	.049	.101	−.008
Unemployed during 1970	−.135	.207	−.651	−.040
Parents Ever Poor	−.115	.119	−.963	−.074
Making Regular Payments Debt	−.001	.039	−.026	−.001
Black	−.257	.245	−1.048	−.083
Education	.150***	.047	3.194	.386
Age	.042***	.014	2.975	.470
Constant	−2.130	.950	−2.242	

Estimated R^2 = .352 −2*Log Likelihood Ratio = 417.298 N = 368.
Percent Predicted Correctly: Probit: 67.1 Null: 53.5.
*** $p < .01$ ** $p < .05$ * $p < .10$.
[a] Effect calculated at maximum value of 56 for age, between 2 and 4 for parents poor, and between $6,000 and $22,000 for family income.

problems. Americans have long been tinkerers, amateur scientists, and we have worshiped technological advances that will expand our control over our destinies (Wright 1957, 226; Lafollette 1990, 127; Uslaner 1993, 71–2). Confidence in science, then, reflects the optimistic belief that we can solve our problems if we only try hard enough. And people who have confidence in science are 13 percent more likely to be trusters (1987 GSS).

Even more powerful are more direct measures of personal control. People who believe that you can only get ahead by knowing the right people, and not by your own deeds, are less likely to trust others.[15] If

[15] The differential is 19 percent in the 1987 GSS and 8 percent in the 1971 Well-Being Pilot.

TABLE 4-5. *Probit Analysis of Trust from Niemi-Jennings Parent-Child Panel: Child Sample 1965*

	Coefficient	Standard Error	MLE/SE	Effect
Parent Trust	.259**	.114	2.274	.089
Influences Family Decision about Self	.173**	.094	1.845	.120
Can Determine Own Friends/Activities	.116**	.054	2.125	.078
Parent: Sometimes Disagrees with Child	.144*	.111	1.300	.048
In-group Trust	−.002	.004	−.478	−.035
Out-group Trust	.012***	.004	3.331	.357
Teachers Are Unfair to Respondent	−.317***	.105	−3.003	−.109
Will Life Be as Wished	.372****	.107	3.466	.125
Black	−.607***	.197	−3.077	−.218
Sex	−.299***	.103	−2.895	−.101
Constant	.358	.226	1.581	

Estimated R^2 = .281   −2*Log Likelihood Ratio = 839.521   N = 711
Percent Predicted Correctly: Probit: 69.1   Null: 64.5
*** $p < .01$ ** $p < .05$ * $p < .10$.

you think that luck works against you, you are more than 20 percent less likely to trust others. Young particularized trusters are much more likely to think that they have mostly bad luck (Niemi-Jennings).[16]

Measures of control are particularly important for young people. Renshon (1975, 76) reported that the amount of autonomy young people have in shaping their own lives is about as important a determinant of children's trust as is parental trust. In the Niemi-Jennings survey, high school students who believe that they can influence family decisions are 12 percent more likely to trust others. Choosing your own friends boosts trust by 8 percent, and feeling free to disagree with your parent by another five percent.[17] If you believe that your teachers are unfair, making success in school beyond your control, you are 11 percent less likely to trust others. *The measures of control have an average impact greater than 10 percent.*

[16] A more ephemeral measure − whether the poor have less chance to get ahead − has a more modest effect of −.076 (1971 Well-Being). So does one of the "standard" measures of "internal political efficacy," that people like me have no say in politics (1992 ANES).

[17] The report of disagreement comes from the *parent*, not the student.

TABLE 4-6. *Regression Analysis of Stranger and Friends/Family Factors from 1996 Pew Metropolitan Philadelphia Survey*

	Stranger Factor		Friends/Family Factor	
	Coefficient	t Ratio	Coefficient	t Ratio
Income	.014	.984	−.010	−.583
Age	.012****	6.000	−.008***	−3.178
Black	−.137**	−2.317	.741****	10.613
Education	.057****	3.696	−.043***	−2.354
Talk to Neighbors	.085**	1.900	−.105**	−1.962
Can Turn to People for Support	.090***	2.327	−.177****	−3.863
Have People Can Rely on	.005	.353	−.044***	−2.572
Could Get Neighbors to Work Together	.059***	2.333	−.021	−.687
Can Have Impact on Community	.078***	2.717	−.004	−.115
Parents Warned Not to Trust Others	−.061***	−2.823	.064***	2.506
Parent Victim of a Crime	−.022	−.462	.096**	1.724
Feel Safe at Home at Night	.067*	1.551	−.228****	−4.444
Feel Safe Walking in Neighborhood	.168****	4.401	−.001	−.017
Constant	.041	.224	−.044	−.203

For Stranger Factor: R^2 = .270   Adjusted R^2 = .256   S.E.E = .564   N = 703
For Friends/Family Factor: R^2 = .329   Adjusted R^2 = .317   S.E.E. = .669   N = 703
**** $p < .0001$ *** $p < .01$ ** $p < .05$ * $p < .10$.

Closely connected to control are measures of authoritarianism and particularized trust. There is a only a fine line between the idea that you can control your own life and the belief that most other people have sinister motives and would trample over you for the slightest reason. The 1987 GSS asked whether people would only work harder if they were paid more and whether they earn higher degrees only to get larger salaries. Both questions reflect the cynical views of human nature that mark the authoritarian personality – both also point to less trust in other people.[18] A similar question – posed in reverse in the Well-Being Pilot – is whether you want a fulfilling job or one that simply pays well. And people who want a satisfying position are almost 25 percent more likely

[18] The effects are −.072 and −.094, respectively.

TABLE 4-7. *Regression of Composite Measure of Particularized Trust from 1992 ANES*

Independent Variable	Coefficient	Standard Error	t Ratio
Fundamentalist	2.259**	.991	2.279
Religion Important	3.18***	1.092	2.948
Catholic	5.597****	.920	6.086
Children: Self-reliant vs. Obedient	-.377**	.218	-1.729
Inequality Not a Problem	1.110****	.313	3.546
People in Government Crooked	.852***	.310	2.749
Family Income	-.062	.071	-.865
Inflation Gotten Worse/Better	1.044**	.442	2.360
Standard of Living Better in 20 Years	.205	.216	.948
College Education	-.090*	.057	-1.591
Black	10.379****	1.221	8.502
Asian	15.140****	3.654	4.143
Contextual Trust	-14.731****	4.255	-3.462
Constant	5.380*	3.295	1.632

$R^2 = .153$ Adjusted $R^2 = .145$ S.E.E. = 14.416 $N = 1425$.
**** $p < .0001$ *** $p < .01$ ** $p < .05$.

to trust others – beyond age and education, the biggest impact on trust in this equation.

Finally, authoritarians believe that those who would exploit them must not be tolerated. Even if the deck is stacked against us, they say, we should teach our children respect for our values and help them resist heretical ideas. So we encourage them to behave in an orderly manner and to fight the temptation to become open to alternative interpretations of the world. So authoritarians prefer their children to have good manners rather than curiosity and to be well-behaved rather than considerate (Adorno et al. 1964, 255). And antiauthoritarians prefer curious and considerate children, who see strangers as the source of new ideas. *Across these five measures, authoritarians are 13 percent less likely to trust others.*[19]

---

[19] People who want children to be curious and considerate are 7 and 9 percent (respectively) more likely to trust others (1992 ANES). People who prefer their children to be obedient rather than self-reliant are likely to be particularized trusters (1992 ANES). If you believe that the government is crooked, you are much more likely to be a particularized truster (1992 ANES).

TABLE 4-8. *Regression of Composite Measure of Particularized Trust from the 1965 Youth Sample of the Niemi-Jennings Socialization Study*

	Coefficient	Standard Error	t Ratio
Parental Particularized Trust	.235****	.039	−6.008
How Close to Father	−2.049**	.980	−2.091
Father's Education	−.057**	.032	−1.791
Parent Fundamentalist	5.115****	1.337	3.825
Bible as Literal Word of God	.327**	.108	2.101
Friend from Opposite Race	−4.388***	1.354	−3.242
All Governments Should Be like U.S.	.673**	.341	1.976
Life Will Be as Wished	−2.817**	1.330	−2.118
Have Mostly Good Luck	−5.151***	2.149	−2.397
Constant	15.474****	3.495	4.427

$R^2 = .200$ Adjusted $R^2 = .187$ S.E.E. $= 15.272$ $N = 561$.
**** $p < .0001$ *** $p < .01$ ** $p < .05$.

I could only compute measures of in- and out-group trust for the 1992 ANES and the Niemi-Jennings surveys. When available, these measures are powerful determinants of generalized trust, though not always in the same ways. For high school students, attitudes toward out-groups are by far the strongest predictor of generalized trust. Young people with the most positive views of people who are different from themselves are 36 percent more likely to trust others than their cohorts with negative views of different folks. But in-group attitudes have no significant impact on generalized trust. For adults, the linkage is reversed. Attitudes toward out-groups are now insignificant, while in-group feelings are the second strongest predictor of trust in others, following only college education. People with the most positive attitudes toward their own group are 27 percent *less* likely to trust others than respondents who are most reserved toward their in-group.

Early on, your view of people different from yourself matters most. Later on, your attachment to your own group shapes your willingness to place trust in others. It is hardly surprising that the attitudes of younger people are shaped more by views of people who are different from yourself. This is, after all, the basis of trust in strangers.

Ethnic and religious attachments often become stronger as we get older, so how much our attitudes harden determines our level of trust later in life. In the 1987 GSS, we find another indication that in-group affinities matter for adults. Fundamentalists who are active in their churches (compared to liberal Christians active in their churches, who occupy the other extreme) are 16 percent less likely to trust others. *Particularized trusters are, on average, 17 percent less likely to trust strangers.* And religious fundamentalism is a key determinant of particularized trust.[20]

These four groups of variables – generalized optimism, a sense of control, authoritarianism, and particularized trust – are the strongest and most consistent predictors of trust in other people across a variety of surveys. Other variables do seem to matter a lot. We see a "Lake Wobegon" effect in the 1987 GSS. Living in the most trusting state (Minnesota) makes you 19 percent more likely to place faith in others than residing in the least trusting state (Mississippi).[21] Only one survey, the 1992 ANES, has good questions about egalitarian beliefs. And the impact of these sentiments is modest for generalized trust, though much more powerful for particularized trust.

Across all of the surveys I examined here, there is only *one* measure of civic engagement – being active in professional societies in the 1987 GSS – that has a significant effect on trust.[22] Even this coefficient ranked just 12th of 15 in the model. There is also mixed support at best for the role of informal social networks in producing trust: In the 1992 ANES and the Pew Philadelphia survey, people who talk to many of their neighbors are more trusting. And it is difficult to work out the direction of causality between feeling good about your social life and generalized trust in a single-equation model. I estimate simultaneous equation models in Chapter 5 in an attempt to sort out the direction of causality.[23] There are also mixed results for trust in government. Trust in gov-

---

[20] Fundamentalists and people who say that religion is important are much more likely to be particularized trusters (1992 ANES). Young people whose parents are fundamentalist, who believe that the Bible is the literal word of God, and who believe that other countries should emulate the United States, are all more likely to be particularized trusters; on the other hand, young people with a friend of the opposite race are less likely to be particularized trusters (Niemi-Jennings).

[21] In the 1992 ANES, contextual trust is also significant for particularized trust, though not generalized trust. Other estimations using the GSS show powerful effects for context (see below), so it seems reasonable to argue that your social environment does matter, usually substantially. The greater significance of contextual trust for the GSS may reflect the greater precision of the statewide estimates, which come from the entire 1972–96 GSS data base. I am grateful to Robert Putnam for providing the state-level codes.

[22] The 1987 GSS has a module that takes us beyond group membership to how active people are in their organizations, thus accounting for both this question and the one on fundamentalists active in their churches.

[23] But the strongest relationships are for satisfaction with your social circle (your friendships and your support networks in the 1987 GSS, and your community in the Pew

ernment had powerful effects in some surveys, but not others. I return to this question in Chapter 5.[24]

GENERALIZED TRUST AND REAL LIFE

The demographics of trust vary from survey to survey, in large part because they are correlated with many of the values and social ties included in the equations. The most consistently large effects for any demographic variable are found for age.[25] The effect of age on trust is well-known and is at least partially responsible for the strong downward trend in faith in other people: The older "long civic generation" of trusters is dying out and giving way to younger people who don't have as much faith in other people (Putnam 1995a, 2000, 140).

The surveys are mostly united in showing strong effects for race.[26] Race is the *most powerful* determinant of particularized trust for both the Pew survey and in the composite measure from the 1992 ANES.[27] African-Americans believe that most other blacks can be trusted, but are much more wary about their dealings with whites. Not surprisingly, Asian-Americans – at least in the 1992 ANES – are also more likely to be particularized trusters (see Table 4-7).

Beyond age and race, the only demographic variable that has large effects in most estimations is education (cf. Putnam 1995a; Brehm and Rahn 1997). But it is harder to get a coherent hand on education than other variables, perhaps because it is interrelated with optimism, control,

survey). There is middling evidence that reading newspapers builds trust. There is a modest effect (.072) for newspaper readership in the 1992 ANES. But it does not show up in the 1987 GSS (or the full GSS sample examined in Chapter 5) or among high school students.

[24] Trust in government is significant in two surveys: the 1987 GSS and the 1992 ANES, but failed to reach significance for the Niemi-Jennings survey, the Pew Philadelphia survey discussed later, or the full GSS sample.

[25] Seventy-five-year-olds are 31 percent more likely to be trusters than 18-year-olds in the 1987 GSS; the effect for the 1992 ANES is just half that. But there is an even bigger effect (.470) for a smaller range (19–56 years old) in the Well-Being Pilot. And age is the strongest predictor of generalized trust in the Pew Philadelphia survey, though its impact on particularized trust is not quite so powerful (and indeed, it is insignificant in a composite measure of particularized trust from the 1992 ANES in Table 4-7).

[26] Blacks are less trusting than whites: by 9 percent according to the 1987 GSS (7 percent for the larger sample in Chapter 5), 8 percent in the Well-Being Pilot (though this effect is not significant), but by much larger margins in the 1992 ANES and the Niemi-Jennings survey (18 and 22 percent respectively).

[27] Race is not significant for the measure of particularized trust in the Niemi-Jennings survey, even though it is a powerful predictor of trust in people more generally.

and authoritarianism. Sometimes its effects are powerful, sometimes they are not. Sometimes college education matters a lot more than high school education, sometimes it does not.[28]

Otherwise, the biggest story of the many estimations is how little (aside from race) real life experiences matter for generalized trust. Gender is significant in only one equation (Niemi-Jennings for generalized trust). And there is virtually no impact for *any* aspect of real resources. For the 1992 ANES, home ownership is significant but with a modest impact. *In no estimation is family income a significant predictor of interpersonal trust.* I included it in the equations for generalized and particularized trust from the Pew and 1992 ANES surveys, but it wasn't significant there either. None of the measures of trust depend on "real life experiences" as we traditionally understand them (save for race and education).

The 1971 Well-Being Pilot provides an excellent venue for testing my claim that optimism rather than objective life circumstances drives generalized trust. This survey contains a wealth of questions on both objective and subjective measures of well-being. In the Well-Being study I employ five measures of optimism, control, and authoritarianism, three indicators that are a combination of optimism and objective status, and ten variables that reflect how well people actually fare along several dimensions of economic security. I include the five measures of optimism that are significant at $p < .10$ or better in the equation. While this is a bit ad hoc, there are almost 30 indicators of optimism available in the survey and there are no clear grounds for choosing among them. I have already summarized the measures of optimism, control, and authoritarianism: whether people think about the future or only the present and several indicators of control; whether they believe that luck works against them; whether people only get ahead by having the right connections; whether the poor have less of a chance to get ahead; and

---

[28] In the 1992 ANES, both types of education matter, but college education has almost double the effect (.354) of additional years in high school (.191). For the 1987 GSS, only college education matters – and not that much (effect = .023). And the Well-Being Pilot shows a strictly linear effect for education, with no special "college" bump. But it is a powerful impact (.386). There are also linear effects in the Pew Philadelphia survey – more education makes you more likely to be a generalized truster and less prone to be a particularized truster – a finding weakly reinforced for college education in the 1992 ANES. In Chapter 5, the analysis of the full GSS sample shows no significant impact for either high school or college education. For the 1987 GSS, mothers' education matters, with an impact (.103) that is *five times as large* as the number of years in college that the respondent has attained.

whether you want a fulfilling job as a measure of both optimism and personal satisfaction.

There are also many available measures of objective economic circumstances; I have chosen the most "obvious" contenders. And most of these objective measures are *not* significant, not even overall satisfaction with your financial status, nor family income, unemployment or the fear of it, home ownership, having a pension plan, making debt payments, or having poor parents. There are some sporadic significant relationships: People who save their money for the future are more likely to trust others. So are people who say that their standard of living is comfortable or who have stocks or savings.

Overall, subjective measures matter a lot more than objective ones. Collectively, the most optimistic person – who wants a fulfilling job, thinks about the future, and believes that she can make it regardless of luck, connections, or current economic circumstances – is 36 percent more likely to trust others than the most convinced pessimist. The most prosperous person – with a relatively high family income, who owns his own home, has savings and a pension plan but does not have to make debt payments, whose parents were well-off, and has neither been laid off nor worried about losing his job – is 2 percent *less* likely to trust others than people who do not fare so well economically. Clearly your worldview, not your resources, determines whether you will trust other people. These clear results obviate the argument that the measures of optimism are self-selected. Only one objective measure of well-being achieves significance, compared to five subjective indicators – collectively, there is no net impact of objective measures on trust.

There is a similar dynamic for the fear of crime and actually confronting it. In neither the 1987 GSS nor the larger sample examined in Chapter 5 did victimization matter. Robbery and burglary mattered, once measures of optimism and control were in the equation (but cf. Brehm and Rahn 1997). Being the victim of a crime had no effect on either generalized or particularized trust in the Pew Philadelphia survey, although people whose *parents* had been victimized were more likely to withdraw into their friends and family (though they were no less likely to place confidence in strangers). Fear of crime does matter, both for generalized trust and particularized trust (1987 GSS and the Pew Philadelphia survey).

The evidence strongly supports my claim that generalized trust reflects an optimistic worldview: Trusters believe that things are going to get better, that they can help make it so, and that people of different backgrounds most likely share the same values that underlie the inevitable march to progress. Trusting people live in trusting worlds – not primarily because the world around them is benign (though it is likely to be so), but because optimism and trust are contagious.

Optimism and trust set in early. Your early family life has a big impact on your trust. High school students whose parents trusted others are 9 percent more likely to place their faith in strangers in the Niemi-Jennings survey. This effect is likely underestimated by the very high trust percentages for both student and parental trust. If your parents warned you not to trust others, you are more likely to become a particularized than a generalized truster, the Pew Philadelphia data show.

The most important finding comes from the Niemi-Jennings study. I earlier reported moderate effects for four measures of personal control over your environment. Together with parental trust, they *cumulate* to produce trusting young people. If a young person has trusting parents, can influence family decisions, can determine his own friends, and feels free to disagree with his parents, he will have a strong probability (.767) of becoming a truster. Someone with mistrusting parents, little influence on family life, and who does not sometimes disagree with parents has only a .428 probability of trusting others – a difference of .339. Similarly, an optimistic youngster who believes that teachers are generally fair is also likely to have faith in strangers (.759), while a pessimist who sees teachers as unfair will be less likely to have confidence in others (.532, for a difference of .235).

Altogether, an upbeat young person with benign parental influence is almost certain to trust other people (.857), while her pessimistic counterpart is unlikely to do so (.296, for a difference of .561). Each element of optimism – be it in the young person's worldview or what she takes from her parents – seems additive. So the warmest parents produce the most trusting young people.

As I shall show in Chapter 6, most of the determinants of trust in the high school students as young adults 17 years later are *not* contemporaneous values or life experiences. Instead, the greatest effects come from their own values and their parents' ideals many years earlier.

Overall, then, lots of things predict trust in other people. Yet only a handful of variables has moderate-to-large effects across surveys. Race, age, and education are almost always important. Not only African-Americans, but also Asians are likely to be particularized trusters (1992 ANES; cf. Yamigishi and Yamigishi 1994). Beyond these variables are three components of optimism: expectations for the future, a sense of control over your future, and antiauthoritarian values. Measures of particularized trust and the overall level of faith in others in your environment also matter. There is also evidence that the dynamic begins with a nurturing family. Across many different indicators and a wide range of surveys, a general sense that tomorrow will be better than today and the belief that you can make it so have consistently powerful effects on trust in other people.

Of course, it is possible that the causal chain works the other way. Maybe optimistic people don't become trusters, but people become optimistic about the future if they are surrounded by lots of trustworthy people.[29] This is what we would expect from a strategic view of trust, which emphasizes life experiences. There is some support for this view in a simultaneous equation model from the 1972–94 General Social Survey I estimate in Chapter 5, but there is even more evidence for the generalized trust framework I advocate. The impact of optimism on trust is almost twice as great as that of trust on optimism. I turn now to a comparison of generalized and particularized trust.

Particularized trusters are the mirror image of generalized trusters, the Pew Philadelphia survey (Table 4-6) shows. The latter are white, older, and well-educated. They see themselves as part of a supportive community where people can come together to solve collective action problems. They are secure in themselves and their neighborhoods and had parents who encouraged them to place their faith in strangers. Particularized trusters are more likely to be black, younger, with less education, fearful for their safety, loners without social support systems, and the children of parents who worried about other people. The correlation between the predicted values of generalized and particularized trusters is −.822.[30]

Second, once again life experiences don't seem to matter beyond the standard three demographic variables (age, race, and education). Personal life histories – such as being married rather than divorced, having divorced parents, being the victim of a crime, employment status – have no bearing on either type of trust (except for father's education in the Niemi-Jennings sample). Neither does participation in your community in any of a wide range of activities; not even for giving time at homeless shelters, much less attending town meetings, contacting public officials, participating in union activities, or joining with co-workers to solve

---

[29] Robert Putnam (private conversations) has made this point to me many times.
[30] This is substantially higher than the correlation between the two factor scores (−.386).

problems. And there is no spillover from trust in government. Context also matters: When you live in a state with few generalized trusters, you are more likely to look inward. Generalized trusters are optimists who believe that they can control their lives. Particularized trusters are pessimists who feel that others govern their fates. And this leads them to withdraw from contact with strangers (see Chapter 5).

TYPES OF TRUST

The story of this chapter is simple: Trusting intentions reflect a basic sense of optimism and control. Trusting others is not so much a reflection of your life experiences as of what you were taught when you were young.

Throughout eight separate estimations, I have driven this point home. There are lots of findings presented in this chapter, perhaps a dizzying array. So I summarize the impacts of the most important predictors in Table 4-9. The strongest impacts on both generalized and particularized trust come from optimism, control, and authoritarian values. Personal experiences such as marital status, parental divorce, income, and victimization play a very limited – mostly insignificant – role in shaping interpersonal trust. Yes, some experiences matter, such as the belief that you are safe in your home and your neighborhood. Education clearly does reflect life experiences. So does age, though it must be a surrogate for something else (see Chapter 6). And race is preeminently about experiences that might make only the most cockeyed black optimist trust white people.

TABLE 4-9. *Summary of Results on Generalized and Particularized Trust*

Predictor	Overall impact
Optimism	Optimists are most likely to be generalized trusters, less likely to be particularized trusters
Sense of Control (sense of luck, authoritarian attitudes, youth who can determine their own activities/friends, can influence family, see teachers as unfair, think people are motivated by selfish reasons)	People who think that they can control their lives are more likely to be generalized trusters and less likely to be particularized trusters

Predictor	Overall impact
In-group Ties	Fundamentalists more likely to be particularized trusters, active fundamentalists less likely to be generalized trusters. In-group trust shapes generalized trust for adults, not youth.
Out-group Ties	Out-group trust affects generalized trust for youth, not for adults. Young people with friends of different race less likely to be particularized trusters.
Parental Influence	Strong impact when available for both adults and youth, on both generalized and particularized trust. Direct influence of both parental trust and indirect influence of parenting style and close relationships of children and parents.
Trust in Government	Sporadically significant for generalized trust
Group Membership	Only significant for active involvement in professional societies.
Informal Socializing	Mostly not significant for generalized trust. Stronger impacts for generalized and particularized trust in Pew surveys.
Race	African-Americans less likely to be generalized trusters and more likely to be particularized trusters.
Education	Highly educated people (especially with college education) more likely to be generalized trusters, less likely to be particularized trusters.
Age	Young people are less trusting and more likely to be particularized trusters.
Income/Financial Resources	Rarely significant as predictor of trust.
Personal Life History	Neither divorce, parental divorce, nor being robbed (among other experiences) shapes trust, though perceptions of neighborhood safety do.

But beyond these demographics, it is control and especially optimism for the longer term future that lead people to trust one another. It is not *primarily* trust in government, though there are sporadic and sometimes large effects for this variable. And it does not appear that civic participation increases trust consistently. There are somewhat greater impacts of informal social networks on trust: People with support networks, who talk to their neighbors, and who are satisfied with their friendships are more trusting. But the direction of causality is not clear. Might trusting people have stronger social networks to begin with? Stolle (1998b) refers to "self-selection" effects – where you need trust to start the causal chain leading to civic involvement and then again to more trust. I take up this cudgel in the next chapter for both formal and informal organizations. Must you bring trust into an organization to take trust out? What happens if you begin with a group of misanthropes and put them into a voluntary organization? I also consider whether trust in government translates into generalized trust in Chapter 5.

You are likely to get particularized trusters – pessimists who believe that *others* control their lives. Seeing strangers as threatening, they will withdraw into their own civic institutions, if they participate at all. The path to civic engagement and good works rests with those generalized trusters. How so we shall see in the next chapter.

5

Trust and Experience

I guess it would seem to me it depends on what group of people you are talking about. In my personal life or work life I would have the tendency to lean towards trust. When it comes to political issues I would probably have the tendency to not trust.

Most people can be trusted, not all people but some, most people can though. Experienced a few people in his life where he trusted them and got shafted.

Sometimes getting too close with feelings toward people you trust them and sacrifice things for them and they can surprisingly shaft you, but they were serious enough that you never forget the experience. The past is the past and you should live for the day and of course you never forget the experience but its not healthy to dwell on it.

Most people can be trusted although they have a renter who hasn't paid in two and a half months. They gave [the renter] an eviction notice today. Everybody else needs to pay their bills.

– Respondents to the 2000 ANES Pilot Study "think aloud"
question on trust

When we decry the decline in trust from almost 60 percent in 1960 to barely more than a third of Americans in the late 1990s, we naturally begin to wonder what we can do to rebuild confidence in other people. Optimism, self-control, and good parenting don't offer much guidance in how to increase trust. How do we make people feel better about themselves and how do we make them better parents?

But there are two routes to interpersonal trust that offer greater hope for social engineering: formal and informal socializing, on the one hand, and government on the other. Putnam (1993, 2000) and others argue that when we get involved with friends and neighbors, we become more trusting. And Levi (1998) Rothstein (2000), Stolle (1999a), and others have argued that a well-functioning state can lead to greater interpersonal trust (see Chapter 2). Yet the evidence so far suggests that experience – with other people and with government – translates only weakly into generalized trust. There are few people who claim that declining trust in government actually *caused* the decline in interpersonal trust (even though there are many who say that government can rebuild trust). But advocates for civic engagement link the drop in trust to the withdrawal of Americans from social life (see especially Putnam [1995a]). In this chapter, I step back a bit and look at both questions in greater depth.

Putnam (1993, 180) and Stolle (1998b, 507) argue that trusting people are more likely to join organizations (cf. Uslaner 1998a, 1998b). But Brehm and Rahn (1997, 1017) and Shah (1998, 488) argue that organizational membership has a much stronger effect on trust than faith in others has in leading people to civic engagement.[1] All of the evidence is not in and there are reasons to be skeptical that involvement with others can produce trust.

Packed into Putnam's argument are two key assumptions. First is the reciprocal relationship between social ties and trust. I shall suggest that Putnam's (1993, 180; 2000, 137) "virtuous circle" of trust, civic engagement, and informal social networks is at best a "virtuous arrow," where, *if there is any connection at all*, the causal direction goes from trust to civic engagement rather than the other way around. You just can't put people in groups and expect them to become more trusting. As Newton (1997, 577) argues, "It is difficult to see how social networks can be created unless there is trust to start with" (cf. Wuthnow 1997, 29; Stolle 1998b). Second is the presumption that the causal arrow usually goes *somewhere*. Some social connections might even reinforce particularized, rather than generalized, trust. But most of the time social networks, both informal and formal, are moral dead ends. They neither consume nor produce trust. They just happen.

There is more plausible support for the argument that trust leads to civic engagement. The tale of Carol Erhard in Chapter 4 tells the story of the causal arrow going from optimism to trust to civic engagement. Your

---

[1] Shah, like Putnam, uses the DDB Needham Life Style data. So he also uses honesty as a surrogate for trust; see Chapter 3 for a discussion of the difficulties in using this measure.

optimistic worldview makes you a generalized truster and your trust in strangers makes you willing to engage in civic activities with them. When you see people giving of themselves, you are looking at people who already trust people who are different from themselves. They may gain an extra boost (the "warm glow") by doing good deeds, but this extra currency is only available to people who already have faith in others.

Putnam (1993, 115) links the development of trust in northern Italy to the many choral societies, soccer teams, and bird-watching societies that sprang up there compared to the sparse social life in the south. In the United States, he focused on bowling leagues and membership in voluntary organizations in his early work (Putnam, 1995a). His more comprehensive study (Putnam, 2000) includes: political participation; membership in unions, churches, and synagogues; attendance at religious services; volunteering; giving to charity; blood donation; and many different forms of informal social connections, including, but hardly limited to, visiting bars and restaurants, visiting neighbors, eating dinner with your family, and playing cards. Putnam's message is simple: A civil community is composed of many different types of voluntary organizations, civic activities, and informal socializing. A civic community depends more on *how many* organizations people join (Putnam 1993, 90) than the types of associations (Putnam 1993, 90; Wollebaek and Selle 2000, 32). Trust seems to be an all-purpose elixir. And many different, and often not very demanding, activities can produce generalized trust.

Some activities are more important in building generalized trust: Formal organizations are better than informal socializing, since they put you in contact with more people and require more effort (Putnam 2000). Organizations that hold meetings are better than those that "merely" require people to write a check and get a membership card and a magazine (Putnam 1995). And "bridging" organizations, composed of people from different backgrounds, are better than groups with homogeneous memberships (Putnam 1993, 93). Hierarchical organizations, such as the Mafia or the Italian Catholic church, which are run from the top-down, might even discourage popular participation (Putnam 1993, 111, 175). Horizontal organizations, which are run democratically, promote civic engagement. Associations that cut across social cleavages are best, but any horizontal group, and even informal socializing, will help create a civic community (Putnam 1993, 175; Putnam 2000, 21, chs. 3, 6).

There may also be a spillover from confidence in government to trust in other people. Lane (1959, 165–6) sees trust in government as part of the same general outlook as trust in people:

[A] person who has faith in people [is] the sociable man with many social contacts, and the man who likes his community is the effective citizen in our democracy. His relationships with his social environment are good. He is in rapport with others. He works for political ends not in a spirit of antagonism but in a spirit of cooperation.

Putnam (1993) argues that trust in people helps produce the social cooperation that is necessary for government to function well, and to be trusted in turn.

Others suggest a more complex dynamic: States can build trust among people by expanding rights, providing a social safety net for the less well-off, and enforcing contracts between people (Levi 1996, 1998). In each case, the government acts as a buffer and neutral arbiter between contending individuals and groups, ensuring everyone that all will be treated fairly (Levi 1996, 1998; Offe 1996, 33). Brehm and Rahn (1997, 1008) extrapolate from the correlation between trust in people and democratic institutions: Interpersonal trust is higher in democracies (see also Inglehart 1997, ch. 6). Following Levi (1996), Brehm and Rahn argue that democratic government can lead to generalized trust and that interpersonal trust will in turn make people more likely to have confidence in their government. Stolle (1999b, 9) elaborates on this linkage, which she expects to be particularly strong for local governments:

Citizens who feel that they are taken seriously by politicians, listened to, and respected, may also develop a belief in other people or people in general. If they perceive politicians to act fairly, honestly, and responsively, they feel more secure and encouraged to trust others. Surely, there must be a connection between those realities and perceptions of local political life, political life, and generalized trust.

I am skeptical of these linkages. Most types of social connections don't bring us into contact with people who are different from ourselves and few of us spend enough time in civic groups to change our values. Some activities – volunteering time and giving to charity – do connect us with people who are different from ourselves. They also call upon our ethical ideals that tie us to the idea that we have a responsibility for people in our moral community. But most types of civic activity don't (and can't) produce trust in people who are different from ourselves. The linkage between trust in people we know and strangers is rather weak.

Trust in government is more ephemeral than trust in people (see Chapter 3). But there is some evidence linking the two types of trust, so it is important to consider the linkage. Most of the evidence to date suggests that confidence in government depends upon trust in people rather than the other way around. So people who have faith in others will extend this trust to the political system (Brehm and Rahn 1997; Brehm, Rahn, and Carlson 1999). There is, however, also some evidence of a reciprocal relationship (Berger and Brehm 1997). Instead, I suggest that the two types of trust have different foundations. Trust in government rests more on approval of the leaders of the day than it does on deeply seated values.

SCHMOOZERS AND MACHERS

Social contacts breed social trust, Putnam argues. And he distinguishes between *schmoozers* and *machers*, two Yiddish terms representing different aspects of social life (Putnam 2000, 93–4). Schmoozing is hanging out with friends and chatting: whiling away your time in the pleasant pursuit of nothing in particular. A macher "makes things happen" by joining groups, working on community projects, giving to charity, following politics, and the like (Putnam 2000, 93–4).[2]

America at the turn of the century has fewer schmoozers and machers, by Putnam's count (2000, Chapters 2, 3, 4, and 6). We socialize less with friends, eat dinner less with our family, either at home or in restaurants; play cards less; visit less with our neighbors or relatives; go to church and synagogue less frequently; attend fewer club meetings; belong to fewer organizations; no longer join the Parent-Teachers Association; vote less often; attend fewer political rallies; write fewer letters to the editor or elected representatives; and sign fewer petitions. Putnam (2000, 291) suggests that our withdrawal from social life is strongly connected with the decline in social trust (Putnam 2000, 291). Even if it is difficult to sort out what is cause and what is effect, there is clearly a

---

[2] Well, sort of. A macher makes things happen, but more like a "rainmaker" than someone who is simply involved in his or her community. Rosten (1968, 216) defines a "macher" as "someone who arranges, fixes, has connections; a big wheel, an 'operator' " who does things "miraculously." Obviously, whether community leaders are trusting is a different question than whether members of civic groups are.

syndrome of withdrawal from others in our community. We are now a nation of "homebodies" and we don't think other people are quite so worthy.

What Putnam has shown us is that states that have high levels of formal and informal socializing and political participation are also more trusting. But it is less clear that the trends for all of these activities track each other so closely, and, even more critically, that there is some connection at the individual level between being either a schmoozer or a macher and trusting others.

I leave the question of whether our withdrawal from social life follows the same trend as the decline in trust to Chapter 7 (hint: it doesn't). First, I examine the individual-level connections. I shall present tables for only a few of the analyses that I discuss. The story of the book is trust, not group membership or volunteering or any other consequence of faith in other people. So presentation of tables for the consequences of trust would whet the reader's appetite for a discussion of what drives each of the dependent variables. That would take me quite far afield from trust. So, aside from a few selected tables, I shall instead describe the consequences of trust and show how faith in other people affects them. I shall list the other predictors in the models in the appendixes.

There are several reasons to doubt that an individual-level connection exists. First and foremost, most of our social connections involve people very much like ourselves. When we attend religious services, we congregate with people who believe in the same ideals that we do. When we join civic organizations, we also meet people with similar interests. When we get involved with politics, we work with people with similar ideologies and party affiliations as ourselves. Most critically, virtually all of our schmoozing involves people we know well. So it is unclear how we transmit trust in people like us to people who are different from us. Second, do we spend enough time in socializing or group activity to make us more trusting? Third, not all socializing will foster trust. Often, perhaps usually, we take political action to defeat someone else, not to try to reach some common ground. Political action may well thrive on a healthy degree of mistrust (Barber 1983, 166, 169; Hardin 2000, 223). We know that fundamentalists are more likely to be particularized than generalized trusters, so it is far from clear that religious devotions will always lead us to be trusting of fellow citizens. Membership in ethnic organizations might also reinforce in-group ties and make us less tolerant of people different from ourselves.

DOES SOCIAL INTERACTION LEAD TO TRUST?

There is lots of speculation about the impact of both informal and formal social connections on trust, but there are very few studies that have tried to sort out what causes what.[3] Putnam's early analyses (1995a, 1995b), Brehm and Rahn (1997), and Stolle (1998a, 1998b) all find that people who join civic groups *are* more trusting than stay-at-homes (but see Damico, Conway, and Damico 2000, 344–6). Putnam (1993, 180; 2000, 137) argues that trust and social connections form a "virtuous circle": Trusting people join groups and social life makes us more trusting. But he does not test this claim. Brehm and Rahn (1997) confirm Putnam's thesis in their analysis of General Social Survey data from 1972 to 1996. Civic engagement is even more likely to produce trust than faith in others is to lead to participation in group life, they report.

Stolle's survey of group members (and some nonmembers) in the United States, Germany, and Sweden asks people how long they have belonged to each type of group. And she finds that neither the simple fact of group membership nor the length of involvement makes people more trusting. So the trust gap between engaged and disengaged people is attributable to "self-selection." Trusting people join groups, she argues, but group life doesn't make people more trusting.

These are all important studies. But none provides a satisfactory answer to whether civic engagement makes one more trusting. If the causal arrow can go both ways, then we should not estimate simple models that test for effects in only one direction, as do Putnam and Stolle.[4] To test the "virtuous circle" hypothesis, we need a statistical technique that lets us test for linkages in *both* directions. And this means some technique of simultaneous equation modeling. The estimates from more simple statistical techniques (such as ordinary least squares regression) may lead to erroneous conclusions.

[3] Torcal and Montero (1999) show that trusters are more likely to join voluntary organizations in Spain. Wollebaek and Selle (2000) find the same relationship in Norway. And Whiteley (1999) finds that the more organizations people join, the more trusting they are, using the first two waves of the World Values Survey, with 92,000 respondents in 45 countries. He also reports significant effects of group membership on trust in separate analyses for the United States, France, Great Britain, and Italy (though not for Germany).

[4] Putnam (2000) does not test for connections between trust and social interactions at all, other than creating an aggregate scale including both.

Brehm and Rahn do estimate a multiple-equation model, allowing for possible connections among civic engagement, trust in people, and trust in government. But their analysis has two different problems. First, their measure of generalized trust is a scale that also includes perceptions of fairness and helpfulness (see Chapter 3). Second, and more critically, what you get out of a statistical model depends heavily on what you put into it. And their model is very thin on measures of optimism and control. It is far from clear that measures of civic engagement would still matter in a more elaborate model. I shall present a more comprehensive test of the argument about trust and social connections by examining a wide range of types of informal and formal ties, linking them to trust, and determining what causes what through simultaneous equation estimation (see Appendix A for lists of variables included in the models).[5]

We know more than a little about the connections between group membership and trust. Yet we know far less about the link between being a schmoozer and a truster – or about the ties between activities that might bind you more to people who are different from yourself, such as volunteering time and giving to charity. There may be good reason to assume that this type of "bridging" activity might make you more trusting of strangers. There is less reason to believe that "bonding" with people very much like yourself – folks in groups you join and *especially in your social circle* – would make you more likely to trust strangers.

Some forms of schmoozing may foster distrust rather than faith in strangers. Putnam (2000, 101) argues that Americans are going to neighborhood bars less frequently than in the past and worries that the goodwill and socializing at "the real-life equivalent of *Cheers*, the neighborhood bar 'where everybody knows your name' . . . is becoming a thing of the past."[6] Others, including Sergeant John Kaminski of the Cleveland, Ohio Police Department, have a different view (Butterfield 1996):

Back when Sgt. . . . Kaminski started out in homicide in the 1960s, the most common murder cases were barroom brawls. There was a bar on every street

---

[5] In some cases, when the bivariate relationships are weak, I don't estimate more complex models.

[6] *Cheers* was a fictional bar in Boston on a television show of the same name in the United States during the 1980s. It was patterned after a real pub, a place of conviviality, and, in a case of life imitating art, the producers of the television show established a national chain of bars named Cheers, where tourists would pay money for all sorts of souvenirs in a place where nobody knew their name.

corner in Cleveland those days, and the men who worked in this city's steel and automobile plants took the trolley to their jobs, stopping off for a shot and a beer on the way home. In some bars, it was like clock work. . . . After a few drinks a patron would insult the man on the next stool, usually a friend, and pretty soon a knife or a gun would be pulled out and one of the customers would be dead. No more. The factories, the bars, and the way of life are largely gone. "I can't even remember the last bar fight," said Sergeant Kaminski, who is 65 years old and has been a homicide detective for 30 years.

Not every bar has the upscale sociability of *Cheers* or the good fellowship of the English pub.

Both Putnam and Sergeant Kaminski may overstate the societal implications of the neighborhood tavern, but the bulk of the evidence supports the sergeant. There is at best a very modest *positive* relationship between going to bars and trusting others in the 1974–96 GSS. But this doesn't mean that bars are marked by good companionship. People who visit bars daily are twice as likely to be the victims of robbery or burglary and almost six times as likely to have been arrested.[7] Overall, you are better advised to watch your wallet in a bar than to leave it on the counter.[8]

The story is not much more optimistic when we look at other forms of socializing that Putnam (2000) discusses. We schmooze when we eat out, but people who go to restaurants are no more trusting than folks who eat at home.[9] Hanging out at bingo parlors has no effect on trust.[10] Playing cards doesn't lead to trust either, whether you just "play cards"

[7] The simple correlations between going to bars and trusting others are: tau-c = .057, gamma = .098, N = 9285; 4.9 percent of people who go to bars almost daily have been robbed in the past year compared to 2.2 percent who never go to bars (tau-c = .021, gamma = .112), while 12.3 percent of daily visitors to saloons have had their homes burglarized, compared to 6.1 percent of those who never go to bars (tau-c = .030, gamma = .098). Thirty-four percent of almost daily visitors to bars have been arrested at some point in their lives, compared to 6 percent of people who never go to bars (tau-c = .173; gamma = .424). This finding is not an idiosyncracy of one survey. In the 1968 Panel Study of Income Dynamics of the Survey Research Center, the correlation (tau-c) between how often one goes to bars and a slightly different measure of trust (trichotomized to trusting few, some, and most people) is .020 (gamma = .036).
[8] Returning lost wallets is often taken as a sign of a trusting community; see Knack and Keefer (1997).
[9] From the 1988 GSS, the correlations are: tau-b = .022, gamma = .056; see Rothstein (2000) for a similar result for Swedish samples.
[10] The simple bivariate relationship between bingo playing and trust in the 1972 ANES is minuscule (phi = –.010, Yule's Q = –.027). In the multivariate analysis, people who trust others are slightly less likely to play bingo (by about 12 percent, p < .10) but playing bingo has no effect on trust. Indeed, there is some evidence – from a probit model of playing without reciprocal causation (a reasonable assumption from the simultaneous

or play the very social games of poker and pinochle. People who play cards have more faith in their neighbors – the people with whom they play – but not in strangers.[11]

There is one *possible* exception: playing bridge. Bridge players are *far more trusting* than nonplayers (by 73 to 44 percent) and playing this sociable game makes them *dramatically* more trusting. Do they get there by socializing with people who are beyond their immediate social circle? Not quite. "Social" bridge clubs have a lot of conversation about all manner of things, including politics. But they are composed of people who already know each other and who largely think alike. "Serious" clubs have more diverse memberships, but their members are so single-minded about their passion that all they do at meetings is play bridge and go home (Erikson and Nosanchuk 1990; Scott and Godbey 1992). This possible exception thus lacks a compelling story.

Across a wide variety of social connections – from visiting friends and parents to talking to neighbors – there are at best modest correlations with trust. There is some evidence that trusters are more likely to talk to more neighbors, but they are *less* likely to see their best friends often and *less* likely to spend a lot of time with parents and relatives.[12] They

---

equation estimation) – that bingo afficionados may be substantially *less* trusting (see Appendix A).

[11] People who play cards, according to the 1996 Pew Philadelphia survey, are neither more trusting nor sociable: 50 percent of card players socialize with their neighbors compared to 47 percent of people who don't play cards (tau-b = .022, gamma = .044). And forty-one percent of card players believe that most people can be trusted, compared to 45 percent who don't play cards (tau-b = -.034, gamma = -.071). The relationships don't grow any stronger in multivariate analyses. Poker players are slightly more likely to trust other people (by 52 to 48 percent in the 1972 ANES), but this weak relationship vanishes in a multivariate equation. Pinochle players *are* more trusting (by 56 percent to 45 percent in the 1972 ANES), but this relationship also vanishes in multivariate specifications. According to the Social Capital Benchmark Survey, conducted in 2000, trust in neighbors is a significant (at $p < .05$) predictor of card playing, but generalized trust is not. These results come from a tobit analysis of the frequency of card playing with the following predictors: age; gender; income; education; race (black); the length of a respondent's commute; the number of hours worked per week; the number of hours the respondent watches television and spends on the World Wide Web; whether the respondent is a homemaker; the number of children; frequency of attending religious services; how long the respondent has lived in the community; and the number of friends the respondent has. I used this same model for other measures of socializing discussed below. The Social Capital Benchmark Survey was commissioned by Robert Putnam of Harvard University. It had a national sample of 3,003 and samples in 41 communities of another 26,230. It is available for public download at http://www.ropercenter.uconn.edu.

[12] In the 1974–96 GSS, trusters are slightly less likely to visit with their parents or close relatives (gammas = -.048 and -.075). They are also less prone (according to the 1986

are no more likely to go to parades, sports events, or art shows often; spend a lot of time with friends from work or simply to hang out with friends in a public place; visit chat rooms on the World Wide Web a lot; or even to play lots of team sports. People who trust folks they know – their neighbors – *are* more likely to go to parades and join sports teams frequently. But overall, the major reason why people socialize a lot is that they have many friends, not that they trust strangers. Misanthropes have friends, too.[13]

TRUST AND ORGANIZATIONAL LIFE

There is little evidence that schmoozing either depends upon trust or, more critically, can produce it. What about social interactions through organized groups? Putnam (1993, 115) points to choral societies as one of the types of groups that helps people develop trust in others. The 1993 GSS asked whether people perform music, dance, or drama – about as close as we can come to Putnam's choral societies. Who sings? Young singles who like classical music. Choral societies are dating clubs. They don't generate trust, and they don't depend upon it, either.[14]

Let's look at the evidence more broadly. First, I look at whether trust shapes civic engagement and then move on to whether group member-

GSS) to visit their closest friend daily (gamma = −.127) or to have frequent contact with their best buddy (gamma = −.096). They are more likely to socialize with their neighbors (Yule's Q = .122 for the Pew Philadelphia survey and gamma = .162 for the 1992 ANES and .153 for the 1992 ANES).

[13] These results come from the Social Capital Benchmark Survey. Each measure is the number of times people did a particular activity in the past year. See note 11 for details on the survey and the tobit model used for each form of socializing. The measures I employ are: going to parades, sports, or arts events; visiting family members; having friends over to your home; hanging out with friends in a public place; how many co-workers socialized with outside of work; number of sports teams; and number of on-line internet discussions. Generalized trust is a significant ($p < .05$) positive predictor of how often you hang out with friends outside of work, but this coefficient belies the zero-order correlation with trust of −.005. Trust is not a significant predictor of the number of friends one has. Significant predictors are *happiness, participation in church-synagogue other than services, black (−),* **gender (male), income, being single, being retired,** age, education, number of children, frequency of attending services, how long you have lived in your community, and home ownership. Italics indicate significant coefficients at $p < .001$, bold at $p < .05$; other coefficients are insignificant.

[14] Younger people who are single with higher incomes are more likely to take part in performances. So are blacks. But the effect for taste in music dwarfs all others. No other taste in music – including opera, Broadway musicals, jazz, Latin, new age, oldies, reggae, contemporary rock, big band, bluegrass, blues, folk, gospel, easy listening, rap, or heavy metal – had any effect on performance. There was a slight *negative* impact for country music, but that vanished in multivariate analysis.

ship leads to trust.[15] I examine many different venues for volunteering
and charitable contributions (which show a deeper commitment to community life), as well as types of voluntary organizations across a wide
range of surveys. I estimated single equation models for a wide variety
of types of civic engagement that I summarize in Table 5-1.[16] I classified
each venue as reflecting high trust, middle trust, no effect, negative trust,
and mixed effects based upon the overall pattern for each across the
surveys.[17]

The story is just about what we would expect from the literature on
trust and civic associations: Some of the time group members, volunteers, and people who give to charity are more trusting than folks who
opt out of civic life. But much of the time they are no more trusting
and once in a while, they are even less trusting. The most trusting people
take part in cultural and educational groups and the least trusting in
unions and religious organizations (always taking into account the demographic backgrounds of group members). People who work with others
on civic or political activities are not any more trusting than others.
And perhaps the biggest surprise is the middling level of trust among

[15] This question is really more appropriate for Chapter 7 (where I discuss the consequences
of trust), but given what lies ahead, it fits in much better with the flow of the argument here.

[16] The surveys I used are the GSS (various years), the 1996 Giving and Volunteering Survey,
the 1996 Pew Philadelphia survey, and the 1972 and 1996 ANES. For each venue for
charitable giving and volunteering and each type of membership in voluntary associations, I ran a probit analysis predicting participation from trust, standard demographic
variables (high school and college education, income, age, gender, race, marital status,
being a homemaker) and attitudinal predictors of civic engagement that might be available in different surveys (religious fundamentalism, whether one's parent volunteered,
feelings of efficacy). I treated each year of the GSS as a separate sample; when I ran
one equation across almost 14,000 cases, all of the variables were strongly significant,
perhaps spuriously so.

[17] High-trust activities generally have coefficients significant at $p < .01$ or beyond (all one-
tailed tests). Middle-trust groups usually have coefficients significant at least at $p < .05$
and relatively few insignificant coefficients. No effect is just that: Most of the estimated
coefficients were not significant even at $p < .10$. Negative effects had most coefficients
significant at least at $p < .10$. And mixed effects indicated some significant positive coefficients and some significant negative ones. The survey questions do not make it easy to
figure out what is included in each category. The GSS asks whether people are members
of service groups, but does not give people examples of what would fall under each
category. The 1972 ANES asked about membership in civic groups and the 1996 ANES
listed community groups (which I listed with civic organizations) and neighborhood
organizations, without specifying what any of these associations might do and who
would be eligible to join. The 1996 Giving and Volunteering Survey and the 1996 GSS
both asked about giving time and money to private community and public–society
organizations. But overall, most of the venues don't need much explanation.

TABLE 5-1. *The Linkages between Forms of Civic Engagement and Trust*

Volunteering and Charitable Contributions[a]

High Trust	Middle Trust	No Effect	Mixed Effects
Arts and Culture	Health/hospitals	Informal	Religion
Education	Human services	Private	
	Youth	Recreation	
		Work-Related	
		Politics/Environment	
		Civic Organizations	

Group Membership[b]

High Trust	Middle Trust			No Effect	Negative Effect Mixed Effects
Business/	Service Groups	Women		Labor Unions	Religion
Professional	Sports			Hobbies	Veterans
Cultural/Arts	Self-help			Neighborhood	
Social		Education		Farm	
		Politics		Youth	
		Fraternal[c]		Civic Groups	
		Fraternities/		Ethnic	
		Sororities[c]			

[a] From 1996 General Social Survey, 1996 Giving and Volunteering survey, and 1996 Pew survey of metropolitan Philadelphia.
[b] From 1972 and 1996 ANES, 1996 Giving and Volunteering survey, and General Social Survey for 1975, 1978, 1980, 1983, 1984, 1986, 1987, 1988, 1989, 1990, 1991, 1993, and 1994.
[c] Generally small positive effects, mostly on the borderline of statistical significance.

members of fraternal organizations. Groups such as Rotary Clubs, the Shriners, the Moose, the Odd Fellows, and the Elks had reputations for doing lots of good works (Putnam 1993, 115; Putnam 2000, 20, 117). Their passing reflects "an American society at war with no-longer fashionable notions of community and fellowship," write Hakim and Mitchell (1995, F4; cf. Putnam 2000). Members of fraternal groups *do* volunteer more than other people.[18] But they are barely more trusting than their fellow citizens, once we control for other factors (especially

---

[18] These results come from the 1996 ANES and the 1996 Giving and Volunteering Survey. Members of fraternal organizations are especially more likely to volunteer in health, human services, recreation, and cultural programs Details are available on request.

age). As with socializing, you don't need trust to get people involved in civic groups.

Do people become more trusting once they are in groups? I first focus on the same GSS surveys that Putnam and Brehm and Rahn examine. I report a simultaneous equation model in Table 5-2.[19] The model tests for reciprocal causation among trust, membership in secular voluntary associations, and optimism for the future. I focus on secular organizations because people are likely to have different motivations for joining religious associations. Religious organizations may be havens for particularized, rather than generalized, trusters. I also exclude unions from the calculations, since for many people membership in unions is not voluntary.

The simultaneous estimation allows me to look at reciprocal causation. Does membership in voluntary associations produce trust, consume trust, both, or neither? And does trust depend upon optimism for the future, or does trust lead to optimism?

The model for trust is similar to those in Chapter 4 and so are the results. What is different is that I include membership in secular organizations in the model for trust, and trust is also included in the model for group affiliation.[20] Trust has the strongest impact of any variable in the model for group membership. People with faith in others are Lane's "sociable" men and women. They take active roles in their communities. But civic engagement *does not* lead to greater trust. Simply put, group membership has *no effect on trust*.[21] Trust largely reflects an optimistic worldview (as in Chapter 4), rather than the experiences learned in civic groups. The results in Table 5-2 suggest support for the self-selection thesis: *If there is a connection between civic life and trust, it is through the "virtuous arrow" (from trust to engagement) rather than the "virtuous circle."* You won't become more trusting by joining civic groups.

---

[19] The model is estimated using three-stage least squares.

[20] The equation for group membership includes many standard predictors (see Putnam 1995a; Brehm and Rahn 1997). More highly educated people (especially those with college degrees), people with strong local roots (who lived in the same city as a child), and the very busy who work long hours are all more likely to join voluntary organizations. And people who attend religious services are also likely to join secular organizations.

[21] The coefficient for membership in secular voluntary associations is −.001, and the standard error is 29 times the size of the slope. Other standard predictors such as age and gender were dropped because they were insignificant.

TABLE 5-2. *Three-Stage Least Squares Estimation from General Social Survey*

	Coefficient	Standard Error	*t* Ratio
Membership in Secular Organizations (Excluding Unions)	Model Chi Square = 591.677	(RMSE = 1.706)	
Trust	1.583****	.175	9.055
Frequency Attend Religious Services	.062****	.011	5.451
High School Education	.044****	.012	3.619
College Education	.084****	.010	8.531
Number of Hours Worked Last Week	.005***	.002	2.492
Live in Same City as Child	.130**	.058	2.227
Family Income	.004	.014	.270
Constant	−.799****	.189	−4.218
Trust	Model Chi Square = 588.887	(RMSE = .623)	
Satisfied with Personal Friendships	.016***	.005	3.220
Lot of Average Person Getting Worse	−1.026****	.167	−6.158
Confidence in Science	.031**	.015	1.996
Membership in Secular Organization (without Unions)	−.001	.029	−.023
Black	−.071***	.027	−2.673
Age	.005****	.001	6.133
Afraid to Walk at Night in Neighborhood	−.038***	.014	−2.696
High School Education	.010**	.004	2.237
College Education	.009**	.004	2.253
Contextual Trust	.257****	.066	3.870
Constant	.811****	.131	6.211
Lot of Average Person Getting Worse	Model Chi Square = 279.313	(RMSE = .505)	
Trust	−.554****	.063	−8.830
Age	.002***	.001	3.157
Life Exciting or Dull	.030***	.011	2.704
High School Education	.002	.004	.503
College Education	.000	.003	.000
Satisfied with Job or Housework	−.013**	.007	−2.000
Financial Situation Compared to Others	−.016**	.007	−2.223
Family Income	−.002	.002	−.878
Fundamentalism	.013**	.007	1.901
Constant	.812****	.057	14.266

**** $p < .0001$ *** $p < .01$ ** $p < .05$ * $p < .10$ $N = 3389$.

There is an additional message in this table. The relationship between trust and optimism is not one way. It is reciprocal. Greater optimism leads to more trust and a trusting disposition makes you more optimistic. The causal linkage is not completely clear: It may well be that trusting people become more optimistic by doing good deeds, as the discussion of volunteering and giving to charity suggests. Whatever the causal logic, there is a much more powerful effect of optimism on trust than the other way around. Optimism has more than three times the effect on trust than trust has on optimism.

PRODUCING AND CONSUMING TRUST

Trusters belong to lots of groups (Wollebaek and Selle 2000, 31). Yet I have argued – and presented supporting data in Table 5-1 – that some groups may be more trusting than others. Even assuming that the causal arrow goes only one way – from trust to civic engagement – not all forms of participation depend upon trust. Groups with heterogeneous memberships are likely to have more trusting members (cf. Stolle 1998b, 516). Religious organizations may tap deep feelings of helping others, but fundamentalist denominations may lead to particularized rather than generalized trust. Groups stressing distinct identities – ethnic organizations and veterans' groups – may also lead to mistrust of people who are different. And some organizations may simply lead nowhere: Hobby groups, like choral societies, may bring together people with similar interests who have no intention to do more than build model ships. And, as I argued in Chapter 2, more demanding forms of civic engagement such as volunteering or giving to charity should be more likely to both consume and produce trust.

Now I put the pieces of the puzzle together and test a more comprehensive model of what types of civic participation might produce trust, and how different modes of engagement rely on faith in others. I turn to the 1996 ANES, which has the best overall set of measures of group and informal involvement. The survey asked people whether they were involved in 20 different types of voluntary organizations, encompassing religious, political, cultural, and professional associations, as well as groups addressed to the interests of the young, the old, women, hobbyists, and people seeking self-help. People could say that they belonged to as many as four groups within each category (as opposed to just checking "yes" or "no" for the GSS and most other surveys), though only for business, hobby, ethnic, and education groups did as many as 4 percent

TABLE 5-3. *Summary of Group Involvement Impacts on Trust from 1996 ANES^a*

Independent Variable	Coefficient	Standard Error
Business Group Involvement	.158***	.062
Cultural Group Involvement	.252**	.109
Children's Group Involvement	.094*	.056
Contributed to Charity	.184*	.114
Ever Attend Religious Services	.152*	.107
Ethnic Group Involvement	−.293**	.106
Arts Group Involvement	.022	.122
Elderly Group Involvement	.020	.106
Labor Union Involvement	−.024	.087
Veterans' Group Involvement	.127	.102
Church Group Involvement	−.019	.092
Nonchurch Religious Involvement	.008	.076
Hobby Group Involvement	.039	.070
Fraternal Group Involvement	.147	.127
Service to Needy Group Involvement	.014	.088
Education Group Involvement	.061	.086
Self-help Group Involvement	.127	.184
Political Issue Group Involvement	.023	.098
Party/Candidate Group Involvement	−.216	.202
Civic Group Involvement	−.103	.197
Women's Group Involvement	.136	.430
Other Group Involvement	.064	.119
Volunteered Time	−.010	.088
How Many Neighbors X Talks to	.026	.031

Estimated R^2 = .353 −2*Log Likelihood Ratio = 1394.330 N = 1233
Percent Predicted Correctly: Probit: 71.7 Null: 60.2
*** $p < .01$ ** $p < .05$ * $p < .10$.
^{a} Effects calculated between zero and two for business, hobby, and educational groups, between zero and one otherwise. See Appendix A for other variables included in the model.

select two or more. The ANES also asked about volunteering and donating to charity, as well as talking to neighbors and attending religious services. Overall there are 24 measures of civic engagement and I use them all in a "kitchen sink" model to get a first cut at what might affect trust. I estimate a probit model using the 24 indicators of civic engagement and a series of other predictors based upon the estimations in Chapter 4 and present the results in Table 5-3.

The chief message of the estimation in Table 5-3 is that *very few types of civic engagement lead people to become more trusting.* Only five of

24 measures of involvement make people significantly more likely to trust others: business, cultural, and children's groups, contributions to charity, and attending religious services. And three of these five just pass significance at the generous .10 significance level. Joining a group related to ethnicity makes you *less* trusting. All other forms of civic engagement – including the political, the religious, volunteering, talking to neighbors, as well as groups for education, self-help, women, the elderly, hobbyists, fraternal orders, and veterans – don't make folks more trusting.

This analysis tells but part of the story, since it doesn't allow for trust to shape any of the forms of civic engagement. It does serve an important pruning function, since a full model testing for reciprocal causation among trust and all forms of civic engagement would have 25 equations: one for each variable in Table 5-3 plus another for trust. At best this would be unwieldy and uninterpretable. At worst, the whole thing would be likely to implode.[22]

The model in Table 5-3 suggests dropping all but the significant predictors of trust in the probit and this is what I do. I then estimate a three-stage least squares model of involvement in business, ethnic, cultural, and church groups, as well as charitable contributions and volunteering. Even though church groups and volunteering were not significant in the model in Table 5-3, I included them in the simultaneous equation estimation because they are theoretically important. Volunteering reflects a commitment to others, and religious activities may reinforce particularized trust.[23] The resulting model has eight equations: for business, children's, ethnic, cultural, and church groups, volunteering, giving to charity, and trust. I report the results for the effects of trust on civic engagement and for civic participation on trust in Table 5-4 below.[24]

---

[22] The problem is likely underidentification.

[23] How often you attend services and whether you believe that the Bible is the literal word of God do shape generalized trust in the estimation in Table 5-3.

[24] For cultural involvement, the other variables in the model are: *a dummy variable for being Jewish*, **family income**, being a liberal, **age, gender,** and living in an urban area. For church involvement, the other variables are *frequency of prayer, how often one reads the Bible, a dummy variable for being Catholic, age, family income, being a liberal (negative coefficient)*, **how long one has lived in the community**, and a dummy variable for being Jewish. The variables in the equation for business involvement are *being self-employed, family income*, **a dummy variable for being Jewish, the number of hours worked each week, saying that others' beliefs are similar to your own, and knowing and speaking to neighbors.** The equation for children's groups includes *age*, **number of**

The results are striking. Trust has powerful effects on business and cultural group involvement, as well as on charitable contributions and volunteering. Trust is the strongest predictor of volunteering, with an impact almost double that of its closest rival, knowing and talking to your neighbors.[25] Beyond church involvement, trust has the greatest effect of any variable on charitable contributions (just beating out family income). And trust ranks first for business group involvement and second (behind being Jewish) for cultural membership. But its effects are *not* universally powerful: Trust has a small positive effect on ethnic group involvement, but no impact at all on either church or children's group membership.[26]

Trust matters most for those activities that signify the greatest commitment to your community: donating money and especially giving time. The two organizations where trust has big impacts help build bridges across groups. People make connections in business and professional societies – these friendships are likely to be particularly important to women and minorities in a world traditionally dominated by white

children aged six to nine, being married, being an Early Baby Boomer (born 1946–1955), church involvement, family income, whether it is important to be involved in helping others, and saying that others' beliefs are similar to your own. For ethnic group membership, other variables include *race,* knowing and talking to neighbors, gender, family income, trust in in-groups, and education. For charity, the predictors are *church group involvement, family income,* frequency of newspaper readership, knowing and talking to neighbors, saying that others' beliefs are similar to your own, and business group involvement (negative coefficient that meets conventional two-tailed tests for significance at *p* < .05). For volunteering, the predictors are *knowing and talking to neighbors, saying that we should care about the well-being of others,* a dummy variable for being Jewish, family income, business group involvement, and age. For trust, the equation also includes *trust in demographic out-groups, "people like me have no say in politics" (negative coefficient),* "there would be fewer problems if there were more emphasis on traditional family values," trust in demographic in-groups (negative coefficient), and a dummy variable for Late Baby Boomers. Italics indicate significant coefficients at *p* < .001, bold at *p* < .05; underlined at *p* < 10, other coefficients are insignificant.

[25] I determined the impact by multiplying the regression coefficient by the range of the independent variable. The impact of trust on volunteering is simply the value of the regression coefficient (.410), while the impact for talking to neighbors is .061 (the coefficient) times the range (four), or .244.

[26] Church involvement is largely driven by how often you pray and how often you read the Bible, both of which are slightly related to mistrust. And people who work with kids' groups have more children of their own between the ages of six and nine: 55 percent of adults with young children are involved in kids' groups, compared to 15 percent who don't have young kids. So parents interact with their own children and those of their friends and neighbors; surely a worthwhile enterprise, but not one that builds the bridges that undergird generalized trust.

TABLE 5-4. *Summary of Reciprocal Effects of Trust and Civic Engagement, 1996 ANES: Three-Stage Least Squares Estimates*

	Coefficient	Standard Error	t Ratio
Effects on Trust from:			
Business Group Involvement	.076	.091	.838
Children's Group Involvement	−.155	.088	−1.763
Ethnic Group Involvement	−.088	.247	−.354
Cultural Group Involvement	−.049	.168	−.296
Church Group Involvement	−.435****	.130	−3.358
Charitable Contributions	.669****	.200	3.342
Volunteering	.505***	.163	3.090
Effects of Trust on:			
Business Group Involvement	.554****	.117	4.733
Cultural Group Involvement	.287****	.073	3.919
Church Group Involvement	.109	.088	1.232
Children's Group Involvement	.056	.130	.430
Ethnic Group Involvement	.064*	.048	1.339
Charitable Contributions	.278****	.072	3.851
Volunteering	.410****	.100	4.113
Equation	**RMSE**	**Chi-Square**	**N**
Trust	.590	175.183	998
Business Group Involvement	.681	145.672	998
Cultural Group Involvement	.409	98.094	998
Church Group Involvement	.476	246.222	998
Children's Group Involvement	.639	103.058	998
Ethnic Group Involvement	.251	28.067	998
Charitable Contributions	.388	236.095	998
Volunteering	.502	109.390	998

**** $p < .0001$ *** $p < .01$ ** $p < .05$ * $p < .10$.

males. Cultural organizations can spread ideas that promote understanding of other peoples' music, art, and drama. Associations based on churches, children, and ethnic groups are less likely to build bridges across cultures. They bring you into contact with people like yourself and whom you may already know.

Does civic engagement promote trust? Membership in organizations does *not* increase trust, no matter what the group is. I started with 20 types of associations named in the 1996 ANES and eliminated all but six for the more complex analysis. None of these survived the test of reciprocal causation. Involvement in church groups even *decreases* confidence in others. Involvement in children's groups also seems to depress trust, though I have no ready explanation for this and am wary of putting too much confidence in the negative coefficient.[27]

For most all types of both formal and informal social contacts, trust is *neither a cause nor an effect*. People can form social bonds without drawing on moral resources. People join civic groups, they say, because friends are members, because they want to meet others who can help them in their career, or to help out in their children's activities (Wuthnow 1998, 29). There is nothing wrong with that. It's great that young people who like classical music get together to meet potential mates with similar interests. It's nice that birders bond together to get a peak at the rara avis. And it's fine that people enjoy themselves competing in bowling leagues. But let's not reify these activities as the backbone of a civil society. Trusting societies may be marked by lots of associations, but so may societies lurching toward totalitarianism (Berman 1997, 565–6).

DOING GOOD AND TRUSTING OTHERS

But sometimes civic engagement does promote trust. Both giving to charity and donating time create "warm glows," feelings of doing good. Indeed, for both volunteering and especially for giving to charity, the boost in trust from helping others was greater than the impact of trust on acts of beneficence. Volunteers say, "I'm sure you'll hear this over and over, but I get a lot more than I give" (Bowles 1996, B4). And there is evidence that they do. The impact of volunteering on trust is 20 percent greater than the effect of trust on volunteering. And giving to charity has almost two and a half times the impact on trust that faith in others has on making contributions. But as powerful as giving time and money are, they are *not* the most important determinants of trust, whereas trust does rank at the top of the factors leading to acts of beneficence. So you need trust to get people involved in good deeds, though folks can be trusting without giving of themselves.

But good deeds repay the good samaritans many times over. In the 1996 Giving and Volunteering Survey, trusters take up almost twice as many volunteering opportunities (1.606 versus .856) and charitable options (2.015 versus 1.221) as nontrusters. Volunteers who take part

---

[27] On a two-tailed test, the coefficient would be significant only at $p < .10$, and on a one-tailed test expecting a positive slope, it would be insignificant.

in eight or more organizations are twice as likely to trust others (by 64 to 34 percent), while people who give to seven or more different types of charities are more than twice as likely to put their faith in strangers (by 68 to 30 percent).[28] Had I a cardinal measure of trust I would expect to find volunteers and donors to have much higher scores than people who don't give of themselves. The stranger factor from the Pew Philadelphia survey gives us precisely this type of measure and it shows that people who don't volunteer for any secular organization have a standardized trust score of –.123, while people who give of themselves in five or more types of organizations have a mean score of .187 ($p < .008$).

The lesson seems to be that civic participation can produce trust, but only when there is faith in strangers initially. It cannot make a silk purse of a sow's ear; that is, you can't turn Scrooge into Bob Cratchitt simply by forcing him to volunteer at a homeless shelter or to empty bedpans at a hospital. As an unhappy student said of her mandatory "service learning" program, in which she had to give her time to a worthy cause to graduate from a Maryland high school: "You're just forcing it on us, and people don't get as much out of that" (Cloud 1997, 76).

Granted that it takes trust to make more trust (suggesting that faith in others is truly a form of capital, social or otherwise), there is one finding that seems puzzling. Giving time is more demanding than simply writing a check to a charity. So why should the payback be so much greater for donating money than for devoting time?

My first thought was that there must be something strange about the estimation using the 1996 ANES, so I constructed another, though simpler, simultaneous-equation model using the 1996 Giving and Volunteering Survey. I present this model, which has just three equations, in Table 5-5. Once again, trust is by far the strongest predictor of both volunteering and giving to charity. It even trumps your socializing patterns, whether you help specific people (relatives or homeless people on the street), and how active you were when you were young (being involved in student government, even volunteering with your parents and your family). But there is *no* warm glow from volunteering at all and a big one from giving to charity.[29]

---

[28] All four relationships are significant at $p < .0001$ or better. These findings are replicated, though with slightly weaker findings, for the 1996 GSS.

[29] Trusting others makes you 65 percent more likely to volunteer your time, according to the regression analysis. And you are 52 percent more prone to make charitable

TABLE 5-5. *Three-Stage Least Squares Estimation from 1996 Giving and Volunteering Survey*

	Coefficient	Standard Error	t Ratio
Trust	Model Chi Square = 207.717	(RMSE = .494)	
College Education	.100****	.026	3.799
Black	−.209****	.033	−6.232
Hispanic	−.071***	.028	−2.504
Age	−.001*	.001	−1.569
Worry about Future	.005	.010	.488
Baptist	−.108****	.025	−4.237
Parents Born in U.S.	.035***	.014	2.448
Confidence in Federal Government	.033***	.011	3.131
Volunteer	−.136	.153	−.887
Contribute to Charity	.431**	.194	2.221
Volunteer with Parents/Family	.016	.025	.646
Constant	.254****	.073	3.481
Volunteering	Model Chi Square = 466.903	(RMSE = .503)	
Trust	.648****	.129	5.016
College Education	.047*	.032	1.488
Active in Student Govt when Young	.049**	.028	1.742
Baptist	.064**	.036	1.789
Attend Services	.061****	.012	4.941
Volunteer with Parents/Family	.139****	.022	6.474
Spend Time with Friends from Work	.027**	.012	2.266
Spend Time with Friends from Church	.041***	.013	3.224
Spend Time with Friends from Sports	.025***	.010	2.362
Gender	.041**	.022	1.891
Have Helped Relatives	.196****	.025	7.730
Helped Homeless	.047**	.028	1.651
Constant	.275***	.087	3.166
Charitable Contributions	Model Chi Square = 354.513	(RMSE = .455)	
Trust	.520****	.088	5.936
High School Education	.140****	.041	3.427
College Education	.146***	.047	3.125
Family Income	.010****	.002	4.592
Attend Services	.056****	.009	6.059
Volunteer with Parents/Family	.067****	.018	3.699
Age	.002****	.001	4.061
Spend Time with Friends from Church	.032****	.009	3.501
Have Helped Relatives	.113****	.020	5.693
Constant	.283****	.063	4.521

**** $p < .0001$ *** $p < .01$ ** $p < .05$ * $p < .10$ $N = 1714$.

There is no easy way to solve this quandary, but I speculate that we may be more likely to volunteer with our own kind. Even putting religious volunteering to the side, we may give time with people like ourselves: in our schools, with our children's youth groups, and the like. As Sara Mosle (2000, 25) wrote: "A lot of what passes for volunteering used to be called simply 'parenting': people helping out in their own children's schools or coaching their own children's soccer teams. Kids with parents who already have resources end up benefitting the most."

Our charitable horizons may be more expansive. We may read about a faraway needy cause in the newspaper or see a story about it on television. We give aid to victims of natural disasters such as hurricanes or earthquakes. We are more likely to donate to homeless shelters than to spend time there. Many people spend time looking for "worthy causes" when they decide to give to charity, but may give of their time at the first and most convenient opportunity, which is likely to be among people they know. Giving to charity, except in the most unusual cases, involves helping people who are different from yourself, at least in class terms. Volunteering, even as it is more demanding, may not extend our horizons to strangers. If this argument is correct, no wonder we get more of a warm glow when we give money to strangers than when we give time to our children and neighbors.[30]

There is both circumstantial and more direct evidence for my argument. In the 1996 Pew Philadelphia survey, both generalized and particularized trusters are more likely to volunteer in schools, for environmental groups, with youth organizations, and for the elderly. Volunteers for the arts and in hospitals are more likely to be generalized trusters. And people who do good works through religious organizations are considerably more likely to be *particularized trusters*. Mainline (or "liberal") Protestant and Catholic churches do reach out to provide social services to the broader community. But white fundamentalist

---

contributions, with trust once more having bigger effects than helpful behavior in both childhood and adulthood, income, and even attending religious services, weekly attendance at which makes you 24 percent more likely to give to charity. The coefficient for volunteering on trust is slightly negative, though insignificant. Charitable contributions, on the other hand, remain more powerful, raising trust by 43 percent. In this model, trust has a bigger effect on charity than vice versa, but charity once again has a bigger impact on faith in strangers than does volunteering.

[30] Three graduate students (Kimberly Cull, Sebastian Gagnon-Messier, and Randi Macks) in my seminar on social capital suggested alternative explanations. People may have some bad experiences volunteering, but since there is no personal contact in giving to charity, donors will remain full of hope.

churches "do not embrace social service provision as an essential part of their mission [and] concentrate their energy on evangelism or meeting the immediate needs of congregational members" (Greenberg 1999, 19–20). Much religious volunteering draws on one's "strong" ties to people one knows (Granovetter 1973) rather than on weaker bonds to the larger community.[31]

The Social Capital Benchmark Survey, conducted in the summer and fall of 2000, provides even stronger evidence (see note 11). This survey separated donations to charity by whether their source was religious or secular, and volunteering by beneficiary. *Generalized trust has no effect on religious giving, but a significant impact on secular donations. Religious donations stem from particularized trust (trust in your coreligionists), while secular donations do not.* Most people who trust nobody still contribute to religious causes. Generalized trusters and people who *only* trust people of their own faith are equally likely to give to religious causes. A bare majority of mistrusters, however, give to secular causes, compared to 63 percent of people who only trust others of their faith and 76 percent of generalized trusters.

Similarly, much of the good works we do for volunteering benefit our own kind. People give time to the arts because it interests them (they are highly educated), not because they trust others. Going to religious services and participating in your house of worship, not trust, leads people to give time to spiritual causes. Having kids, rather than being trusting, engages people in volunteering for young people. *On the other hand, some volunteering does reach out, most notably giving time to the poor or elderly, for health care or fighting disease, or for a civic group. The type of volunteering that reaches out to others depends upon generalized trust; in contrast, people who primarily trust their coreligionists shy away from helping strangers. And people who only trust people of their same ethnic background are less likely to engage in almost all kinds of volunteering than generalized trusters, even at their houses of worship.*[32]

---

[31] Note, of course, that the friends and family factor includes people in your church.

[32] There are too many results to spell them all out. I estimated identical probit models for volunteering for arts, health, the needy and elderly, civic groups, religion, and youth. The predictors, in addition to the two measures of trust, include: age; gender; family income; education; attending services; participation in other activities in your house of worship; owning your own home; being a student or a homemaker; the number of hours a day you watch television; weekly hours working; the number of children living at home; the time you spend commuting each day; and a dummy variable for race (black).

Do these findings represent a general syndrome of civic engagement by generalized trusters and withdrawal by particularized trusters? No! Some particularized trusters will participate only in groups of their own kind. Fundamentalist Christians, for example, don't participate much in secular civic groups (see the citations in Chapter 2). Yet there is less evidence that particularized trust leads to opting out more generally. People who only trust their own ethnic group generally participate at similar levels to generalized trusters in 17 of the 18 types of groups in the Social Capital Benchmark Survey. People who only trust their coreligionists are just as active as generalized trusters in 15 of the 18 forms of association.[33] Particularized trusters primarily opt out of the more demanding forms of civic engagement that might link them to people who are different from themselves. They can – and do – form their own self-help, hobby, and youth groups (among others). And so do misanthropes. Mistrusters do participate less than either particularized or generalized trusters, but the differences are generally minuscule.[34] As

Trust in coreligionists leads to *more* participation only for volunteering for religion and the arts, and for *less* participation for the needy, health, and civic groups. Generalized trust is significant only for the needy, health, and civic groups. I constructed a measure of overall trust from the generalized trust question and the question about trusting coreligionists. People who answered positively to the generalized trust question and who said that they trusted their coreligionists a lot were classified as generalized trusters. Generalized mistrusters who trusted coreligionists a lot or some were classified as particularized trusters. People who trusted neither were classified mistrusters. Eighty-seven percent of generalized trusters, compared to 83 percent of particularized trusters and 72 percent of mistrusters, contributed money to religious causes; 76 percent of generalized trusters, compared to 63 percent of particularized trusters and 53 percent of mistrusters, contributed to secular charities. I also constructed a more complex measure of particularized trust, using the mean scores for trust in racial and ethnic in-groups (whites, Asians, African-Americans, and Hispanics). The measure is similar to that for coreligionists, but because of differing marginals, I used trust "a lot" or "some" of in-groups in building the measure of generalized trust. The results show that generalized trusters are 5–9 percent more likely to volunteer *in each of the areas*, including religious venues, with the exception of giving time to the arts. Each of these differences was significant at $p < .0001$ or better.

[33] The 18 groups are: religion; sports; youth; parent-teachers; veterans; neighborhood associations; elderly; charity; service; unions; professional; ethnic; political; literary; hobby; self-help; and internet. Generalized trusters are very slightly more likely to participate in service groups compared to people who only have faith in their own ethnic groups. And they are slightly more likely to participate in political groups than folks who only trust people who share their faith. The relationships, however, are stronger for professional associations and service groups. People who only trust their own ethnic group are slightly less likely to join service groups.

[34] When I cross-tabulate the composite measures of trust against group membership, *none* of the tau-c correlations is above .10 for ethnic-based particularized trust. Only

misanthropes have friends, they also seem to have groups. They may be dour sorts, but misery does seem to love company, too.

REACH OUT AND TOUCH SOMEONE

It seems tempting to draw a sharp line between the social ties that depend upon trust and those that don't. If an act draws upon a sense of compassion, then it will be based upon trust. If the social tie is mainly for your own enjoyment, it has no ties to trust. This is too simplistic an argument. There are all sorts of reasons for doing good deeds beyond the sense of generalized faith in others, ranging from a commitment to people who are close to you (family and friends) to a basic sense of human decency that most people share. Random acts of kindness won't produce trust, since faith in others is not based upon reciprocity. Helpful behaviors may not even be good guides to who is trustworthy and who is not. Some good deeds produce a warm glow, while others are mere fireflies in the realm of trust, lighting up one's faith in humanity for a brief second before fluttering away.

There are some data fragments that directly address the question of whether trust depends upon reciprocity. The 1996 Giving and Volunteering Survey asked respondents whether they had been helped by someone else when they were young, whether their family had helped someone, or whether someone they admired had helped someone. If trust depends upon reciprocity and experience, then being helped or seeing someone close to you assist others should matter mightily for your own views. But they don't: 38.5 percent of people who had been helped by someone when they were young believe that most people can be trusted compared to 38.3 percent who were not the beneficiaries of beneficence; 38.7 percent of people whose family helped someone when they were young trust others, compared to 37.8 of people whose family provided no assistance. And marginally fewer people who saw someone they admire provide aid place their faith in others (38.5 percent compared to 38.8 percent).[35]

In most cases, there is no clear linkage between receiving help, or even seeing someone you admire give assistance, and whether you volunteer

charitable groups, professional societies, and service groups have tau-c's above .10 for faith-based particularized trust. Details are available on request.

[35] For "being the beneficiary of beneficence," tau-b = .002, gamma = .004; for "family helped someone when you were young," tau-b = .008, gamma = .020; for "someone you admire helped someone," tau-b = −.003, gamma = −.006.

now. In a few cases, there are moderate correlations, but they tend to reflect volunteering activities that may help out people you know (youth-related volunteering and giving time through work).[36]

Nor does the link between helping and trust depend upon who the beneficiary is. You can help a neighbor or give a homeless person some spare change – in neither case are you likely to be more trusting than others in the society. Helping strangers is not a fail-safe guide to a trusting disposition.

In the summer of 1998 my family took a break from the Delaware shore. We visited Australia and rented a motor home (and didn't take a cooler with us). Somewhere between nowhere and nowhere else we had a flat tire. We barely knew where we were and had no idea where the spare tire was located. I saw a small house down the road and my son and I walked there to see if we could ring the emergency road service for help. A woman answered the door, took pity on this father and son with strange accents, and let me call both the road service and the owner of the motor home company. We thanked her for her kindness and walked back to the van to wait the hour or so it would take the road service to appear.

Five minutes later a truck whizzed by in the opposite direction, stopped suddenly, made a U-turn, and pulled up to our motor home. The same woman and her husband got out and he immediately squeezed under the vehicle, located the spare, got his jack from his truck, and began changing the tire. He continued working hard even when the road service arrived (thankfully in just fifteen minutes) and didn't leave until we were road-ready once more. Then, he and his wife (who stood directing traffic around us) got back in their truck, waved, and took off like the Lone Ranger and Tonto.[37]

Why did the Australian couple help us? It was clear that they didn't expect any reciprocity from me. I offered to pay for the phone calls. They declined. It was highly unlikely that they would expect some favor from me in the future, since we were returning to the States in three days and they did not appear prosperous enough to make the trip to the Washington area. Even if they somehow wound up in my

---

[36] These data come from the 1996 Giving and Volunteering Survey. Details are available upon request.
[37] *The Lone Ranger* was a children's Western television program in the United States in the 1950s. The ranger wore a mask to conceal his identity. He and "his faithful Indian companion," Tonto, would ride the range looking for people in trouble. He would help them out, and then he and Tonto would ride away without identifying themselves.

neighborhood, they were in a particularly poor situation to demand reciprocity since (like the Lone Ranger) they didn't even ask our names (or give us theirs).

Here was a couple who could have turned us away. They could have demonstrated their fine character by simply letting us make the two long-distance calls. But they chose to come back and find us and help us out, even when the road service was working on the tire. This seems like a wonderful trust story. But it may not be. All sorts of people, trusters and mistrusters, are willing to help people that they can identify.

In both the Giving and Volunteering Survey and the Niemi-Jennings parent sample, generalized trusters reserve their good deeds for *organized* volunteering rather than person-to-person assistance. And these good works have a big impact on their children. Parents who take part in organized volunteering have more trusting children. And this impact is lasting. If your parents volunteered, you will be more trusting as a young adult, as well.[38]

Individual acts of beneficence, including helping family, neighbors, the homeless, or other needy people you see on the street are uncorrelated with trust.[39] Informal helping does reflect your personal experience: People who were helped when they were young or who saw someone they admire help someone when they were young are more likely to give to a *specific individual* who needs help. But they are not any more prone than others to do organized volunteering or donate to charitable organizations. This is where trust comes in. It takes generalized trust to give either time or money to help people you don't know and will likely never see (cf. Amato 1990, 31). Good works toward your own kind or at least to people you can identify is based upon personal experiences and reciprocity. Good works toward people you can't identify depends upon your moral sense, and not upon your life history.[40]

Helping people you can see is not quite the same thing as helping your own kind, but the psychological logic seems similar. Once we make eye

---

[38] Seventy-one percent of high school students whose parents volunteered are trusters compared to 63 percent whose parents did not (gamma = .179). Seventeen years later (in 1982), 70.3 percent of young adults whose parents had volunteered in 1965 said that most people can be trusted compared to 60.3 percent whose parents did not volunteer (gamma = .220).

[39] In the 1996 Giving and Volunteering Survey, these activities are correlated (gammas) with trust at .014, -.033, -.051, and -.033, respectively.

[40] These results are based upon a three-stage least squares estimation of models for trust, volunteering, giving to charity, helping the homeless, and helping other needy people from the 1996 Giving and Volunteering Survey. Details are available upon request.

contact, we seem to treat beneficiaries as different from the "generalized" stranger. We think back to our experiences when others helped us and we react in kind. The Australian couple who helped us may have taken pity upon us when I walked up to their house, with my son, then eight years old, looking at them expectantly. Perhaps someone had helped one of their children. Reciprocity may lead us to do good deeds. But it won't lead us to trust and it will lead us to do different sorts of good deeds than will trust.

We may readily jump to the conclusion that people who help others, like the husband and wife who helped fix the flat tire on our van in Australia, must be generalized trusters since they perform good deeds. But this isn't the case. I didn't ask whether they believe that most people can be trusted and they didn't volunteer whether they have a positive view of human nature. But, upon reflection, there was little reason to expect that they were generalized trusters. People in small towns and rural areas may depend upon such acts of reciprocity – the couple who helped my family may have benefited from others' assistance in the past. Australians who live in rural areas are generally less trusting than urban residents, but they are *more* likely to provide help to other people (Onyx and Bullen 1998).

Neither trust nor civic engagement rest upon reciprocity. And if people don't decide to trust others based upon people they know, they certainly should not make up their minds based upon the purported behavior of people they don't know. Thus, contextual effects are not likely to represent estimates of trustworthiness. Instead, the assumption that they stand for contagion effects seems quite reasonable.

Generalized trust isn't simply an evaluation of how trustworthy others are. But it is far more than a synopsis of how we see ourselves. Almost everyone sees themselves as trustworthy. Fifty-three percent of Americans said that they were "very trusting" persons and an additional 39 percent called themselves "somewhat trusting" in the 1998 GSS. In the Pew Philadelphia survey, more than 90 percent of people said that "most people trust you." Yet our upbeat views of ourselves don't translate readily into favorable views of others. A majority of "very trusting" people (56 percent) says that "you can't be too careful in dealing with people." And a majority (51.7 percent) who say that "most people trust you" also urge caution in dealing with others.[41]

---

[41] People who say that they are less trusting are also less likely to have faith in others, but the relationship is not strong (tau-c = .086, gamma = .167). And people who say that others trust them are also more likely to say that most people can be trusted, but again the relationship is not overwhelming (phi = .174, Yule's Q = .627).

FROM PEOPLE WE KNOW TO STRANGERS

Most of our social connections neither depend upon trust nor produce it. They are "moral dead ends." For a few activities, you need trust (the "virtuous arrow") and for even fewer there is evidence of a "virtuous circle." Even when social ties can produce trust, they depend even more heavily upon it. Most of the time, you can't get there (trust in strangers) from here (trust in people you know).

There is reason to be skeptical of the linkage between trust in people you know and a generalized faith in others. As Rosenblum (1998, 48) argues:

There is the tendency to adopt a simplistic "transmission belt' model of civil society, which says that the beneficial formative effects of association spill over from one sphere to another. . . . The "transmission belt" model is simplistic as a general dynamic. It is one thing to say that within face-to-face rotating credit associations "social networks allow trust to become transitive and spread: trust you, because I trust her and she assures me that she trusts you," and quite another thing to show that habits of trust cultivated in one social sphere are exhibited in incongruent groups in separate spheres.

In Japan, there is evidence of such a "transmission belt" of trust – from your immediate family to the school to the workplace – and then it stops. Particularized trust doesn't spread to strangers in Japan; indeed, "when Japanese people are taken out of . . . settings" where trust has developed because of personal ties, "they tend often to behave in highly aggressive and exploitative ways" (Eisenstadt 2000, 61). Stolle (2000, 233) argues that civic groups amount to "private social capital," providing benefits only to members that "are not universal and cannot be generalized to other settings."

The 1999 *New York Times* Millennium Survey asked the generalized trust, fairness, and helpfulness questions, as well as whether people they know were fair or helpful. And the 1996 Pew Philadelphia survey asked the generalized trust, fairness, and helpfulness questions, as well as whether friends and family were trustworthy (see Chapters 2 and 3). These surveys offer an opportunity to examine the reciprocal effects of expectations about people we know and trust in strangers. I estimated simultaneous equation models for the three measures of generalized trust, fairness, and helpfulness and the two knowledge-based indicators for the *New York Times* Millennium survey and for the same three measures and the trust in friends and family factor for the Pew survey. I present diagrams of the key relationships in Figures 5-1 and 5-2 (see Appendix A for the full models).

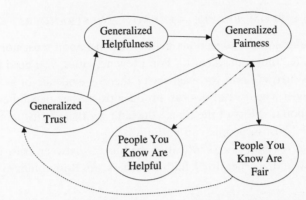

FIGURE 5-1. The Relationship between Generalized and Strategic Trust in the 1999 *New York Times* Millennium Survey. Connected lines reflect statistical significance at $p < .05$ or better. Dashed lines reflect statistical significance at .10. Mixed long and short dashes indicate a significant relationship at $p < .10$ between "people you know are helpful" and generalized fairness and a significant relationship at $p < .05$ between generalized fairness and "people you know are helpful."

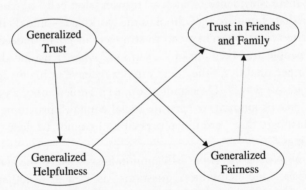

FIGURE 5-2. The Interaction of Generalized and Strategic Trust from the 1996 Pew Metropolitan Philadelphia Survey. Connected lines reflect statistical significance at $p < .05$ or better. Dashed lines reflect statistical significance at .10.

For the *Times* Millennium Survey, I constrained the linkages among the three generalized measures: Trust could shape fairness and helpfulness, but not the other way around. This is arbitrary, but allowing for complete reciprocal causation led to nonsensical results where nothing caused anything else. The story in Figure 5-1 is that interpersonal trust is related to the other generalized measures (hardly a surprise since many people use them as part of the same scale). But it has only weak relationships to the knowledge-based measures.

Trusting strangers doesn't make you more likely to believe that people you know would be helpful or fair. We are much more likely to say that people *we know* are both helpful (85 percent) and fair (90 percent), compared to people we don't know (59 percent helpful, 35 percent fair, and 40 percent trusting). As Hardin (2000, 80) argues, we restrict most of our interactions to people we know are trustworthy.[42] We have so much confidence in people we know that our personal relations are a rather poor guide to how we feel about strangers. There is, to be sure, a link between knowledge-based fairness and generalized trust, but it is rather weak and is barely significant, even at the generous .10 level.

The results of the 1996 Pew Philadelphia survey are even more pointed. Here I estimate just two equations, one for interpersonal trust and the other for particularized (knowledge-based) trust in our friends and family. Generalized trust shapes generalized helpfulness and fairness. Generalized fairness, *but not generalized trust*, makes people more likely to have faith in friends and family. But there is *no reciprocal relationship* from knowledge-based trust *to any of the generalized measures of trust, fairness, or helpfulness. You simply can't get there from here.* We don't transfer trust in people we know to strangers. So the weak links between trust and socializing with people like ourselves stem from the lack of a broader connection.

The Pew Philadelphia study shows why trust in one domain doesn't translate easily into the other. Among the most important factors shaping generalized trust are a sense of personal control (I can have an impact on my community) and parental warning not to trust others (see Appendix A). Personal connections such as support networks have no role in predicting generalized trust. But they are critical for particularized trust. How you feel about your friends and family depends upon how long you have lived in your community, whether you think that you can turn to people for support, whether you have people you can rely upon, if you are a union member, whether you have volunteered for a secular organization, and especially your race.

---

[42] This comparison shows that Hardin is wrong when he interprets the standard trust question as reflecting our personal knowledge.

Particularized trust reflects your immediate life experiences far more than generalized trust.

These results are *not* specific to one culture. Gibson (2001, 61) reports a correlation of virtually zero between trust in strangers and trust in people in your social network *in Russia*. As in the United States, the overwhelming majority of people place trust in their acquaintances and only a minority have faith in strangers.

TRUST IN PEOPLE AND TRUST IN GOVERNMENT

If neither trust in friends nor recpirocity makes us more trusting of strangers, might government do the job? Do attitudes toward government shape our relations with fellow citizens? Is the well-documented decline of faith in government in the United States responsible for the waning of interpersonal trust?

Lane (1959, 164) argues, "Trust in elected officials is seen to be only a more specific instance of trust in mankind." Advocates of a link between the two types of trust maintain that strong government performance makes people feel better about government, and, ultimately, more willing to cooperate with each other (Misztal 1996, 198; Berger and Brehm 1997; Brehm and Rahn 1997, 1008; Stolle 1999b). Citizens can rest easier when dealing with strangers if they know that government will enforce contracts. We don't have to be quite so wary in dealing with each other if we know that there is a neutral arbitrator to resolve disputes (Levi 1998). Rahn, Brehm, and Carlson (1997, 24) argue that when people trust their government, they are more likely to believe that they can influence it. This growing sense of efficacy makes people more likely to trust each other.

But Americans' sense of efficacy has not grown. As we have lost faith in each other, we also have far less confidence in government. In 1964, almost 80 percent of Americans trusted the federal government to "do the right thing" always or most of the time. By 1994 the percentage of trusters had fallen to barely more than 20 percent before bouncing up again in 1996 (to 29 percent). We became much more likely to believe that government is run by big interests (from 31 percent in 1964 to 72 percent in 1996); that government wastes taxes (from 48 to 61 percent); that many in government are crooked (from 30 to 43 percent); that government officials don't care about the common person (from 75 percent in 1960 to 25 percent); and that "people like me have no say" in politics (from 30 percent in 1960 to 45 percent).

Distrust of government may well be a rational response to a venal political system. Fifty or more years ago, a lobbyist asked Louisiana Governor Earl Long how he should explain a broken campaign promise on a tax break for business. Long replied, "I'll tell you what to tell them. Tell them I lied" (quoted in Liebling 1970, 41). Several decades later, then-Representative (now Senator) John Breaux (D-LA) was asked if his vote could be bought. No, he replied, "but it is available for rent" (quoted in Barone and Ujifusa 1997, 621). In between one president was forced to resign for lying about a burglary and another was forced to forsake reelection because he had not told the truth about a war many thousands of miles away. Later, another chief executive lost an election for going back on his solemn pledge not to raise taxes, while a second president was impeached for lying to a grand jury about indiscretions with an intern.

Distrust is the citizen's tool to try to keep political leaders honest; some skeptics see exhortations to trust our leaders as strategies by the powerful to keep the masses in their place (Barber 1983, 167–70). Leaders lie to us about things big and small.[43] They may manipulate the economy to get themselves reelected (Tufte 1978). No wonder we have less trust in our elected leaders.

Is our withdrawal of faith in other people part of the same syndrome as our decline in faith in government? At the aggregate level, trust in people and confidence in government go together. The two trends track each other quite closely, with a simple correlation of almost .800 (see Figure 5-3).[44] Looking at survey responses, Brehm and Rahn (1997) find support for the linkage at the individual level, as well. Their examination of GSS data shows a reciprocal relationship between the two types of trust. Confidence in government was *the most important factor shaping faith in other people* – a finding replicated by Berger and Brehm (1997, 22) using the 1972-74-76 ANES panel.

Yet there is reason to be skeptical about the link between the two types of trust. If trust in government rests on perceptions that our leaders are out of touch or even crooked, it is not clear that we should expect generalized trust to follow the same path. Trust in people is not primarily based upon the assumption that other people, much less our politicians,

---

[43] Which is which depends upon where you stand on the political spectrum.
[44] The trust-in-government question is the standard ANES query about how often you can trust the government in Washington to do the right thing. The strong correlation reflects the time trend (downward) common to both trust items. When I detrend both, they are not so strongly related ($r = .413$).

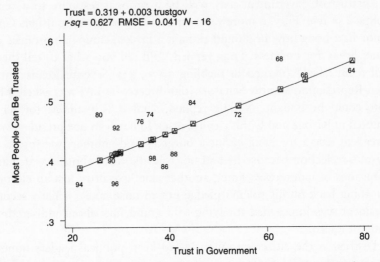

FIGURE 5-3. Trust in Government and Trust in People in the United States, 1964–98.

are trustworthy. If confidence in government depends more on our evaluations of specific institutions and their performance (Citrin 1974; Hetherington 1998), there is even less reason to expect similar roots for trust in people.

In the analysis in Chapter 4, sometimes trust in government was a significant predictor of generalized trust and sometimes it wasn't. It reached significance in surveys that lacked good measures of general optimism (the ANES and the Giving and Volunteering Survey), but was insignificant where there were good measures of hopefulness and control (the GSS). So the connection between the two types of trust may reflect a common foundation of positive feelings.

Even then, there is less of a syndrome of positivity than Lane (and others) may have imagined. Trust in people and trust in government are *not* strongly correlated at the individual level in the United States (Orren 1997, 85), in Russia (Gibson 2001, 64), or formerly Communist countries more generally (Mishler and Rose 2001). Nor is there a significant linkage cross-nationally (Newton 1999). I spell out the bivariate relationship measures in Table 5-6. I also compare the more standard ANES question (see note 40) with the GSS measure on confidence in the executive branch. The correlations between interpersonal trust and confidence in government are generally rather modest. The average tau-c for the ANES measure is .117, the average gamma .261. For the GSS question, the averages are .094 and .175.[45]

So why do other studies find such powerful reciprocal effects between the two types of trust? The time period that Berger and Brehm (1997) examine, the early-to-mid 1970s, is highly atypical. This period of Watergate and Vietnam had unusually high correlations between the two types of trust. The correlations (tau-c) range from .207 in the 1976 ANES to .227 for the 1972 survey, by far the most powerful in the eleven measurements and more than twice as great as the mean for other years. There is much the same pattern, though slightly less pronounced, for gammas. And we see the same pattern for the GSS data: The correlations for 1973–1976 are higher than almost any others. When I remove the surveys from 1972 to 1976, the mean tau-c with interpersonal trust falls by 31 percent for the ANES measure and by almost 10 percent for the already-lower GSS question.

Interpersonal trust is far more stable in the 1972-74-76 ANES panel than confidence in government: 73.4 percent of people had the same general level of trust in people over four years, compared to 56.9 percent for trust in government (see Table 3-3 in Chapter 3). More than twice as many young people had consistent responses to trust in people from 1965 to 1982 than stayed the same on confidence in government (63.9 percent compared to 29.9 percent in the Niemi-Jennings youth sample). The gap was only slightly less pronounced over these 17 years for their parents: 71.7 percent compared to 44.8 percent (see Table 3-4 in Chapter 3).

Trust in people is a long-term value, while confidence in government reflects our evaluation of how well government performs, especially on the economy (Citrin 1974; Lipset and Schneider 1983; Hetherington 1998). When people think that the government is doing a good job, they say that they trust government. How well the government is doing can change in a relatively short period of time. The mid-1970s were a good example of how political turbulence can weaken trust in government. In

---

[45] The GSS also asks about trust in the legislative branch. Since attitudes toward Congress play a large role in shaping generalized trust in government, I also examined the correlations between confidence in the legislature and trust in people. The average tau-c is .041 (.037 with 1972–6 excluded) and the average gamma is .084 (.080 with 1972–6 excluded). The aggregate correlation ($N = 19$) over time between confidence in the legislative and executive branches is .759. The individual-level tau-c's range from .304 in 1974 (when Congress and the president were virtually at war) to .485 in 1978. The gammas range from .493 to .759.

TABLE 5-6. *Correlations between Trust in People and Trust in Government: 1964–96*

ANES Question Wording[a]			GSS Question Wording[b]		
Source	tau-c	gamma	Source	tau-c	gamma
1964 ANES	.143	.268			
1966 ANES[c]	.160	.251			
1968 ANES	.122	.227			
1972 ANES	.227	.408			
			1973 GSS	.119	.215
1974 ANES	.220	.430			
			1975 GSS	.124	.234
1976 ANES	.207	.426	1976 GSS	.165	.313
			1978 GSS	.097	.189
			1980 GSS	.095	.175
			1983 GSS	.107	.201
			1984 GSS	.118	.213
			1986 GSS	.055	.103
1987 GSS[c]	.136	.252	1987 GSS	.105	.193
			1988 GSS	.071	.133
			1989 GSS	.092	.171
			1990 GSS	.127	.232
			1991 GSS	.026	.049
1992 ANES	.076	.158			
			1993 GSS	.125	.239
			1994 GSS	.075	.144
1995 Washington Post[c]	.046	.100			
1996 ANES					
Preelection	.117	.244	1996 GSS	.048	.092
Postelection	.085	.177			
1998 ANES	.098	.194	1998 GSS	.038	.075
Mean	.117	.261		.094	.175
Mean Excluding 1972–1976	.084	.208		.084	.158

[a] "Do you trust the government in Washington to do the right thing?"
[b] Confidence in the executive branch of government.
[c] Four-point scale employed.

1972, 57 percent of Americans said that they could trust the government in Washington to do the right thing all or most of the time; by 1974, as Watergate, Vietnam, energy crises, and racial problems dominated national politics, just 38 percent gave government the benefit of the doubt most of the time. The ANES panel showed virtually no change in the aggregate share of people who said that "most people can be trusted."

It is easy to see why there are differences. Our evaluation of government depends upon specific performances: how much we like the president, the Congress, and even the Supreme Court. But it is not simply about our preferences for abstract institutions. Confidence in Washington reflects our evaluations of the men and women who lead the nation. It also reflects how well people think things are going in the country *now*. Trust in government, then, largely reflects our experience with our political world and how we evaluate specific performance. It is partly about seeing government as trustworthy, but even more about how well we think our leaders are doing their jobs. As a friend remarked at a social capital conference: "I have a lot of trust in other people, but I see no reason to trust my government because I don't agree with what it is doing."[46]

Our evaluation of government is, in Levi's words, always contingent. And that means that trust in government is *strategic* trust.[47] Confidence in government reflects our experiences with specific leaders and institutions, rather than abstract ideals. We evaluate the performance of government in many of the same ways that we judge the performance of contractors. Our expectations for leaders are simple: They should keep the economy humming along and keep the country out of war. They should pursue policies in accord with public opinion, or at least attitudes in their own constituencies (Fenno 1978; Patterson and Caldeira 1990; Hibbing and Thiess-Morse 1995, Chapter 5; Stimson et al. 1995; Kimball and Patterson 1997). And they should foster an image of trustworthiness. People base their evaluations on both performance and on specific knowledge of government decisions – whether they like them or

---

[46] This quote is from Per Selle of the University of Bergen at the European Consortium for Political Research Workshop on Social Capital in Copenhagen, April 2000. The quote may not be exact.

[47] Hardin (1995, 25; 2000, 221) argues that we don't know enough people in government personally to determine whether we should trust them. But apparently a large number of Americans feel comfortable evaluating political leaders and institutions and using these judgments to express trust or mistrust about government. Ninety-four percent of Americans in the 1996 ANES were willing to place President Bill Clinton on a left-right scale and just 16 percent said that he was a conservative. Ninety-one percent could rate Republican presidential nominee Bob Dole on the left-right scale and just 13 percent said he was a liberal. Overall, most people seem to know enough about the political leanings of their leaders to make judgments about them.

not. There is even some evidence that popular approval of the Supreme Court reflects agreement with its decisions (Caldeira 1986). We may not know the people in government personally, but we believe that we have quite enough information to make judgments about them and the institutions in which they serve.

The public shows what we might consider common sense when it evaluates specific departments in the government, according to a survey by the Pew Research Center for The People and The Press. The Postal Service, the Park Service, the Centers for Disease Control, the Defense Department, and the Food and Drug Administration get the most favorable evaluations, while the Department of Housing and Urban Development, the Central Intelligence Agency, and the Internal Revenue Service fall at the bottom (Baer 1998). The top ratings seem to go to agencies that provide services – usually with considerable efficiency – or protect people against disease and contamination. The public is most skeptical about investigative bodies or other agencies that consistently get negative press. There seems to be some factual basis for Americans' evaluations of their government departments.

One of the best ways to demonstrate the differences between the two types of trust is to estimate models for each and then see how well the trust-in-people model accounts for confidence in government (and vice versa). I use the 1996 ANES to estimate models for each variant of trust based upon the theory I have developed for interpersonal trust and upon the extant literature for how we evaluate government.[48] I present these models in Tables 5-7 and 5-8 below.

The trust-in-people model (Table 5-7) includes a workable measure of particularized trust (in-group trust for whites, African-Americans, and Hispanics minus out-group trust), as well as measures of long-term optimism and control, religiosity, egalitarianism, efficacy, and standard demographics.[49] The trust-in-government model (Table 5-8) includes specific evaluations of officeholders (Bill and Hillary Clinton), institutions (the Supreme Court, the Congress, candidates for Congress), knowledge about government (knowing the majority party in Congress), political efficacy, and standard demographics. This model also includes both long-term and short-term evaluations of the economy, since our feelings about government may reflect how well we think that it is

---

[48] I dichotomized the trust-in-government measure.
[49] The 1996 ANES asks about trusting each group, not simply thermometer scores; see Chapter 7.

TABLE 5-7. *Probits for Trust in Government and Trust in People: 1996 ANES (Trust-in-People Model)*

	Trust in Government			Trust in People		
	Coefficient	Standard Error	Effect	Coefficient	Standard Error	Effect
Particularized Trust (In-group Minus Out-group)	.038	.036	.113	-.142****	.038	-.412
Too Much Attention Paid to Other's Well-being	-.082**	.037	-.108	-.073**	.037	-.099
Bible Literal Word of God	-.001	.059	-.001	-.101**	.058	.069
Not a Problem That Others Have Equal Chance	-.036	.033	-.047	-.105***	.034	-.144
Living Standards Better in Future	.232****	.045	.158	.168***	.045	.081
Days Read Daily Newspaper Last Week	.010	.014	-.049	.042***	.014	.100
People Like Me Have No Say in Politics	.153****	.032	.200	.162****	.031	.226
Black	-.181*	.130	-.057	-.595****	.142	-.191
Hispanic	-.054	.142	-.018	-.490***	.149	-.159
Family Income	-.021***	.006	-.166	.024***	.006	.141
Education	-.011	.015	-.060	.018*	.015	.104
Constant	-.583**	.286		-2.449****	.296	

Government: Estimated R^2 = .295 $-2*$Log Likelihood Ratio = 1441.168 N = 1241
People: Estimated R^2 = .287 $-2*$Log Likelihood Ratio = 1474.406 N = 1242
Percent Predicted Correctly: Probit: 70.2 Null: 70.1 Percent Predicted Correctly: Probit: 69.8 Null: 60.1
**** $p < .0001$ *** $p < .01$ ** $p < .05$ * $p < .10$

155

TABLE 5-8. *Probits for Trust in Government and Trust in People: 1996 ANES (Trust-in-Government Model)*[a]

	Trust in Government			Trust in People		
	Coefficient	Standard Error	Effect	Coefficient	Standard Error	Effect
Bill Clinton Feeling Thermometer	.007**	.002	.205	.001	.003	.051
Hillary Clinton Feeling Thermometer	.006**	.003	.182	.003	.003	.097
Supreme Court Feeling Thermometer	.010***	.003	.255	.001	.003	.041
Approval Of Congress	.173****	.036	.195	-.075	.032	-.042
Democratic House Candidates Feeling Thermometer	.005*	.003	.125	-.001	.003	.107
Know Republicans Have Majority In House	.064*	.039	.074	-.023	.037	-.033
Living Standards Better In Future	.162***	.060	.093	.116**	.056	.084
Better Off Than Last Year	.202****	.054	.217	.114***	.047	.163
People Like Me Have No Say in Politics	-.161***	.044	-.176	-.150****	.039	-.218
Politics Too Complicated	-.025	.045	-.028	-.152****	.040	-.221
Hispanic	-.192	.196	-.051	-.522***	.186	-.179
Black	-.749****	.192	-.174	-.550***	.172	-.189
Age	.012***	.003	.190	.007**	.003	.138
Family Income	-.012*	.009	-.078	.025****	.008	.205
Constant	-1.940****	.442		-2.107****	.406	

Government: Estimated R^2 = .499   -2*Log Likelihood Ratio = 810.212   N = 815
People: Estimated R^2 = .201   -2*Log Likelihood Ratio = 1012.248   N = 812.
Percent Predicted Correctly: Probit: 73.7   Null: 70.7   Percent Predicted Correctly: Probit: 65.2   Null: 54.7.
**** $p < .0001$ *** $p < .01$ ** $p < .05$ * $p < .10$.
[a] Effects for age calculated between .18 and 75.

156

performing now, while the optimism that underlies generalized trust is more long-term.[50]

The two types of trust clearly have different foundations. The most important variable in the trust-in-people model is by far particularized trust. The more you trust your in-group compared to out-groups, the less likely you are to trust other people. Particularized trust has *the wrong sign* for trust in government. Race is far more important for trust in people, and so are egalitarian beliefs and religious values. Only efficacy ("people like me have no say in politics") and a sense of control ("too much attention is paid to others' well-being") are strongly significant in both equations.

The most important factors in the trust-in-government model are evaluations of specific institutions (the Supreme Court and the Congress; cf. Feldman 1983; Luks and Citrin 1997; Hetherington 1998) and leaders (Bill and Hillary Clinton). Feelings about candidates for office (Democratic House candidates) and political knowledge (which party controls the House) also matter. *None of these factors is significant for trust in people* – two (approval of Congress and know which party has the majority) have the wrong sign. Evaluations of the economy are significant for both types of trust, and, as expected, short-term personal evaluations have a stronger impact for trust in government. Measures of efficacy and many of the demographics are significant in both equations.

The trust-in-people model is based largely on abstract ideas: how we view in-groups and out-groups, interpretation of the Bible, and social egalitarianism. True to my claim that trust is a moral ideal, faith in strangers reflects these deeply held values. Trust in government, in contrast, is a summary evaluation of how pleased we are with our leaders and institutions. The trust-in-government model performs very well for confidence in our institutions, but not nearly as well for trust in people.[51]

For the trust-in-people model, I calculated joint effects for particularized trust, interpretation of the Bible, social egalitarianism, race (the dummy variable for being black), and Hispanic identification.[52] Someone

---

[50] It might seem reasonable to include trust in people in the trust-in-government model and vice versa, but this would make it impossible to estimate the models in Tables 5-7 and 5-8.

[51] The estimated R^2 = .499 for the trust-in-government model, compared to .201 for the trust-in-people model.

[52] The minimum value I used for particularized trust was −.548 and the maximum 2.468, representing the fifth and ninety-fifth percentiles.

who ranks high on out-group trust, endorses a liberal interpretation of the Bible, and is strongly concerned about social egalitarianism is 34.6 percent more likely to trust others than a person who ranks low on out-group trust, who places a low value on social egalitarianism, and endorses a literal interpretation of the Bible. The composite effect for trust in government is 8.8 percent.

When I repeat the same exercise for the trust-in-government model, the results are almost as striking. Here I used the six institutional-personal variables that shape trust in government. A respondent with positive evaluations of both Clintons, who strongly approved of both the Supreme Court and the Congress, who knew which party had majority control of the House, and who strongly approved of House Democratic candidates was 74.1 percent more likely to trust government than someone who strongly disliked the president and the First Lady, had little confidence in the Court or the Congress, who didn't like Democratic House candidates, and who could not say which party controlled the House. The composite effect for trust in people is 26.6 percent.[53] If there is anything remarkable about these findings, it is that these specific evaluations have a measurable impact at all for trust in people.

The broader message is that trust in government and trust in people don't have much in common. When I estimate a model allowing for each type of trust to cause the other, neither type of trust has an impact on the other.[54] This null finding is rather remarkable since both questions (at least in the ANES wording) include the word "trust" and both types of confidence depend upon a sense of efficacy.

REPRISE

Once more, we have seen evidence that trust in people largely *doesn't* depend upon our experiences. Neither people we know nor government makes us trusting of strangers. And this makes sense: We trust people

---

[53] The signs are reflected for approval of Congress, the House Democratic feeling thermometer, and knowledge of which party controlled Congress. For the Clintons, the minimum was zero and the maximum 100; for House Democratic candidates, it is 15 and 85 (see note 8 above).

[54] I estimated a two-stage least squares model for both trust in people (using the variables in the model in Table 7-2) and trust in government (using the variables in the model in Table 7-3), making each type of confidence endogenous to the other. Trust in people was not significant in the confidence-in-government model and vice versa.

we know because they have proven themselves trustworthy. We trust government when it works well and produces results and policies that we like. In both cases, our experiences are the most important factors shaping our confidence. Yet trust in strangers can't be based upon our experiences. So it shouldn't be surprising that these worlds of trust are quite different, if complementary.

Generalized trust is also more stable than trust in government. Yet this does not mean that it never changes. Trust in people has fallen dramatically from its high of almost 60 percent in 1960 to the mid-30s in the 1990s (before inching back up again to the 40s). When looking for the causes of the decline in trust, we now have some clear directions, and they point away from our personal lives and point more to collective experiences. I turn next to this question.

6

Stability and Change in Trust

You can't be too careful, times have changed. We are living at a faster pace and people go at their own speed. We live in a Microsoft-type hot bed and people are anxious to get ahead naturally.
– Respondent to the 2000 ANES Pilot Study "think aloud" question on trust

Trust is one of the most stable values, but it also has fallen sharply from its high in the boom years of the 1960s. In this chapter I look at both stability and change, though mostly the latter. Trust has fallen from 58 percent in 1960, the first time the question appeared on a national survey, to about 36 percent in 1996 (before rising to about 40 percent in 1998 and 1999). Something important is going on and we can learn some important lessons about the prospects for cooperation by looking at the dynamics of trust.

At one level stability and change may be quite consistent. Putnam (1995a, 1995b, 2000) argues that America has become less trusting because each succeeding generation has less faith in others. Our collective loss of trust stems from population replacement. There is much support for Putnam's argument, but a generational argument doesn't explain why younger people are less trusting. And it also cannot do justice to one remarkable countertrend: The generation that supposedly started the unraveling of trust, the Early Baby Boomers, shifted direction in the late 1980s. Soon they were to become the most trusting generation.

Even in the face of aggregate stability, there was some systematic shuffling of individual-level trust in the 1970s. And people responded in precisely the ways that my account of trust suggests that they should.

The Vietnam War tore apart a lot of intergenerational goodwill as young college students chanted in the streets: "Don't trust anyone over 30." And many of them didn't. The Vietnam War polarized the society and those who opposed it were particularly likely to lose faith in other people (Barone 1990, 392).

As destructive to the social fiber as the war was, something else was happening during the 1960s and 1970s that helped build some bridges and tear others down: the civil rights movement. The movement began in an era of high trust and became a strong moral crusade. Chong (1991, 1) called it "the quintessential example of public-spirited collective action of our time."

Yes, much of the struggle for civil rights was confrontational, but it also built bonds between people of different backgrounds and, for many people, laid the foundation for greater trust. It led others to become less trusting, but the overall impact on faith in others was positive. Volunteers in the civil rights movement, in particular, became more committed to establishing bonds across racial lines and to pushing for other goals, such as reducing poverty and ending the war in Vietnam (Demerath, Murwell, and Aiken 1971, Chapter 5). They came into the movement with high levels of faith in others and throughout the 1970s and 1980s remained far more trusting than the overall population. Seventy-nine percent of civil rights volunteers agreed that "most people can be trusted" in a 1965 survey; eight years later, this figure dropped marginally to 72 percent, and then rose to 83 percent in 1982, compared to a national sample in which just 58 percent said that others were trustworthy.[1]

The Baby Boomers came of age during the civil rights movement and much of the increase in trust for this cohort stems from their greater tolerance for out-groups. The Early Boomers were not only the most

[1] This trust question does not offer the alternative "you can't be too careful in dealing with people," so the mass public findings from the 1983 General Social Survey are higher than we find for the standard question. The civil rights volunteer data come from the Dynamics of Idealism surveys conducted by Michael T. Aiken, N. J. Demerath III, and Gerald Marwell in 1965, 1973, and 1982 at the Department of Sociology, University of Wisconsin, Madison, Wisconsin and available for downloading at http://dpls.dacc.wisc.edu/Idealism. See Demerath et al. (1971) for a more detailed analysis of these data. I looked for changes in civil rights volunteers' trust levels, but the skewed distributions, small samples, and moderately high rates of attrition across the panel make such inferences very hazardous. I am grateful to Megan Henly (and the Undergraduate Research Assistant Program at the University of Maryland) for putting the Dynamics of Idealism data set together for me.

trusting. They were by far the least committed to their own in-group. Both the Vietnam war and the civil rights movement established "collective memories" that had profound effects on trust (cf. Rothstein in press, for a similar argument about Sweden).

Beyond Vietnam and the civil rights movement is the omnipresent problem of optimism. Interpersonal trust reflects an optimistic worldview and as Americans became less optimistic they became less trusting. Yet optimism is not the entire story. As at least two of my colleagues have remarked, the problem with an account based just on optimism is that trust is "all in peoples' heads." Trust, a value, depends upon optimism, a way of looking at the world. Your worldview comes from your parents. But where do your parents get their ways of looking at the world? Sooner or later, I must come to grips with the real world. And even though people's trust doesn't reflect their personal life histories or resources, as I showed in Chapter 4, *collectively* the level of trust in society depends upon how economic goods are distributed. There is clearly a link between personal fate and collective outcomes. Yes, trust has gone down as economic inequality has risen, but the Early Baby Boomers have become more prosperous and more trusting.[2]

The experiences of Vietnam initially made the Early Boomers less trusting, but the effects of civil rights and optimism for the future pushed the Boomers toward greater trust. No other group became as tolerant as the Early Boomers. And certainly no other cohort fared so well economically. But it was not just how well the Early Boomers did, but how evenly their wealth was distributed. The post-World War II generation grew up in an era of great expectations and more of them "made it" than their parents or those who were born later. Tolerance, plus a more equitable distribution of resources, led one cohort to become more trusting, even as others lost faith in their fellow citizens.

THE DURABILITY OF TRUST

How stable is trust and how lasting are the effects of nurturing parenting? The Niemi-Jennings socialization study offers an opportunity to examine these questions since it contains data on young people and their parents at three points in time. The first survey, conducted in 1965, examined young people when they were in high school. By 1982, 17

---

[2] See a similar argument by Putnam (2000, 359–60) based upon a cross-sectional examination of the American states.

years later, the high school students were young adults in their mid-30s. Were they still trusting? In Chapter 3, I noted that 64 percent of young people had the same level of trust in 1982 that they did in 1965. In Chapter 4, I showed that high school students' trust reflected both their parents' faith in others and how nurturing their parents were. Trusting young people were more likely to have parents who let them determine their own friends and influence family decisions. They were also more likely to say that they sometimes disagreed with their parents (according to reports by the parents).

Seventeen years later, parental nurturing still paid off. Young adults whose parents let them determine their own friends when they were in high school were more likely (by 8 percent) to trust other people in an equation I estimated from the 1982 wave of the youth sample (see Table 6-1). In 1965 students who felt free to disagree with their parents were more likely to trust other people. As young adults, this relationship was reversed: Now young people who said that they largely agreed with their parents (in 1965) were more likely to become trusting adults. Young people value freedom from their parents. But if parents serve as role models, agreement with parents might be even more useful in transmitting values than tolerance of opposing viewpoints. Nurturing still matters later on, but in a different way: Young adults who find common bonds with their parents are more likely to trust others.

Parental trust also matters, though the effects don't seem quite as long-lasting as nurturing style. Whether you have faith in people depends upon your parents' confidence in others from nine years ago, rather than 17 years earlier. Young adults whose parents trusted other people in the past (1973) are more likely to trust others now. There may also be an indirect link from parental trust through education. Parental education (in 1965) shapes both parents' trust and young adults' trust, even 17 years later. Indeed, it is the strongest determinant of young adults' faith in others.[3]

The other major predictors, as measured by the effects, of young adult trust are young peoples' attitudes toward out-groups, and young peoples' own trust, all measured in 1965. Early tolerance of out-groups strongly promotes later trust. In-group attitudes don't matter quite so much.[4] The

---

[3] Young adults with highly educated parents are 23 percent more likely to trust others than their cohorts with parents who have little education.

[4] These findings parallel those in Chapter 4 for the Niemi-Jennings sample, though estimates using the same measures of in-group and out-group trust with ANES samples show much more powerful effects for in-group attitudes.

164 *The Moral Foundations of Trust*

TABLE 6-1. *Probit Analysis of Trust from Niemi-Jennings Parent-Child Panel: Child Sample 1982*

	Coefficient	Standard Error	MLE/SE	Effect
Trust (1965)	.472****	.109	4.339	.166
Parental Trust (1973)	.284***	.116	2.460	.098
Parent Education (1965)	.037**	.019	1.939	.225
Can Determine Own Friends/Activities	.121**	.055	2.184	.082
Parent: Sometimes Disagrees with Child	−.237**	.111	−2.127	−.081
In-group Trust (1965)	−.001	.004	−.203	−.015
Out-group Trust (1965)	.007**	.004	1.899	.213
Frequency Parent Service Attend (1965)	.144***	.052	−2.748	.145
Fundamentalist Church Member (1965)	−.178*	.110	−1.620	−.060
Life Will Be as Wished (1982)	.387****	.104	3.717	.131
Black	−.381**	.210	−1.814	−.133
Constant	−.602*	.288	−2.092	

Estimated R^2 = .281   −2*Log Likelihood Ratio = 806.963   N = 684.
Percent Predicted Correctly: Probit: 69.0   Null: 61.8.
**** $p < .0001$ *** $p < .01$ ** $p < .05$ * $p < .10$.

direct effect of parental trust and the indirect effects of nurturing style and the level of parental education are not the whole story. In the 1960s, before the current wave of fundamentalism, religiosity boosted interpersonal trust.[5]

Optimism for the future is a key determinant of trust and I showed in Chapter 4 that this result also holds for the Niemi-Jennings youth sample in 1965 with just about the same impact. People who said that their life hopes would be fulfilled were substantially more likely to trust other people. And again, African-Americans are less likely to trust others.

Overall, race, current levels of optimism, the legacy of parental nurturing and background, and values held 17 years previously are good

[5] Young adults whose parents had regularly attended religious services in the 1960s were 15 percent more likely to become trusting adults. Belonging to a fundamentalist church worked the other way – young adults who had been affiliated with such a church while in high school were 6 percent less likely to trust others.

predictors of trust as a young adult. The strongest predictors are *not* contemporaneous measures, but indicators that go back to high school (and perhaps college) years.[6]

A young adult who was trusting in 1965 had parents who placed confidence in others nine years earlier, and who gave high marks to out-groups, had a .769 probability of trusting others, compared to a .377 probability for a respondent who was not trusting 17 years earlier, did not have a trusting parent, and ranked out-groups negatively.[7] Add to the "trusting" profile four years of graduate education for a parent and the probability rises to .818. And then say that the parent attended religious services at least weekly in 1965 and the probability jumps further to .848. In contrast, consider the young adult at the other end of the scale: As a high school student, he didn't trust others and had negative views of out-groups. His parent in the sample had just a seventh-grade education, never attended services when he was in high school, and did not trust others nine years earlier. This young adult would have just a .209 probability of being a truster. A positive home environment, together with early trusting views, makes it almost inevitable that high school students will become Lane's "sociable" adults.

CHANGING PATTERNS OF TRUST

Trust may be stable, but it is not immovable. In the 1972-74-76 ANES panel, about a quarter of the respondents took a different position on trust from one wave to another, and slightly more than a third did so in the Niemi-Jennings youth sample over a longer period, 1965 to 1982. By now, we have a pretty good idea of what shapes trust: optimism for the future. The two trends track each other quite well in the GSS time series, as I show in Figure 6-1.[8] But rather than focusing on stability, I look at how people have changed their attitudes over time, which exploits one of the great advantages of panel studies (cf. Uslaner and Conway 1985). I thus concentrate on people who *don't* fit the

---

[6] The probit model in Table 6-1 correctly predicts 69 percent of the respondents (compared to 61.8 percent for a null model predicting that everyone would be a truster). This is a pretty solid result, virtually the same as the 1965 model for high school students using contemporaneous predictors.

[7] The boundaries for the effects are −22.7 and 25.0.

[8] The observation for 1980 is an outlier, since trust is higher than in proximate years. There is also an uptick in trust in 1976, 1984, and 1992, all presidential election years. I discuss this in Chapter 7.

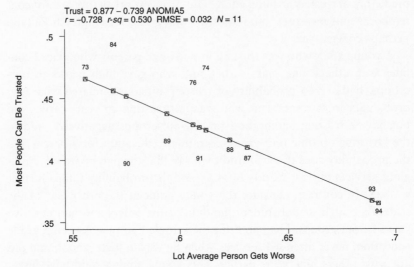

FIGURE 6-1. Trends in Trust and Optimism from General Social Survey. The year 1980 is excluded as an outlier. With 1980 included, $b = -.453$, $R^2 = .223$, RMSE = .042.

standard pattern of consistent behavior that is largely shaped by optimism, education, attitudes toward out-groups, fundamentalism, and a few other key indicators. I use both the ANES panel and the Niemi-Jennings youth sample from 1973 to 1982 to estimate models for changes in trust.[9]

The models I estimate for changes in trust are based upon two basic types of variables. The first type includes the determinants of trust I have employed throughout: attitudes toward out-groups, religiosity, and optimism for the future. The second is based upon the key events of the period during which trust fell most sharply: the civil rights movement and the war in Vietnam. I expect that people who became more favorable to civil rights would become more trusting, while those who opposed the war in Vietnam would become less trusting. The dependent variable is the direction of change in trust, from trust to distrust or from distrust to trust.[10] I estimate models for changes in trust from 1972 to

---

[9] I estimated some models for the Niemi-Jennings adult panel, but they were not terribly informative compared to the ANES panel. Similarly, there was nothing of note to report for changes in trust for 1965 to 1973 for the Niemi-Jennings child panel.

[10] People who moved from distrust to trust were coded "1," while those moving in the opposite direction were coded as "0."

TABLE 6-2. *Changes in Trust from 1972 to 1974 from ANES Panel*[a]

	Coefficient	Standard Error	MLE/SE	Effect
Change in In-group Trust 72–76	−.012**	.005	−2.281	−.329
Change Rights Leader Thermometer	.009**	.004	2.335	.251
Change Civil Rights Too Fast	−.110*	.068	−1.624	−.157
School Busing Scale	.137***	.058	2.354	.270
Change In Contextual Trust	5.324***	1.772	3.005	.366
Science May Upset Beliefs	−.069*	.043	−1.619	−.098
Gender	−.389**	.174	−2.229	−.140
Constant	1.226	.449	2.731	

Estimated R^2 = .206   −2*Log Likelihood Ratio = 304.738   N = 244.
Percent Predicted Correctly: Probit: 66.0   Null: 54.5.
**** $p < .01$ ** $p < .05$ * $p < .10$.
[a] Effect ranges are truncated from −40 to +40 for civil rights leader thermometer and from +2 to +2 for change in civil rights too fast.

1974 and from 1974 to 1976 using the ANES panel and from 1973 to 1982 for the Niemi-Jennings youth sample. I present the results in Tables 6-2, 6-3, and 6-4, respectively.[11]

The changes in trust in the early 1970s are largely due to the civil rights movement. The model in Table 6-2 reveals seven variables that significantly shape changes in trust from 1972 to 1974, and four of them either directly or indirectly stem from the civil rights movement. Apart from changes in contextual trust, the most powerful determinants of changes in trust are variations in in-group trust, changes in the feeling thermometers for civil rights leaders, changing evaluations of civil rights progress, and attitudes toward busing to schools.

People who became less insular toward their own groups, more favorable to civil rights leaders, less likely to say that the pace of civil rights was too fast, and who supported school busing for racial integration were overwhelmingly likely to become more trusting. A person who

---

[11] Once more a caveat is in order. The ANES and Niemi-Jennings panels can't help us determine what led to the decline in interpersonal trust. The Niemi-Jennings study showed no decrease in trust over time and the ANES panel actually had an increase in faith in others. But they do give us some insight into the forces that led to changing patterns of trust in the 1970s and 1980s. These panels also lack good measures of optimism, so I may underestimate the role of expectations for the future when I analyze these samples.

TABLE 6-3. *Changes in Trust from 1974 to 1976 from* ANES *Panel[a]*

	Coefficient	Standard Error	MLE/SE	Effect
Change in In-group Trust 72–76	–.012**	.006	–1.860	–.207
Change in Out-group Trust 72–76	.018***	.007	2.359	.277
Oppose U.S. Role in Vietnam (1976)	–.107**	.050	–2.133	–.139
Military Thermometer Change 74–76	.012***	.005	2.353	.223
Change in Contextual Trust 74–76	6.501***	2.113	3.077	.432
Safe to Walk Street at Night (1976)	.384**	.203	1.887	.127
Change in Service Attendance 74–76	–.137*	.093	1.478	–.136
Gender	.446**	.198	2.254	.146
Constant	–.574	.416	–1.378	

Estimated R^2 = .334   –2*Log Likelihood Ratio = 243.116 N = 213.
Percent Predicted Correctly: Probit: 70.4   Null: 64.3.
**** $p < .01$ ** $p < .05$ * $p < .10$.
[a] Effect ranges are truncated from –30 to +30 for military thermometer change 1974–6 and from –2 to 1 for change in service attendance from 1974–6.

supported busing and otherwise was becoming more favorable toward the civil rights movement and its leaders and less committed to her own in-group was almost certain to change (if she needed to at all) toward generalized trust. The probability of a change toward more trust is .968. People who opposed busing and became more insular and less supportive of civil rights were almost as certain to become mistrusters (probability of becoming a truster = .152).

Beyond the civil rights movement, there is evidence that fundamentalist values lead people to become less trusting. If you are worried that science might upset your religious beliefs, you were likely to move away from generalized trust.[12]

The civil rights movement energized the country's moral reserves. It might not have succeeded if it were simply a protest by African-Americans against centuries of discrimination. The movement would not have achieved the widespread support that led to changes in laws and behavior in the 1960s. And it most emphatically would not have built

[12] The impact here is 10 percent in Table 6-2. There is also a significant and powerful effect for gender: Men became less trusting, although the reason why is unclear.

TABLE 6-4. *Changes in Trust from 1973 to 1982 from Niemi-Jennings Parent-Child Panel: Child Sample*[a]

	Coefficient	Standard Error	MLE/SE	Effect
U.S. Did Right in Vietnam (1973)	−.431**	.239	−1.804	−.141
Change in Black Thermometer 65–82	.008**	.005	1.738	.374
These Are Best Years of Life (1982)	.721***	.305	2.366	.235
Change in Business Thermometer 73–82	.029****	.007	4.041	.565
Had Friend of Opposite Race (1965)	.520**	.258	2.015	.162
Constant	−.293	.315	−.930	

Estimated R^2 = .382   −2*Log Likelihood Ratio = 170.314 N = 151.
Percent Predicted Correctly: Probit: 72.2   Null: 58.9.
**** $p < .0001$ *** $p < .01$ ** $p < .05$.
[a] For changes in business thermometer, effects truncated to between −30 and +30.

bridges across races. No other social movement – and certainly no voluntary organization – so explicitly called forth the message of forging trust across groups that were visibly different but who shared so many other values in common. Overall, Americans became slightly more supportive of civil rights from 1972 to 1974, leading a few more people to become trusters than to shift the other way.[13]

The civil rights movement had become less central to American political life by the mid-1970s. Other big events, from the war in Vietnam to Watergate to the energy crisis, displaced it on the national agenda. Each tore apart America's social fabric, but only the war in Vietnam had big effects on social trust. Watergate didn't divide the country as Vietnam did. It was a political crime. Compared to the Vietnam conflict, which lasted almost a decade, it was over and done with rather quickly. And Americans were not as badly divided over Watergate issues as they were on Vietnam – or later on the impeachment of President Clinton. The energy crisis (later crises) did lead to much incivility (cf. Uslaner 1989).

[13] There was a modest shift toward greater in-group trust (.054), a small shift toward more support for civil rights leaders (a mean of 1.198, for an overall range of 145), and a slight shift (.165 on an eight-point scale) toward support for faster progress on civil rights.

But it too was over quickly, perhaps too quickly for people to learn from one energy shortage to the next.

Vietnam was different. It was the first war that the United States "lost." For many, it was literally a matter of life and death. And it divided families, political parties, and social groups. No wonder that it affected trust. What is surprising is that there was no big effect on trust until the war was close to its close. There were no significant Vietnam effects in the first two waves of the 1972-74-76 panel and the war had no effects on changes in trust over the first two years. From 1974 to 1976, however, both overall attitudes toward the war in 1976 and a change in attitudes toward the military had significant effects on trust. People who opposed the war were less trusting, as their rhetoric suggested. And people whose opinions of the military became more positive between 1974 and 1976 were more likely to put their faith in others. The effect for changes in attitudes toward the armed forces was large – .216, the fourth largest in the model. Overall, people with positive views on Vietnam on both measures were very likely to become more trusting. Their probability of changing toward higher trust was .809. Opponents of the war who became less supportive of the armed forces had only a .474 probability of becoming a truster.

By the mid-1970s, civil rights beliefs had no direct effect on changes in trust. There were, however, indirect effects through the two measures of particularized trust. Apart from contextual trust, two of the three biggest effects came from changes in particularized trust. When we developed more favorable views of out-groups and less affect for our own kind, we became more trusting. The other major force affecting changing trust was a person's position on the Vietnam war. People who became more supportive of the military also became more trusting. Opponents of the war in Vietnam really were less likely to place confidence in other people, not just those over 30.[14]

Altogether, people who became considerably more trusting of out-groups and less enamored with their own in-groups were almost certain (probability = .849) to become trusters.[15] In the 1970s the two measures on the war in Vietnam were almost as powerful.[16] When I combine the effects of particularized trust and attitudes on Vietnam, the impacts are

---

[14] The key effects are: .277 for out-group change, −.207 for in-group change, .223 for change in the military thermometer, and −.139 for opposing the war in Vietnam.

[15] People who shifted the other way were not at all prone to become trusters (probability = .379).

[16] Supporters of the war who became more pro-military had a .830 likelihood of becoming trusters, compared to a .478 probability for opponents who found the armed

striking. Consider a supporter of the war and the military who also was becoming more tolerant of out-groups and less insular. She would have a .952 probability of changing from mistrust to trust, compared to a .222 chance for someone with the opposite ideas.

The effects of both Vietnam and civil rights lingered for years to come. In the Niemi-Jennings 1973 and 1982 youth samples, there are still significant impacts for both the war and the crusade for racial justice. Yet the strongest determinant of changes in trust from 1973 to 1982 is change in the feeling thermometer toward business, which may reflect both the better economic times of the 1980s and the waning of the liberalism of the 1960s that spurred the activism against the war in Vietnam. People who were optimistic about life were also substantially more likely to shift toward trust. But the second biggest effect was change in affect toward blacks. And whether one had a friend of the opposite race while in high school also contributed significantly to becoming more trusting. Attitudes toward minority groups and having friends of the opposite race as a child led young adults to become more trusting.

Vietnam still was important, but in a very different way than we have seen so far: People who opposed the war were becoming more trusting.[17] This result seems curious initially. The Niemi-Jennings youth sample consists of Early Baby Boomers, the generation noted for opposition to the war in Vietnam (though it actually wasn't more antiwar than its elders) and its lack of trust.[18] When they became young adults, those who were critics of the war were more likely to change from mistrusters to trusters.

BOOMERS BOOMING

Why has trust dropped from almost 60 percent in 1960 to around 40 percent today? The decline in civic engagement is *not* a promising place

services more distasteful. The ANES panel shows some other, perhaps surprising, effects for other variables. Men had become more trusting from 1972 to 1974. Now they became less trusting than women. There is some evidence that religiosity and trust were becoming less compatible, perhaps because of growing fundamentalism. People who went to religious services less often from 1974 to 1976 became more trusting (effect = −.136), though barely ($p < .10$). And finally people who thought it was safe to walk the streets at night became more trusting.

[17] A two-tailed test of significance might be more appropriate, but the coefficient would still be significant at $p < .10$.

[18] In the 1972-74-76 ANES panel, 52 percent of people born after 1945 opposed the war compared to 54 percent born earlier (phi = −.037, Yule's Q = −.078, not significant).

172 The Moral Foundations of Trust

to look. Most types of civic engagement are not at all related to trust – as either cause or consequence. And those that do consume, rather than produce, trust and show no evidence in the GSS time series of atrophying. Membership in cultural (literary) organizations is relatively steady over time – inching up to 11.5 percent in 1993 from 9.4 percent in the 1970s, before slipping back to 9.8 percent in 1994. And membership in professional organizations has increased sharply – from 13 percent of the population in the 1970s to 19 percent in 1994 – an increase of more than 40 percent. Participation increased from 19 percent to 26 percent among generalized trusters. But it doubled among mistrusters – from 7 to 14 percent. The connections between trust, overall group membership, secular group membership (excluding unions), literary associations, and professional groups are all *negative*, and some of these correlations are of more than modest size. Multivariate analysis confirms that trust has either no effect on group membership, or, perhaps a negative impact.[19]

An alternative thesis is generational. Since most people are either consistent trusters or mistrusters, the aggregate changes in trust are likely to reflect changes due to population replacement. Younger generations are less trusting than their elders were. Putnam (2000, 140) attributes "most, if not all of the decline in American social trust since the 1960s . . . to generational succession." Early Baby Boomers (born between 1946 and 1955), who were the most vocal protestors of the war, were the demarcation between the "long civic generation" born between 1910 and 1940 and their less trusting successors born after World War II. Putnam (1995b, 676; emphasis added) argues: "It is as though the post-war generations were exposed to some mysterious X-ray that *permanently and increasingly* rendered them less likely to connect with the community" (cf. Brehm and Rahn 1997).

[19] The simple correlations over time (1974–94) between trust and group membership are: −.272 for all associations, −.530 for secular organizations (excluding unions), −.288 for literary associations, and −.510 for professional groups. I estimated models that also included aggregate measures of education, service attendance, and overall confidence in government institutions (the means for the army, the legislature, the executive, and the judiciary). In simple regressions adjusting for serial correlation, neither trust nor confidence in government was significant in any of four regressions (overall group membership, membership in secular organizations excluding unions, joining professional associations, or membership in literary groups). For autoregressive integrated moving average (ARIMA) models with a single lag, trust in people had negative coefficients for all groups and secular organizations excluding unions (where confidence in governmental institutions was also negative and significant). Membership in professional associations and literary groups did not depend upon either type of trust.

Of course opponents of the war in Vietnam didn't trust other people. They didn't believe that their political adversaries shared their values. Many rejected the dominant culture in favor of a new "counterculture." A new, less trusting generation emerged and you could hope against hope that the Baby Boomers might become more trusting (and participatory) as they grew older. In the past, people became more trusting as they aged. This link has been broken.

Putnam got it right – but he missed by a decade. Yes, the postwar generations became less trusting and, yes, for most of them there has been no sign of a mid-life renaissance. One cohort stands out as a dramatic exception – the "first" uncivic generation, the young people who first came of age with television and who were the most vociferous protesters of the war in Vietnam. These Early Boomers started out just where we would expect them to be – the least trusting cohort. But by the 1980s something happened: Boomers began to become more trusting, though erratically so. As it is declared in the Bible, "the last shall be first," so had it become for the Early Boomers by the late 1980s. Or, as an assistant professor of philosophy at my undergraduate institution prophesied after he was denied tenure during the heyday of the counterculture: "All the potheads will become department heads."[20] The Early Boomers *permanently and increasingly* became the new, and perhaps last, trusting cohort.[21]

Throughout all of the 1990s the Early Boomers were markedly more trusting than *any other cohort* – in virtually every survey, be it from the GSS, the ANES, *Washington Post*, or the INDEPENDENT SECTOR.[22] I present

---

[20] The philosopher in question was Daniel Bennett. The institution was Brandeis University and the time was circa 1965–66.

[21] Putnam (1995b) missed the trend because he used five-year rolling averages in his analysis, which meant that he would have picked up only a small portion of the shift in the late 1980s. Brehm and Rahn (1997) used the entire GSS as a single sample. For the *entire* GSS sample (excluding 1996, which was not available when they did their analysis), the Early Boomers were less trusting than the Pre-Boomers (42.2 percent compared to 46.3 percent, $p < .0001$ either with or without the Post-Boomers in the analysis).

[22] There is a smidgen of contrary evidence. Trust rose slightly in both the ANES and the GSS in 1998 (to 39 percent and 39.9 percent, respectively). In each survey, the Early Boomers were no longer the most trusting: the 1930s generation was. In the GSS, 51.4 percent of the 1930s generation were trusters, compared to 48.6 percent of Boomers. In the ANES, 46.8 percent of the 1930s generation trusted others, compared to 48.1 percent for the Early Boomers (the most trusting cohort). I thank Robert Putnam (personal communication) for bringing the 1998 problem with the GSS to my attention. In the 1999 *New York Times* Millennium Survey, Early Boomers were the *least* trusting cohort (at 36.1 percent), while Post-Boomers were the *most* trusting cohort (43.2

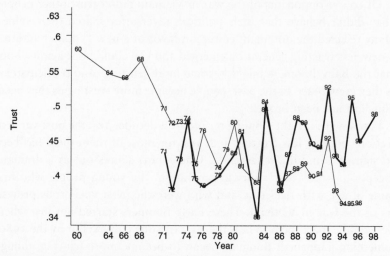

FIGURE 6-2. Overall Trust and Early Baby Boomer Trust, 1960–98. Thin line: overall trust; thick line: Early Baby Boomer trust.

the trends for overall trust (thin line) and Early Boomer faith in others (thick line) in Figure 6-2. Early Boomers were generally less trusting than the entire population throughout the 1970s. They spurted ahead in 1981 before falling substantially below others in 1983. They tracked the overall population in 1984 and 1986 (there are no trust data for 1985). In 1987 Early Boomers began to outpace the population (by 2.7 percent). By the next year, they had become considerably more trusting (by 7.3 percent) and even overtook Pre-Boomers (by 48 to 43 percent). Early Baby Boomers were becoming more trusting in their middle age.[23]

The trends are put in sharper relief in Figure 6-3, where I plot trust over time for three different cohorts: the Early Baby Boomers, the highly civic generation born in the 1920s (called the "last suckers" by sociologist Charles Tilly [Putnam 1995b, 675]), and people who were born in

percent), a result not found elsewhere. The 2000 ANES Trust Pilot Study, with 51.9 percent trusters, once more had Early Boomers as the most trusting cohort (61.2 percent) compared to 51.1 percent for Pre-Boomers and 48.4 percent for Post-Boomers.
[23] The correlation between the difference in trust between Early Boomers and the entire public and time is .848.

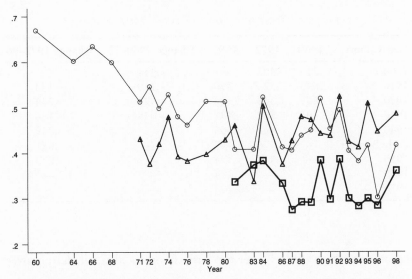

FIGURE 6-3. Trends in Trust by Cohort. ○ 1920s generation; △ Early Boomers; □ 1960s generation.

the 1960s. In one sense the expectations of the conventional wisdom are fulfilled: The 1960s generation is (with one exception) far less trusting than the Early Boomers. The average gap is 13 percent and it is fairly consistent over time. On average, 30.9 percent of the 1960s generation agree that "most people can be trusted" from 1980 onward, compared to 43.8 percent of Early Boomers. And the succeeding cohort, people born in the 1970s, are even less trusting (averaging 23.7 percent from the first measurement in 1990). And, in contrast to the Early Boomers, the 1970s generation is becoming *less* trusting as they grow older. So succeeding generations have less faith in others and there is no sign of any recovery as they age.

The 1920s generation began as by far the most trusting cohort. In each year of the 1960s 60 percent or more believed that most people can be trusted. By the early 1990s this cohort was *less* trusting than the Early Boomers and by 1996 it had barely more faith in others than the 1960s generation. Over the 24 time points from 1980 onward, the "last sucker" cohort was 2 percent less trusting than the Early Boomers. The 1920s generation lost on average two-thirds of a percentage point of trust every year from 1960 onward, as faith in others fell from 66.9 percent to 30.2 percent in 1996, before recovering to 42 percent in 1998. And the civic

TABLE 6-5. *Trust by Cohort in 1960, 1972, and 1996*

Year/Cohort	1960	1972	1996	Change 1960–72	Change 1972–96
1900	.513	.402	—	–.111	—
1910	.643	.523	.390	–.120	–.133
1920	.669	.546	.302	–.123	–.244
1930	.605	.567	.441	–.038	–.126
1940	—	.444	.503	—	.059
Early Boomer	—	.376	.447	—	.071
1950	—	.317	.394	—	.077
1960	—	—	.284	—	—
1970	—	—	.203	—	—

generation's "advantage" over the Early Boomers also fell sharply over time.[24]

The attrition in trust is *not* confined to the "last" civic generation. With the exception of the Early Boomers, *every cohort* for which there are time series data became less trusting over time, and all recent generations have become less likely to place faith in others than their elders. I present selected trends in Table 6-5.[25] The 1920s generation had the biggest drop in trust over time, in part because it started so high. But there are notable downturns for cohorts born in 1900, 1910, and 1930. The increases in trust for the 1940s and 1950s generations are entirely due to the Early Boomer (1946–55) effect.

Why did the Early Boomers go against the grain from the late 1980s onward? I estimated probit models for trust for Early Boomers in the "early" (1972–87) and "later" periods (1988–94) using the GSS (see Table 6-6).[26] I estimated identical models for the two eras for Pre-Boomers (born in 1945 or earlier) and Post-Boomers (born since 1956) and report just the probit effects and levels of statistical significance in Table 6-7.

[24] The correlations of trends in trust and time are –.739 for people born in the 1970s, –.827 for the 1920s generation, and –.681 for the 1930s cohort.
[25] I end with 1996 because the 1998 data show irregular spikes upward for several cohorts that seem atypical of the more general time trends since the 1980s. Before we conclude that these represent a new direction, we need additional time points.
[26] I use the 1988 cut-off for the later period because that is the first year that the Early Boomers became the most trusting of all cohorts. The time series ends in 1994 rather than 1996 since the measures of optimism were not asked in the 1996 GSS.

TABLE 6-6. Probits for Trust for Early Baby Boomers in Early and Later Eras from General Social Survey 1972–96[a]

	Early Period (1972–87)			Later Period (1988–96)		
	Coefficient	Standard Error	Effect	Coefficient	Standard Error	Effect
Contextual Trust (by State)	1.229***	.489	.201	1.175*	.722	.180
Lot of the Average Person Worse	-.321****	.094	-.111	-.376***	.144	-.121
Not Fair to Bring Child into World	-.252***	.099	-.086	-.413***	.147	-.136
Officials Not Interested in Average Person	-.248***	.091	-.085	-.443***	.154	-.143
Confidence in Scientific Community	.224***	.072	.150	.071	.109	.044
People Get Ahead by Luck vs. Hard Work	-.004	.058	-.003	.299***	.092	.181
Tolerance Factor Score	.090**	.052	.088	.309****	.087	.285
Satisfied with Friendships	.160****	.036	.303	.096**	.057	.178
Afraid to Walk at Night in Neighborhood	-.097	.085	-.032	-.157	.138	-.049
High School Education	.024	.022	.093	.076**	.035	.245
College Education	.031**	.017	.212	.061***	.026	.373
Age	.021***	.009	.142	.039**	.019	.181
Black	-.457****	.127	-.152	-.318*	.213	-.101
Constant	-.481	.438		-1.516*	.939	

Early: Estimated R^2 = .302 −2*Log Likelihood Ratio = 1258.488 N = 1069 *Later:* Estimated R^2 = .381 −2*Log Likelihood Ratio = 530.122 N = 483.
Percent Predicted Correctly: Probit: 67.8 Null: 55.3.
Percent Predicted Correctly: Probit: 71.6 Null: 50.7.
**** $p < .0001$ *** $p < .001$ ** $p < .01$ * $p < .05$ * $p < .10$.
[a] Effects for age calculated between 21 and 41 for early period and between 33 and 48 for later period.

177

TABLE 6-7. *Probit Effects for Trust for Pre-Boomers and Post-Boomers in Early and Later Eras from General Social Survey 1972–96*[a]

	Pre-Boomers		Post-Boomers	
	Early Period	Later Period	Early Period	Later Period
Contextual Trust (by State)	.176***	.100	.218***	.322***
Lot of the Average Person Worse	-.067***	-.037	-.015	-.100**
Not Fair to Bring Child into World	-.091****	-.108***	-.064**	-.027
Officials Not Interested in Average Person	-.146****	-.088**	-.095***	-.058*
Confidence in Scientific Community	.121****	.067	.128***	.071
People Get Ahead by Luck vs. Hard Work	.048**	.073*	.070**	.056
Tolerance Factor Score	.125****	.147***	.151***	.196***
Satisfied with Friendships	.304****	.202***	.053	.207***
Afraid to Walk at Night in Neighborhood	-.083***	-.128****	-.089***	-.070
High School Education	.181****	.188****	.072	.287**
College Education	.300****	.321****	.305***	.475***
Age	.085***	.120**	.096	.140**
Black	-.203****	-.328****	-.179****	-.177****

**** $p < .0001$ *** $p < .01$ ** $p < .05$ * $p < .10$.

a Effects for age calculated between 35 and 80 for Pre-Boomers in the early period and between 45 and 85 in the later period. For Post-Boomers, effects for age calculated between 18 and 31 in the early period and between 18 and 40 in the later period. For Post-Boomers, the top value for college education (for effects) is 16 years in the early period and 17 years in the later period.

178

The models are much the same as the GSS equations I estimated in Chapter 4 (though many of the questions asked in the 1987 module are not available for the full sample). I add two variables that will prove to be of great import: whether people get ahead by luck or hard work, which appears to tap both optimism and especially personal control, and a "tolerance factor score." This measure is a composite index of whether people are willing to permit atheists, racists, communists, and militarists to speak in public forums, teach, and have their books in libraries. As I argue in Chapter 7, tolerance of unpopular groups is a mark of the truster. I treat it there as a consequence of trust, but the relationship may well go both ways – from an acceptance of people who are different to trust, as well as from faith in strangers to a liberal attitude on civil liberties. It seems like a reasonable surrogate for the particularized trust measures that I constructed from the ANES and Niemi-Jennings surveys but are not available in the GSS measures.

Each model has 13 independent variables and I estimated six equations (one for each era for Pre-Boomers, Early Boomers, and Late Boomers). These 78 coefficients offer lots of room for interpretation. Much of the time the results only repeat what I have already demonstrated about optimism, control, and personal experiences in Chapter 4. Most of the time, when a variable becomes more or less important across time periods, the change occurs for all three age cohorts.[27]

Overall, two things stand out when we compare effects across time and cohorts. First, for both Pre- and Post-Boomers, the links between feelings of optimism and control and interpersonal trust become weaker over time. For Early Boomers, on the other hand, optimism and control became *more important* determinants of trust.[28] Second, for every cohort, tolerance becomes more important in the later period. For Early Boomers, tolerant attitudes became far more important than for either Pre- or Post-Boomers. Indeed, tolerance ranked only behind college education in shaping Early Boomers' trust.[29] The effect of tolerance for Early

---

[27] See in particular, the increasing importance of college education, where the probit effect increases from .300 to .321 for Pre-Boomers, .212 to .373 for Early Boomers, and from .305 to .475 for Post-Boomers.

[28] Of five measures of optimism and control, three increase over time for Early Boomers in Table 6-6, one decreases (confidence in the scientific community), and one remains about the same over time. For Pre-Boomers, three become weaker, one stays about the same, and one gets stronger (though less significant). For Post-Boomers, four of the five measures become weaker.

[29] The probit effects are .285 for the tolerance factor score and .373 for education (see Table 6-7).

Boomers is 45 percent greater than the impact for Post-Boomers and almost twice as great as the effect for Pre-Boomers.

The Early Boomers were at least as optimistic as other cohorts.[30] But their optimism goes further in generating trust. Trusters are also more likely to have a college education, and this leads to greater trust. They are *far more tolerant.*[31] And their tolerance goes further. The Early Boomers grew up during the civil rights movement and have a legacy of optimism and tolerance that makes them view people different from themselves as part of their moral community.

The Boomers may have damned the system during Vietnam and Watergate. Yet they came of age during the early 1960s, the years of the "American High," when everything seemed possible (O'Neill 1986). The Boomers may not have come around to this realization until they had made it themselves, with comfortable incomes and a happy family life. They might be the last generation to buy into the expectation of the promise of Disneyland: "There's a great big beautiful tomorrow."

For each cohort the American Dream came true. The 1920s generation began the time trend at the top of the economic heap. But in the mid-1970s, their economic prowess began to fade. By 1977 their children, the Boomers, had surpassed them in family income.[32] In the 22-year period from 1973 to 1996, the 1920s generation family income rose from approximately $9,000 to around $19,000 (based upon the GSS categories). Surely much of this was eaten away by inflation. The Boomers saw their income rise from about $7,500 to almost $25,000. *The Boomers had made it, more so than any other cohort in America. They were better educated and had higher incomes. And they were the last, at least in this time series, to earn more than their parents.* As their income matched their expectations, they regained faith in their fellow citizens. The Post-Boomers of the 1990s earned slightly more than their parents. The generation of the mid-1940s and early 1950s had outpaced its predecessors and was running away from its successors.

---

[30] They are slightly less confident in science than Post-Boomers, and substantially more likely to disagree that it is "unfair to bring a child into the world" than either cohort. But both of these results may reflect age effects. For the other measures of optimism, there are no cohort effects in the later period.

[31] The mean tolerance factor scores (with positive values being more supportive of civil liberties) are: −.336 and −.160 in the early and later periods for Pre-Boomers, .126 and .272 respectively for Post-Boomers, and .287 and .355 for Early Boomers. The difference between Early Boomers and Post-Boomers in the later period is significant at $p < .008$.

[32] I cannot say by how much – the GSS categories are rather crude.

The Boomers became optimistic because the American Dream came true for them, more so than for any other generation in recent memory. The Pre-Boomers overcame the Great Depression and gained a sense of national purpose and destiny in World War II. But they later saw their income stagnate. The Post-Boomers' incomes rose slowly, up to the levels of their grandparents. They did not fare as well as their parents. It wasn't supposed to be that way.

FRATERNITÉ AND EGALITÉ

Optimism, not income, is the driving force behind generalized trust. Trust cannot thrive in an unequal world. People at the top will have no reason to trust those below them. Those at the top can enforce their will against people who have less (Seligman 1997, 36–7). And those at the bottom have little reason to believe that they will get a fair shake (Banfield 1958, 110). The rich and the poor have little reason to believe that they share common values, and thus they might well be wary of others' motives.

The Early Boomers weren't optimistic simply because they made more money than either Pre- or Post-Boomers. Rather, their incomes were distributed more evenly. What matters is not *how rich a country is, but how equitable is the dispersion of income*. The standard deviation tells us how equitably incomes are dispersed. Incomes seemingly became more equitable for each group over time, though this is a mirage due to category creep.[33] But category creep alone can't explain why Early Boomers *consistently have the lowest standard deviations of any cohort*.

For every comparison, both the early and later periods and for each specific year (1973, 1984, 1988, and 1996), the Early Boomers had a more equitable distribution of wealth than any other cohort. From self-reports in the GSS, I present standard deviations of incomes for the early and later periods, and also for selected years, in Table 6-8. Another common measure of the dispersion of wealth is the Gini index of inequality. The measure ranges from zero (complete equality) to one (where a hypothetical economic tyrant would control all wealth). The distribution of income has become more unequal since the 1960s. In the 1960s, the

---

[33] The GSS has used the same twelve-point scale since it first asked the income question in 1973. Back then 22 percent of Americans said that they earned $5,000 or less, compared to less than 5 percent in 1996. In 1973 less than 7 percent of Americans earned $25,000 a year or more, compared to 63 percent in 1996. As incomes rise to the top category ($25,000 or more), the standard deviation will necessarily decline.

TABLE 6-8. *Standard Deviations of Income by Age Cohorts*

	Pre-Boomers	Early Boomers	Post-Boomers
Early Period	3.161	2.898	3.114
Later Period	2.630	2.029	2.698
1973	3.063	3.033	—
1984	2.936	2.408	3.196
1988	2.758	2.229	3.196
1996	2.463	1.861	2.456

Source: General Social Survey.
No Post-Boomers were in the 1973 survey.

Gini index ranged from .348 to .364.[34] By the 1994–96 period, it increased to between .421 and .426.

Only a handful of people pay attention to aggregate statistics such as standard deviations of income or Gini indices. How meaningful are the distributions of income to average folks? You don't need to be an economist to determine whether the rich are getting richer and the poor are getting poorer. Most of us have a pretty good idea where we fit in. The people with the highest incomes and lowest standard deviations, the Early Boomers, see themselves as faring best. From 1988 onward, Boomers say that they are about as well off as anyone else, while both Pre- and Post-Boomers (and people born in the 1960s, in particular) see their income as somewhat below average.[35]

We have two ready sources of information: how well we are faring and the information we get from the media, mostly television. People look at others in their reference group to determine how well they are doing financially (Mutz and Mondak 1997). So it seems reasonable for Early Boomers to look at others in their cohort to figure out their place on the economic ladder. Television, too, plays an important role in our perceptions of success. We see visions of the good life on television. Television shows often glorify the "life-styles of the rich and famous," but

[34] The Gini indices of family income come from the United States Department of Commerce (1998) Bureau of the Census (Report C-30), available at http://www.census.gov histinc/index.html.
[35] This result comes from the GSS question on relative financial status (FINRELA). The average score on a five-point scale (with higher scores being more positive about how well you are doing) is 2.984 for Early Boomers from 1988 onward, 2.891 for Pre-Boomers, 2.847 for Post-Boomers, and 2.829 for people born in the 1960s.

news programs also pay a lot of attention to people lining up at home-less shelters when things are bad.[36] It doesn't take too much imagination for people to determine how they are doing. I estimated a model for how well people see themselves doing as compared to others.[37]

People who watch a lot of television are more likely to think that their own economic situation is worse than average. In part the difference between the cohorts who see themselves falling behind and those who think that they are doing relatively well lies in media effects. The more television people watch, the more likely they are to think that they are doing relatively poorly; except, that is, for Early Boomers, for which group television has no effect. And the Early Boomers watch the least television, anyway.[38]

Television is only part of the story and it pales by comparison to the "real world": people's actual income, the best predictor of your relative financial situation. Overall, we make reasonable distinctions. In the aggregate, people are more likely to think that hard work won't be sufficient to get ahead in the world when income equality is high. The GSS trend in how people get ahead – by hard work (lower scores on a three-point scale) or luck (higher scores) – tracks income inequality well. There is a slightly better fit with a lagged Gini index than with a con-temporaneous measure: We may wait to see how lasting the bad news is before we reassess their assumptions about how people get ahead (see Figure 6-4).[39] The level of economic inequality also shapes another key measure of optimism: whether people see life being better for their chil-dren than for themselves (cf. Chapter 4). When economic inequality is growing, people fear that their kids won't fare as well as they have (see Figure 6-5).[40]

---

[36] This is the name of a popular television show in the United States during the 1980s and 1990s that focused on the high living of famous people.
[37] The model for relative financial situation, estimated from the GSS for the 1988–96 period, also includes: frequency of newspaper reading; income; high school and college education; a dummy variable for being black; gender; whether people get ahead by luck or hard work; and whether people see the lot of the average person as getting worse. The coefficient for newspaper readership suggests that the more often people read news-papers, the better off they think they are. Newspaper readership, however, was not sig-nificant in any of the specific cohort estimations.
[38] They watch 2.62 hours per day compared to 3.24 for older respondents and 2.85 for Post-Boomers.
[39] The correlation with the lagged measure is $-.723$ ($r^2 = .535$), with the contemporane-ous measure $-.624$ ($r^2 = .389$).
[40] The simple correlation is $-.840$ ($r^2 = .705$). The data on expectations for children's lives come from the Roper Center and are reported in Ladd and Bowman (1998, 63). The

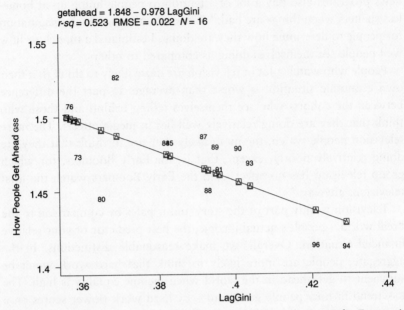

FIGURE 6-4. Trends in How People Get Ahead and (Lagged) Economic Inequality, 1973–96.

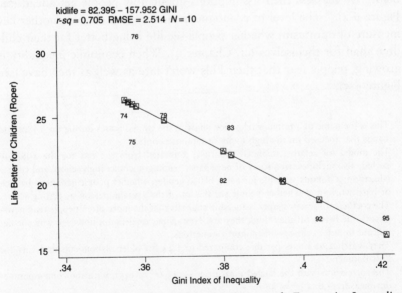

FIGURE 6-5. Expectations for Children's Lives and Economic Inequality, 1973–95. *Note:* r^2 with 1976 excluded = .811.

Early Boomers responded to their own economic well-being and not to the trends for the entire country. Boomers (in the aggregate) say that they are doing well as they make more money, and as the standard deviation of their income distribution falls.[41] As the overall level of inequality in the country (the Gini index) increases, the Boomers became more satisfied with their own financial status. The Boomers' income rose – and became more equal – as wages for the rest of the country fell.[42] No wonder the Boomers became more trusting as the rest of the country's faith in others fell.

Some, perhaps much, of the growing income gap is generational, as with the trust gap. The Boomers moved away from the general trend of trust as they became well-off. This is a direct piece of evidence that real life matters. Yes, we get much of our information about how well we are doing from television. But we get even more from observing how well our circle of friends and associates are doing. This is the most direct evidence we have about inequality. So Early Boomers got a mixed message – one from their own environment (optimism) and the other about most of the rest of the country (pessimism). But it was still a far more upbeat message than other cohorts were hearing. So the Boomers were more optimistic than most, but still less trusting than the Pre-Boomers in earlier years.

observation for 1976 seems to be an outlier. Deleting it raises the r^2 to .811. In none of the other measures of optimism Ladd and Bowman report (1998, Chapters 2–3) does 1976 appear exceptional, so it is possible that the "high" level of 31 percent optimistic in 1976 reflects measurement error.

[41] There is no clear relationship between how well people think that they are doing and trends in the aggregate economy because the relative financial situation variable seems to have an implicit norm embedded in it. It doesn't vary much from one year to the next, so that some people think that they are doing well and others say that they are below average. The aggregate correlation between how well Boomers think that they are doing and their mean income is .734. The correlation is −.770 for the standard deviation of Boomer income. Relative Boomer financial status is also correlated with the overall inflation rate at −.573 and the national unemployment rate at −.414. It has no relationship with the change in the gross domestic product ($r = -.100$). Because the income level has a strong upward trend and the standard deviation a powerful downward trend, I generated residuals from regressions of income and standard deviations on the consumer price index. The correlations with Boomers' relative financial status are .483 and −.556, down considerably from the simple measures, but still impressive.

[42] The correlation between the Gini index and Boomers' satisfaction is .711. The correlations with the Gini index are .887 for Boomer income and −.867 for the Boomers' standard deviations of income ($r = .554$ and −.561 for the residualized measures described in note 20).

Samuelson (1995, xiii, 54, 129) argued that the extraordinary economic performance raised people's expectations unrealistically. No matter what else happened, he said, we could not replicate the go-go years of the booming sixties. So Americans became pessimistic about the future even as things continued to get better, albeit more apace. But the growing economic inequality shows that not everyone has prospered in recent years. Looking only at overall growth hides the reason why Americans have become less optimistic. *Optimism may not depend upon your own income, but rather it is more closely linked to how well you expect to do* (Mutz and Mondak 1997, 300). Perhaps the 1960s raised expectations to unrealistic levels. But, based upon the level of economic inequality in the country, these hopes did not seem out of line at the time. The political commitment of the "war on poverty" further boosted aspirations.

Optimism provides the link between perceptions of prosperity and trust. Economic well-being in and of itself does not explain variations in trust. The rates of unemployment and especially inflation have little to do with the state of trust.[43] Economic growth also has but modest effects on trust. Yet there is a direct linkage between trust and economic inequality in the United States, as I show in Figure 6-6. Economic inequality has a much stronger effect.[44] The regression equation predicts a decline of trust of 14 percent based on the rise of economic inequality in the United States from 1960 to 1996. Trust actually fell 22 percent, but economic inequality's contribution is substantial. Changes in the Gini index alone account for almost two-thirds of the decline in trust (see also Chapter 8 for cross-national evidence).[45]

The level of economic inequality is the prime mover of generalized trust. Vietnam and especially the civil rights movement clearly played a big role in shifting many people's levels of trust. But, for most people, trust is a stable value, so the level of individual change is not likely to be great. There is also little evidence that individual changes tilted heavily in either direction across the surveys I examined. And it is difficult to measure aggregate changes attributable to either Vietnam or the civil rights movement, since there are not good time-series data on attitudes toward Vietnam or even on the civil rights movement.

[43] The correlations are −.401 and −.013, respectively.
[44] The correlation of trust with economic growth is .349, with economic inequality, −.736 ($r^2 = .542$).
[45] See the analyses by Brehm and Rahn (1997) and Alesina and LaFerrara (2000) that show powerful effects for state- and community-level (respectively) economic inequality on individuals' interpersonal trust.

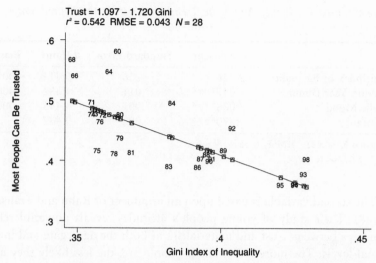

Trust = 1.097 – 1.720 Gini
r^2 = 0.542 RMSE = 0.043 N = 28

FIGURE 6-6. Trends in Interpersonal Trust and Economic Inequality, 1960–98.

In seeking a more general account of why trust has declined, I look first to economic inequality and then to other variables that may lead to both short- and long-term fluctuations in generalized trust. I estimate an equation for generalized trust over time in the United States in Table 6-9. Aside from the Gini index, I include two other variables: a dummy variable for presidential election years and Stimson's (1998) measure of "public mood."[46]

The election year dummy reflects an interesting structural effect, also noted by Rahn, Brehm, and Carlson (1997; see also Uslaner 1999d, 143): Trust in people rises in presidential election years, at least since 1976. People may look to presidential elections as opportunities to change the direction of the country. Elections may forge a sense of community as people participate in choosing their leaders (Rahn et al. 1997, 7).[47]

[46] I report results from an ordinary least squares (OLS) estimation. I also estimated a model using generalized least squares to correct for autocorrelation, but the autocorrelation coefficient *rho* was insignificant (*rho* = .106, standard error = .169, t = 1.162, p < .256). I also estimated a first-order ARIMA model where the autocorrelation was significant (t = 6.479), but the t ratios differed only marginally from the OLS estimates. Because of the small sample size, I estimated the regressions a thousand times using the STATA 6.0 bootstrap command. The "bias" entries in Table 6-9 show what we might interpret as "confidence levels" of the regressions from bootstrapping. None of the bias coefficients is significant.

[47] Ironically, interpersonal trust is more strongly correlated with the election year dummy (r = .476) than trust in government (r = .233).

TABLE 6-9. *Predicting Aggregate Trends in Trust in the United States,*
1960–96

	Coefficient	Standard Error	t Ratio	Bias
Gini Index of Inequality	−2.126****	.226	−9.414	−.008
Election Year Dummy	.047****	.011	4.382	.0003
Public Mood	.006****	.001	4.445	.0000
Constant	.870****	.092	9.437	

Adjusted R^2 = .821   RMSE = .027   N = 27.
**** $p < .0001$.

The second variable is based upon an argument of Rahn and Transue
(1998). Their study of young people's attitudes reveals powerful relationships between trust and materialism at both the aggregate and individual levels: The more materialistic people are, the less likely they are
to trust others. Rahn and Transue (1998, 551) equate materialism with
Tocqueville's "unchecked" individualism. Tocqueville (1945, 98) argued:
"Selfishness blights the germ of all virtue; individualism, at first, only
saps the virtues of public life; but in the long run it attacks and destroys
all others and is at length absorbed in downright selfishness." As materialism increases, then, trust in others should decline. Alas, there is no
measure of materialistic values over time. A surrogate is Stimson's (1998)
measure of public mood. The mood construct is an estimate of the relative liberalism (higher values) and conservatism of the American public
across a wide range of policy issues over time. My logic for using it is
rather simple: Materialism rises in more conservative eras (such as during
the Reagan administration), which are often called by such names as the
"me" generation.

The model performs very well statistically. It accounts for almost all
of the changes in trust over time. And it points to the central role of economic inequality in the decline of trust in the United States. The Gini
index accounts for 81 percent of the fall in trust.[48] The public mood
explains 38 percent of the shift in trust, while the election year dummy
accounts for just 21 percent. Obviously, I have "overpredicted" the
decline in trust, but these variables are correlated with each other,
making it difficult to separate out independent effects. But there is a clear

---

[48] I calculated this by multiplying the regression coefficient for the Gini index (−2.126) by
its range (from .348 to .429) and dividing that figure by the range in trust (from .578
to .357).

message that while election years bring a temporary boost (about 5 percent) in trust, the longer-term trends stem from ideological shifts among Americans and especially from rising income gaps.

REPRISE

There is strong evidence that optimism leads to greater trust and that both depend upon economic equality. This finding eludes individual-level analysis, since there is no direct way to measure inequality at the individual level. The distribution of income is the key to why trust has declined in the United States, but also why one particular group, the Early Boomers, went against the grain and became more trusting. It is also a major reason why African-Americans have less faith in others than whites do, and why the civil rights movement may have boosted peoples' faith in others. The civil rights movement was about equal treatment under the law, but it was also about the deeper legacy of slavery, African-American poverty. It offered hope for economic as well as legal progress and it fit very well with the overall optimism of the "American High" years. Protests over the war in Vietnam offered few expectations that things would get better. And this is why the main effect of the war was to destroy our faith in others rather than to build it up.

More generally, collective experiences shape our willingness to trust strangers (cf. Rothstein in press). They always have roots in "real life," though they don't always reflect our daily life and people we know. Yet, as with economic inequality, we form our impressions of the world by what we see all around us, even if not from our immediate experiences.

In the next chapter, I move to an examination of the consequences of trust. In Chapter 8 I show that economic inequality separates the trusting and the distrusting beyond the United States. And this robust finding will send a big note of caution for people who look for a quick institutional fix to the problem of declining trust.

7

Trust and Consequences

Part of my attraction to [volunteer firefighting] is its vivid clarity: what we do is of immediate unalloyed benefit. The pager jolts into life and we rush to someone's urgent need, achieve a degree of resolution, then go back to what we were doing, having given completely of ourselves.

– Koren (1997, C19)

A lot of what passes for volunteering used to be called simply "parenting": people helping out in their own children's schools or coaching their own children's soccer teams. Kids with parents who already have resources end up benefiting the most.

– Mosle (2000, 25)

Trust matters. People who trust others have an expansive view of their community and this helps connect them to people who are different from themselves. It also leads people to seek common ground when they disagree on solutions to public issues. In this chapter, I trace the benefits of trust both for individuals and the society. I also examine how some of the gains from trust, both public and private, have become more scarce as trust has fallen. In the next chapter, I extend this examination to look at the sources of trust and its impact cross-nationally.

Trust is not an all-purpose solution to society's problems. It won't get people involved in civic groups or in political life. But it does have other, perhaps even more important consequences. Because trust links us to people who are different from ourselves, it makes cooperation and compromise easier. Trusters are substantially more likely to say that most people are cooperative – by 83.5 percent to 54.4 percent for mistrusters in the 1972 ANES.[1] Many experimental studies in game theory have found that people who trust others are more likely to use cooperative strategies (Rotter 1971, 1980; Yamigishi 1986, 1988; Orbell and Dawes 1991; Wrightsman 1991; Yamigishi and Yamigishi 1994).[2]

A civil society is a cooperative society (cf. Putnam 1993, 88, 105, 111). As trust in people has declined since the 1960s, so has cooperation in our body politic (Uslaner, 1993, Chaper 4). Trust may not be the only route to cooperation (Levi 1999, 14). But trust can make it easier to solve recurring collective action problems, since goodwill eliminates much hard bargaining at the outset of each negotiation, and should make it more likely that some compromise will be reached (Putnam 2000, 135).

In a cooperative culture, citizens should be engaged in their communities. They should devote their time and financial resources to improving the lives of others. People who trust others should also be the most likely to endorse the prevailing moral code in their communities. Cooperation and compromise can only flourish when people respect each other, despite their differences. So a trusting community is a tolerant community, where discrimination is anathema.

Generalized trusters have a distinctive view of civil society: They see it as *one* society united by a set of common values. They oppose efforts to split the society into groups that might foster particularized trust, so they don't like attempts to do away with classical education or letting ethnic politicians make appeals primarily to their own communities. Here they face tensions in their own moral values: Trusters want to empower people who face discrimination in the society. Yet they also worry that groups just gaining power will be more concerned with asserting their own influence than building coalitions across the major fault lines (race, ethnicity, gender) in society.

An engaged, tolerant, and committed group of people who believe that others share their values seems the perfect recipe for a cooperative society. Recall the bases of misanthropy and selfishness in the literatures of social choice theory, social psychology, and politics (both scientific and

---

[1] I trichotomized the measure of cooperativeness. The tau-c is .302 and the gamma is .589.
[2] It is more common in the experimental literature for strategic trust to lead to cooperation: When people see that others play cooperative strategies, they are more willing to trust others and will reciprocate cooperative behavior (Deutsch 1958, 1960; Loomis 1959; Giffin 1967; Boyle and Bonacich 1970). But these findings cannot solve the collective action problem of why people cooperate in the first place. And the Boyle and Bonacich study *defines* trust in terms of previous payoffs.

ideographic). The egoist of rational choice theory who seems doomed to suboptimal outcomes will either not cooperate at all or only in response to others' initial positive moves. The misanthrope in social psychology and politics (such as Banfield's Montegrano) is a social hermit who has little faith in human nature. She *may* place her confidence in people like herself and then burrow herself into her own community. But this will make her *less* predisposed to cooperate with strangers. She may feel that events in her community are beyond her control, so it makes little sense to get involved with strangers. People from different backgrounds don't share her values, so working with them can at best lead nowhere and at worst be treacherous. A society with a lot of mistrusters or particularized trusters won't be tolerant, inclusive, or ready to compromise with people who are different from themselves.

I have already demonstrated two of the most important consequences of trust: volunteering time and donating to charity (see Chapter 5). Giving time and money reflects a deeper commitment to your community than simply joining a voluntary association made up of people like yourself. These activities depend upon trust in two ways. First, we do these good deeds *because* we feel a connection to other people. Generalized trust is based upon the notion that those who are less fortunate than ourselves are part of our moral community. Second, since generalized trust has a moral basis, trusters feel a moral responsibility to help people who have less through no fault of their own. People who trust others believe that it is wrong that some people have so much less than others (see Chapter 4). As inequality has increased in society, the need for good deeds has gone up, but the supply of trust has gone down (see Chapter 6). This places a heavier moral burden on people with faith in strangers. Fewer people are doing good deeds because there are fewer trusters, even as the demand for altruism goes up.

Underlying the link between trust and good deeds is a broader set of consequences. Generalized trusters are connected not just to other people, but to their communities. American society, they believe, is held together by a set of common values. Trusters are tolerant of people who are different from themselves. Not only do they give of their own time and money to help the less fortunate, but they also support governmental policies to redress social and economic inequalities. Trusters believe that you should not try to take advantage of your neighbors or the state – that it is imperative that we all fulfill obligations to each other, such as serving on juries (cf. Putnam 2000, Chapter 21). Trust also affects some more routine aspects of daily life: not locking your doors, not using a gun to protect yourself, and not calling in sick when you are well.

Just as trust does not usually lead people to join voluntary associations, it also has little effect on political participation. Putnam (2000, 290-2) reports that states with high rates of political participation also are more trusting. But there is little evidence that people who trust others participate more in politics, or that trends in political activity are linked to the decline in trust.

Trust and political participation are in constant tension. On the one hand, taking part in the political system is itself an act of trust in government. Voting, signing a petition, and writing a letter to a public official all are affirmations of the belief that someone out there is listening and is likely to be responsive. It is an act of trust. On the other hand, political life is necessarily confrontational. People will be more likely to get involved in political life when they get mad and believe that some others, be they other people or political leaders, can't be trusted. When people are upset, they are more likely to take direct action in their communities (Dahl 1961, 192-9; Scott 1985, 44-5) and give money to their favored causes (Hansen 1985). It may be ironic that we need generalized trust to make politics run smoothly, but we need distrust to get people involved in the first place (Warren 1996).

Americans have become less trusting and more insular. We give less of our income to charity and volunteer less (at least for the Red Cross). We give less all around, but particularly to causes that help people who are different from ourselves. As trust has dropped, so has respect for the law (as reflected in the reported crime rate). And so has our ability to get things accomplished in the legislative arena. In both the private and public spheres, a less trusting environment means that it is more difficult to reach out to those who may be different from us or who may disagree with us. But, at least in the United States, there is not much direct support for the argument that trust leads to economic growth.

WHY TRUST MATTERS

Perhaps the most important role of trust in a civil society is its commitment to a set of ideals that all people share. Trusters believe that there is a common set of beliefs. Forty-one percent of people with faith in others agreed with the strong statement in the 1993 GSS that "Americans are united and in agreement on the most important values" compared to 29 percent of mistrusters. No other variable shapes the perception that Americans share a common set of values.[3] Trusters' belief in a common culture is hardly an ultimatum to conform or else. People with faith in others value diversity within the context of common understandings. Trusters are far less likely than mistrusters to be suspicious of people who try to be different from the mainstream culture.[4]

Saying that there is a common culture goes hand-in-hand with a belief that society needs to take steps to include groups that have historically faced discrimination. Among whites, trusters are substantially more likely to admire African-Americans. Indeed, trust is the strongest determinant of admiring blacks.[5] And white trusters are *less* likely to believe

---

[3] Other variables include: race; gender; education; income; subjective social class; evaluation of how well one is doing financially relative to others; religion; religiosity (fundamentalism or frequency of attendance at religious services); region of the country; size of community; political ideology; party identification; or age. Gender *is* significant at $p < .10$, with men more likely to agree that there are common values, but trust is significant at $p < .003$. Relative financial status has a *t* ratio indicating significance, but it is people who see themselves with *below average* incomes who are most likely to find widespread agreement.

[4] This question comes from a 1964 survey on anti-Semitism in the United States conducted for the Anti-Defamation League of B'nai B'rith and available at http://www.arda.tm/archive/ANTSEMUS.html (accessed April 24, 2001). I estimated two-stage least squares models for this and other measures from this survey (see below). Other variables in the model for tolerance of differences are **education, gender (female), a knowledge scale (based upon respondents' ability to identify a range of personalities in politics, entertainment, literature, and sports)**, fundamentalist, income, relative evaluation of Jews compared to parents, black, and service attendance. The trust model for this and other variables includes *fundamentalism (negative), education, black, happiness, whether our lives are controlled by plots (negative), whether you believe that you have the capacity to solve problems when they arise, getting ahead is more a matter of luck than ability (negative)*, age, income, and being more successful than others. Variables significant at $p < .10$ are underlined; variables significant at $p < .05$ are in bold; variables significant at $p < .001$ or better are in *italics*, and insignificant variables are in regular typeface.

[5] There are too many results in this section to report the other variables for each finding so I briefly summarize where each variable comes from and the method of estimation. Details for any of the models are available upon request. The question on admiring blacks was asked in the 1994 GSS and the model was estimated using two-stage least squares with trust endogenous. Whether African-Americans can work their way up the economic ladder and the number of immigrants allowed to come to the United States were estimated by ordered probit from the 1996 GSS. The effects of affirmative action and illegal immigration on job loss and how the government treats whites come from the 1994 GSS and were estimated by ordered probit. The questions on the costs and benefits of immigration come from a factor analysis of these four items in the 1996 GSS and the inclusion of the factor scores in a three-stage least squares estimation that also included trust, trade imports, and a composite measure of American nationalism (the components of which are treated separately, since trust did not affect the overall index). These questions include the importance of being an American, whether other countries should emulate

that African-Americans can overcome prejudice without special assistance. Aside from ideology, trust has the greatest impact on support for affirmative action.

Trusters don't support affirmative action because they are liberals. In fact, as a whole they are not.[6] People who have faith in others *do* see people having shared fates. Trusters are less likely to believe that programs that will benefit minorities will take away benefits – specifically promotions on the job – from their own families. And white trusters believe that their own race gets more attention – and blacks get less concern – than they deserve.

Trusting people are also far less likely to be anti-Semitic. Trust, far more than any other variable, predicted people's attitudes toward Jews in a 1964 survey. Generalized trusters were far less likely to hold a range of stereotypes about Jews compressed into a single scale, and they were also less likely to believe that Jews stir up trouble by their beliefs or that God has punished Jews for refusing to accept Jesus as their Messiah. They were also more likely than mistrusters to

the United States, and whether the United States should go its own way in world affairs. I also estimated ordered probits from the 1996 GSS for questions on why women take greater roles in raising children than do men and from the 1996 ANES on the rights-of-women scale. The evaluations of gays and lesbians came from the feeling thermometer (ranging from zero to 99) in the 1992 ANES, as did the questions on gays and lesbians in the military and adopting children. I estimated seemingly unrelated equations for the two measures, as well as for the gay and lesbian tolerance measures from the 1972–96 GSS. I also estimated SUR models for racist and atheist tolerance measures from the GSS (estimated together). The question on immigrants' success comes from the B'nai B'rith 1964 Anti-Semitism Survey (see note 4) and was estimated by two-stage least squares. The model used the same predictors as those in the model for tolerance of people who are different, but only trust was significant. The anti-Semitism index is a composite measure including beliefs that Jews have too much power in business, are more loyal to Israel than the United States, employ shady business practices, are "overly shrewd" or tricky, care only about other Jews and only hire other Jews, want to be at the head of things, and have many irritating faults. *Blacks* and **parental attitudes toward Jews compared to the respondent** were also significant, but *trust* had the highest *t* ratio. For stirring up trouble, *trust* was the strongest predictor, but **fundamentalism, black,** and *parents' attitudes* were also significant. For God punishing Jews, the strongest determinant was the *frequency of attending services* (positive); also significant were **fundamentalists (positive), the knowledge scale (negative), and black (negative).** Trusters were more likely to vote against an anti-Semitic candidate (at $p < .05$), as are **people more friendly than parents toward Jews, people high on the knowledge scale,** and *more highly educated respondents*.
[6] All trusters in the 1972–96 GSS sample are slightly more likely to be conservative: The mean ideology score on a seven-point scale is 4.144 for trusters compared to 4.100 for mistrusters ($p < .012$, $N = 18,664$). The gap is bigger when I consider only whites: 4.217 compared to 4.126 ($p < .0001$, $N = 15,842$).

say that they would vote against a candidate who made anti-Jewish statements.

People with faith in others are also supportive of immigrants. People with faith in others are not bothered when immigrants fare better than people born in the United States. As with African-Americans, trusters don't see illegal immigrants taking jobs from natives. And they have far more favorable views of *legal* immigrants than mistrusters: Immigrants don't increase crime rates, generally help the economy, don't take jobs away from people who were born in the United States, and make the country more open to new ideas. And trusters don't believe that immigrants can readily work their way up the economic ladder, any more than African-Americans can, without government assistance.

Trusters want to let more immigrants come to America since they are more likely to believe that newcomers share the basic values of people already here. And trusters also favor free trade as a means of boosting economic growth. People with faith in others are less afraid that trading with other countries will permit other countries to take unfair advantage of the United States. Once again, this reflects a greater comfort level with people unlike oneself.

It thus should not be surprising that trusters, whom we know are less authoritarian, should also be less xenophobic. They are less prone to say that being an American is very important to them, that other countries should emulate the United States, and especially that the United States should go its own way in the world.

Trusters also have more positive evaluations of other groups in the society that have faced discrimination. They rate gays and lesbians more highly than mistrusters. Generalized trusters are much more supportive of gays and lesbians serving in the military and adopting children. In each case – general affect, military service, and adopting children – particularized trusters (as measured by the difference in feeling thermometers of out- and in-groups in the 1992 ANES) are far less supportive of homosexuals. Particularized trust is by far the strongest determinant of overall affect and it is also more powerful for military service. Trusters are far more supportive of gays' and lesbians' right to teach and speak in public schools and for the right of libraries to have books by gay and lesbian authors. Since trusters don't fear strangers – or even people they don't like or with whom they don't agree – they are willing to extend the same rights to atheists and racists.[7]

---

[7] Particularized trust is by far the strongest determinant of overall affect and it is also more powerful for military service.

And people who have faith in others are also more likely to endorse greater rights for women and to reject arguments that women are either biologically better suited for raising children or willed by God to take primary responsibility for childcare. Particularized trusters are, in contrast to generalized trusters, less supportive of women's rights.

Although I have looked at affect for out-groups and support for their rights as consequences of trust in others, it is equally plausible to argue (as I did in Chapter 4) that the direction of causality goes the other way. A positive view of out-groups is the hallmark of generalized trusters. Support for women's rights should not, on this logic, precede generalized trust, because women are not "out-groups" in the same sense that minorities are.

TRUST AND THE UNITARY TEMPERAMENT

People who trust strangers are not simply fuzzy multiculturalists. Trusters are tolerant of people who are different from themselves, who may have ideas and lifestyles that are very different from their own. These attitudes make cooperation with others much easier. Trusters are willing to give others the benefit of the doubt and to assume that there are underlying shared values, a unitary temperament.

Trusters want to empower minorities and other groups that have faced discrimination. Yet they worry that disadvantaged groups might be wary of forming broad coalitions. Empowerment might easily lead to fractionalization. This would go against the very lesson that trusting people put highest on their agenda: working to include rather than exclude folks who are different from themselves. So trusters are especially likely to say that ethnic politicians should *not* primarily serve their own communities. And, reflecting their view that there *is* a common culture, trusters are wary of the claim that high school and college students spend too much time reading classic literature. (See Appendix A for the multivariate statistical analyses.)

Trusters thus walk a fine line between empowering minorities and telling them how their politicians should conduct themselves and what the curriculum in their schools should be. This tension is the "price" of a common vision underlying the culture. And it is the very idea of a common vision that makes trust so compelling to so many social scientists. Lane's argument about the trusting person being the "effective citizen" is a rather broad claim. And I have shown that trust produces the sorts of attitudes that are essential for a cooperative society.

Trust is a powerful force shaping civic engagement. But its effects go well beyond volunteering or giving to charity. While these types of engagement are all to the good, they may not be the most important ways in which people can work together cooperatively to solve collective action problems. Agreement on legal norms is a prerequisite for a civil society where people seek to work together to solve common problems. I argued in Chapter 2 that trust is the foundation of a rule of law and shall provide evidence below that crime rates have risen as trust has fallen in the United States. I shall present cross-national evidence in the next chapter that a strong legal system depends upon trust. Here I show that support for the rule of law depends upon trust.

People who trust others are the strongest supporters of the fundamental norms that make for a civil and cooperative society. Trusters are more likely to say that it is wrong to purchase stolen goods, to claim government benefits that you are not entitled to, to keep money you have found, and to hit someone else's car without making a report. Trust and one's own moral code lead people to endorse strong standards of moral behavior – *not* expectations of others' morality. Trust matters most on moral questions when the stakes are highest (in terms of real monetary costs) and when there is the least consensus on what is moral. When everyone agrees that something is wrong – say, joyriding – or when violating a norm has small consequences – for instance, avoiding a fare on public transportation – trust doesn't matter so much. Trust also matters most when a specific person bears the brunt of breaching a norm. Trust is not quite so important for actions affecting the government – say, cheating on taxes or avoiding fares – as it is when we can point to a specific, though unknown, victim, as would be the case when keeping money you have found or hitting someone's car without making a report.

This strong support for a moral code helps maintain a system of rules and laws. Yet trusters do *not* give blanket endorsements to upholding laws under all circumstances. Law must be based upon justice. People who trust others say that it is sometimes acceptable to disobey unjust laws (by 65 percent compared to 52 percent of mistrusters in the GSS). They are also more likely to say that protest demonstrations should be permitted. So trusters are critical supporters of the legal system. We must enforce *just* laws and people must be permitted to protest statutes that they believe are wrong.

Yet trusting people are more supportive of *the legal order*. They are substantially more willing to serve on a jury, where they not only help to run the system of laws but also are likely to interact with people unlike themselves. Generalized trusters are more likely to say that they are willing to serve on a jury. And particularized trust matters even more: People who rank their own in-groups highly are much less likely to say that they would serve, while those who give more favorable ratings to out-groups are much *more* willing to fulfill their jury duty.[8] The measures of generalized and particularized trust are *the strongest predictors* of willingness to serve on a jury. Trusters form the backbone of the legal system because they have the strongest commitment to the values that sustain it.

TRUST AND DAILY LIFE

Beyond values that promote cooperation in dealings with other people, trusters demonstrate their faith in other people in daily life, as well. They may not be more likely to help people they see on the street or their own relatives. But they feel obligated to demonstrate their commitment to society in other ways, and in so doing provide a link between strategic and moral trust. People with faith in others are less likely to call in sick when they are really well. Most of the predictors of fidelity to your employer reflect more "strategic" considerations – how long you have worked for your employer, whether you can make most of your job decisions yourself, and how much you like your job – but trust matters, too, even if not so dramatically.

No one would say that trusters should feel morally obligated to keep their doors unlocked. Perhaps doing so would be foolhardy in many places. But trusters are *far* more likely to say that it is not important to keep your house bolted. Indeed, next to living in an urban area, trust has the biggest effect of any variable on whether people think they should lock their doors. Even being attacked or robbed three times in the last five years doesn't matter as much as being a truster. People with faith in others are also less likely to feel that they must protect themselves from criminals with a gun.[9] In some ways, then, trusters are cockeyed optimists, going well beyond what calculations based upon personal

---

[8] People with faith in others are between 7 and 16 percent more likely to say that they are willing to serve. The effects of in-group and out-group trust are even higher, between 17 and 24 percent.

[9] Only three other variables – living in a border state or the South and whether you or a family member witnessed a crime – have a bigger effect on defending yourself with a gun compared to trust.

experience would presume of them. But maybe only someone with a bit too much optimism and trust can look for cooperative solutions in today's more contentious and less trusting world.

THE CONSEQUENCES OF DECLINING TRUST

If trust brings us lots of good things, then there should be consequences of declining faith in others. And, indeed, there are. Yet we should recall that trust is not a cure-all. Just as trust does not shape much of our social life, neither can it be the villain for everything. Putnam (2000) is concerned that we are not connecting with each other as much as we did in the past. And he is equally worried that we are less trusting than we used to be. Yet he doesn't show any direct links between these tumbling trends. Nor is there any good reason to believe that there *should be* any connection between them. Hanging out with friends is great, but it doesn't make people any more trusting of strangers. And misanthropes are just as likely to socialize with friends as trusting people (see Chapter 5). Outlaw bikers have social circles, too. They may be very different from choral societies, but they are not necessarily more diverse. While we may not be bowling in leagues as much as we used to, we are *hardly* likely to bowl *alone*.

So if we are schmoozing less and joining fewer organizations these days, we cannot lay the blame on declining trust. And if we are less trusting, we cannot trace the cause to fewer social activities with people like ourselves. Across 26 forms of schmoozing in Putnam's data and three more formal measures of group involvement, *there is no evidence that declining trust is either the cause or the effect of trends in our social or civic lives.*

We are doing less of almost everything that involves social interactions these days. We eat fewer dinners or breakfasts with our families, have fewer dinner parties, entertain less at home, and go on fewer picnics. We attend fewer sporting events, go camping and fishing less, spend less time swimming, play less tennis, attend fewer sporting events, and even watch less sports on television (which would surprise the wives of my ESPN-addicted friends).[10] We don't play cards that much and we even don't bowl as much as we once did. Church attendance is down, as is participation at club meetings and work on community projects. As we

---

[10] ESPN is an all-sports cable network (actually, a collection of at least three networks, one of which does nothing but rerun old sporting events) in the United States.

withdraw from social connections, we are more likely to shop by mail than in stores. *Yet we cannot trace the decline of either informal or formal civic engagement to falling trust. And lower levels of trust are not the reason we spend less time with family, friends, or people like ourselves.* In no case does any form of formal or informal participation lead to a decline in trust. In only a handful of cases is there any evidence that trust affects schmoozing. But each time, less trust leads to *more* informal social contacts with people like yourself. As trust has gone down, we are *more* likely to play cards, eat family dinners together, go fishing, and, yes, *go bowling.* Maybe we would be better off if people *did* bowl alone, or at least not so much. These results may be counterintuitive – they may just be statistical flukes.[11]

Our social connections have changed as our families have become smaller and women have entered the workforce (cf. Wuthnow 1998; Putnam 2000). Working mothers don't have as much free time to take part in community projects or go to club meetings or to prepare dinner for either their families or friends. As our families have become smaller, we are less likely to spend time together. We don't schmooze as much because our families are busier than ever and because there are fewer people in our closest circle, the family. Smaller families and working women, not generalized trust, lead to "boiling alone." Trust has little to do with these connections and there is little reason to expect it to be critical in such mundane events as how often we go camping.[12]

---

[11] Sooner or later, if you run enough models, as the famed statistician John Tukey once wrote, the data are bound to say "Merry Christmas!".

[12] See note 30 in Chapter 3 for the data source. I estimated equations for each of these forms of socializing and more formal activity by two-stage least squares, with each form of civic engagement both a potential cause and effect of trust. The trust equation, as in Chapter 6, includes the Gini index of economic inequality, the public mood, and the election year dummy, as well as each measure of socializing in turn. The equation for each type of activity includes trust (significant *negatively* for bowling, playing cards, fishing, and eating dinner as a family), average household size, education level, and the belief that a woman's place is in the home (a proxy for a better measure of women as homemakers). Most forms of socializing depended most heavily upon household size and the proper place for women. We had more cookouts, played more cards, went fishing more, bowled more frequently, entertained more at home, had more picnics, ate more meals as families, went to more movies and sporting events, swam more, and ate more meals together when our family size was larger. As our family size shrank, we went to *more* rock concerts. Almost all of these activities were more frequent when more women were at home, as were church attendance, going to club meetings, and especially working on community projects. Exceptions are eating lunch at restaurants, which is now more frequent as more women are in the workforce. Clearly, changing gender roles

We see a similar pattern (or lack thereof) for political participation. The Roper organization has asked people about a wide range of political activities from 1974 to 1994.[13] Trust in government (specifically in the Congress), not trust in people, leads people to get involved in politics across 12 categories of political actions – and the residual category of no activity, at least in the aggregate. Trust in people does have modest effects for being an officer in a club and serving on a committee within an organization.

Other activities – signing a petition, attending a public meeting, going to a rally or a speech, working for a political party, writing a letter or an article for a newspaper, making a public speech, running for or holding public office, writing a letter to a member of Congress, or joining a good government group – have no relationship to interpersonal trust. Even the trend in refraining from *all of these forms of political activity* does not track trends in trust. People who participate in protest marches are *less* likely to trust strangers; they are more likely to trust people of their own faith. Some forms of political activity thrive on mistrust rather than trust.[14] It is hardly surprising that the link between political participation and faith in others is so weak and sometimes even negative. The cooperative spirit underlying trust stands in stark contrast to the harsh realities of political life. Politics revolves around rallying the faithful for a cause, which may be anathema to seeking common ground with opponents.

have had a major effect on how we spend our time. Other forms of schmoozing not so clearly linked to family structure but also unrelated to trust are: going to bars; playing golf; jogging; attending lectures; skiing; and visiting art galleries (most of which are either increasing or show no time trend). Since these models are based upon time-series data, I also estimated ARIMA models, and they confirmed the two-stage least squares estimates. The forms of socializing and participation selected were based upon the DDB Needham data which had at least 20 years of data available.

[13] The Roper data are taken from a memo by Robert Putnam for the conference, "Is Civil Society Weakening? A Look at the Evidence," sponsored by Pew Charitable Trusts, National Commission on Civic Renewal, and the Brookings Institution, at the Brookings Institution, Washington, D.C., November 25, 1996.

[14] The aggregate regressions also include an aggregate measure of education, taken from GSS surveys. Confidence in the legislative branch is significant in all equations except for working for a political party, writing an article for a newspaper, and joining a better-government group. Attending a rally was negatively associated with trust in the executive branch. I estimated all regressions correcting for serial correlations and also using ARIMA modeling. In the ARIMA models confidence in the executive branch was not significant for signing petitions and writing letters to Congress. When trust in people is significant, it reaches only the $p < .05$ level. The protest march variable is measured at the invididual level in the Social Capital Benchmark Survey. See Appendix B for the other variables in the model.

Yet generalized trust is very important for the two activities that tie people to strangers at the individual level: giving to charity and volunteering time. As interpersonal trust has declined from 1960 to 1996, so has the share of gross domestic product that Americans have donated to charity (cf. Putnam 2000, 123).

The most comprehensive data base on charitable giving, the Amercan Association of Fund Raising Council's (AAFRC) *Giving USA.*, shows a strong relationship with generalized trust ($r^2 = .610$; see Figure 7-1). While trust is a powerful predictor of overall charitable giving, it is not *the most important predictor.* This is not surprising, since the *Giving USA* figures reflect *all types* of charitable contributions, not just those to people who are different from yourself.

There is a stronger link to trust for United Way contributions over time. The United Way is composed overwhelmingly of charities that reach out to the less fortunate.[15] Contributions to the United Way dropped from .087 of Gross Domestic Product to .045 percent. The trends in charitable giving and trust are strongly linked ($r^2 = .804$; see Figure 7-2). Trust has the strongest effect of any variable in a multivariate analysis on United Way contributions.[16] It is also the strongest predictor of donations at the individual level, and the rationale is not hard to understand. Giving to others represents more of a commitment to people unlike oneself.

Time-series data on volunteering are hard to come by. Red Cross officials, however, have kindly put together trends from their annual reports for me. Some caution is in order. The Red Cross has but a small share of the total volunteering population in the United States. The figures never exceed 2 million, while a reasonable estimate of the total volunteering population in the United States might approach 100 million.[17] The Red Cross, like the United Way, comprises a small share of good

[15] See the United Way's web site, http://www.unitedway.org, to get an idea of the specific charities that belong to the United Way in any particular area.

[16] I follow the *Giving USA* convention of adjusting charitable contributions for national wealth (the value of the GDP). Both the United Way and *Giving USA* data are for individuals and thus exclude corporate contributions. I am grateful to Robert O'Connor of the United Way and to Ann Kaplan of the AAFRC Trust for Philanthropy for providing me with their data. The correlation between the two series is .835 ($N = 30$).

[17] This figure comes from estimates in various national surveys, including the 1996 Giving and Volunteering Survey and the 1992 ANES, where about 40 percent of Americans say that they have volunteered. The Red Cross figures were provided by Robert Thompson of the Historical Resources Department and Patrick Gilbo of the Public Affairs Department from figures reported in the Red Cross Annual Reports and in organizational files.

204

The Moral Foundations of Trust

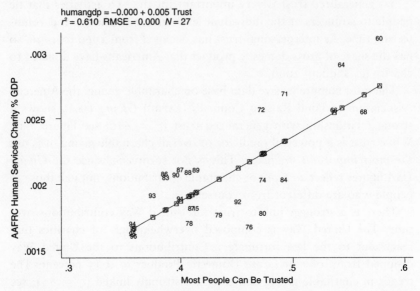

FIGURE 7-1. *Giving USA* Charitable Contributions as Percent of GDP and Trust over Time.

deeds Americans do. Yet both organizations tap moral resources. The United Way is a large umbrella organization where contributions are more likely to go to people you don't know. And Red Cross volunteering is mostly aimed at helping strangers, through such activities as blood donations, humanitarian services (especially in natural disasters), and international assistance.

The share of Red Cross volunteers in the population has decreased as trust has gone down ($r^2 = .796$; see Figure 7-3).[18] This holds in multi-

The Red Cross figures include youth volunteers, but the guess of 100 million volunteers for all causes is still too high because it includes people too young to volunteer. For some years, the figures are precise down to the single volunteer. For other years, the Red Cross only has estimates; for the 1960s the figures are always 2 million while for some later years the numbers are rounded off to the nearest 100,000. But using different break points (e.g., eliminating the early years of the 1960s) and controlling for time trends don't destroy the basic result.

[18] Putnam (2000, 127–9) reports an increase from 1975 to 1999 in volunteering from the DDB Needham Life Style surveys. There are questions, however, about the representativeness of this survey (Putnam 2000, 420–4) that may be particularly severe for demanding activities such as volunteering. Also, the volunteering question Putnam reports does not distinguish among types of volunteering and Red Cross volunteering

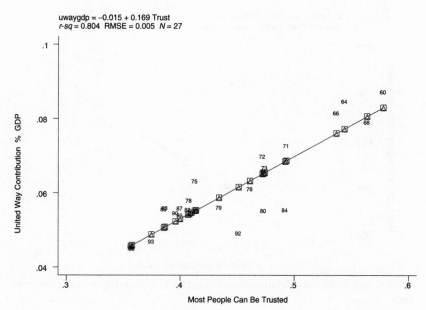

FIGURE 7-2. United Way Charitable Contributions as Percent of GDP and Trust over Time.

variate analyses allowing for simultaneous causation between trust and volunteering. Trust is the major determinant of trends in Red Cross volunteering. There is mixed evidence about whether volunteering increases trust, as well.[19]

is reaching out to people who are different from yourself. Red Cross volunteering as a share of the United States population and United Way contributions as a percentage of gross domestic product are strongly correlated ($r = .907$, $N = 30$). Regressing each against the other yields significant coefficients ($p < .05$) even when controlling for population size, gross domestic product, and time. The partial correlation between the two measures controlling for population, GDP, and time is .334.

[19] Both trust and volunteering as a percentage of the United States population are strongly correlated with time ($r = -.872$ and $-.845$, respectively). The results, however, are robust to including time as a predictor and also to single-equation models estimated with a first-order autoregressive lag through ARIMA modeling, as well as deleting all cases in the 1960s except for 1968 (to take into account errors in estimation of volunteers in the Annual Reports). The coefficient for trust is .020, with a standard error of .004 ($t = 5.661$). The other variable in the equation is the divorce rate ($t = -3.882$): As the divorce rate increased, fewer people had time to volunteer. There is a strong positive coefficient for volunteering as a percentage of the United States population in the trust equation, but it drops to insignificance when I eliminate the early years of the 1960s.

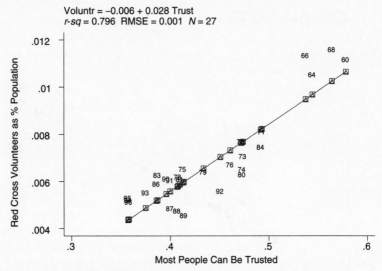

Voluntr = –0.006 + 0.028 Trust
r-sq = 0.796 RMSE = 0.001 *N* = 27

FIGURE 7-3. Red Cross Volunteers as Percent of U.S. Population and Trust over Time.

Two sets of data on charitable contributions allow me to expand on my claim (in Chapter 5) that trust is more important for donations to people unlike yourself than for offerings to your own kind. Both of these data sets separate the two types of contributions by beneficiaries.

John and Sylvia Ronsvalle have divided church-based charitable contributions over time into "benevolences," contributions to strangers, and "congregational" contributions, which support the local church. And their data suggest that giving to people who are different from yourself depends more on trust than contributing to your own kind. Both benevolences and congregational contributions have declined in tandem with trust. Yet trust has a more powerful impact on benevolences, while congregational gifts depend more heavily upon church attendance rates. So reaching outside your church and giving to people different from yourself depends more on trust, while contributions to your own congregation reflect your allegiance to the church itself.[20]

[20] The Ronsvalles divide these church-based charitable contributions as a share of disposable per capita income into "congregational" finances and "benevolences." The trend data from 1968 to 1997 are available at the Ronsvalles' web site, http://www.emptytomb.org/Table2.html (accessed May 31, 2000).

The relationship between trust and benevolences is very strong (see Figure 7-4).[21] As trust has declined, we are less likely to make contributions to people who are different from ourselves. Yet, as we see in Figure 7-5, we are also *less likely to contribute to people who are different when the need is greatest, when the level of economic inequality is greatest.* The correlation between benevolences and the Gini index of economic inequality is both *negative* and extremely strong.[22]

Why do we give less when the need is greatest? As inequality grows, trust declines. The levels of contributions don't depend upon simple economic factors (such as economic growth, inflation, or unemployment) as much as they do on our sense of trust. Benevolences are not the only "good works" that fall when the need is greatest. As inequality grows, Red Cross volunteering, congregational giving, and giving to both the United Way and to charities more generally all fall.[23] The rise in inequality may well tap an increase in materialism among those who are well-off and a corresponding decline in the public-spiritedness that undergirds trust.

The *Giving USA* data even more dramatically show that trust shapes some forms of giving and not others. Trust is the strongest predictor of giving to secular causes over time, but it is *not* a significant predictor for all religious charitable contributions (in direct contrast to the Ronsvalles' data). There are moderate positive correlations between trust and contributions to education and health, but both vanish in multivariate analyses. And trust is *negatively* related to the AAFRC's categories of arts and culture and public-society.[24] "Public-society" may appear to reach out to the less fortunate, and to some extent it does (including civil rights, voluntarism, and community development). But it is dominated by contributions to research institutes in the sciences and social sciences, as well as public utilities and credit unions. In both arts and the sciences, better-off people are making contributions to good causes. But they are not redistributing resources from the well-off to the less fortunate. Instead, we are now contributing more to causes from which we might benefit personally – museums, universities, theater groups.

[21] The correlation is .778; r^2 = .605.   [22] The correlation is −.953; r^2 = .905.
[23] The respective correlations are −.643 (Red Cross), −.648 (congregational giving), and −.771 (United Way contributions), and *Giving USA*'s total contributions (−.446).
[24] The correlations between trust and the AAFRC categories are: religion (.121), education (.323), health (.570), public service (−.566), and arts and culture (−.791), and human services (.781). These data were also provided by Ann Kaplan of the AAFRC.

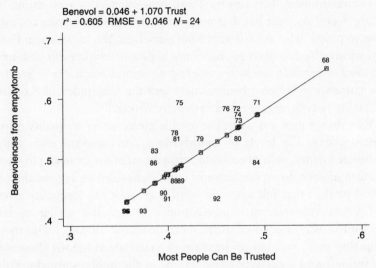

FIGURE 7-4. Benevolences (from emptytomb) and Generalized Trust, 1968–96.

Mosle (2000, 25) writes: "When people talk about giving, they are often talking about contributing to institutions, like the Metropolitan Museum of Art or the New York City Opera, that confer prestige on the donor and improve the quality of life primarily for the middle class. Despite the roaring economy, organizations that work with the poor have actually seen their proportion of the charitable pie narrow in recent years." We are contributing less to human services charities. We gave twice as much of our national wealth to public-society causes in 1960 as we did in 1996. Our arts contributions increased by 82 percent. But we are now giving half as much to human services. We can boast of generosity while making ourselves feel better.

Not surprisingly, trust is the most important factor shaping giving to human services charities. The human services category is a veritable laundry list of good causes: homeless shelters, food banks, vocational counseling, assistance to the handicapped, Meals on Wheels, disaster relief, summer camp for disadvantaged kids, the Boys and Girls Clubs, and the like. Yes, some groups may not have much outreach – for instance, the Boy Scouts, Girl Scouts, Little Leagues, the Grange, and the Farm Bureau. Yet most beneficiaries are different from the contributors.[25]

[25] Public-society contributions increased from .0005 of the Gross Domestic Product in 1960 to .0010 in 1996; arts contributions rose from .0077 to .0014, while human ser-

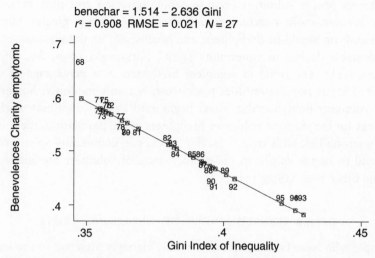

FIGURE 7-5. Benevolences (from emptytomb) and Economic Inequality in the United States, 1968–96.

As Americans' empathy for people who are different has fallen, we have redirected our charitable contributions. We give more to our own kind and less to others. But there is no evidence that we have become less trusting because we see others shunning the less fortunate. The direction of causality goes from trust to charitable contributions, the aggregate data suggest (see Appendix B). Charitable contributions do lead to a warm glow for those who do good deeds. But they depend upon trust in others in the first place, so they cannot be responsible for the decline in trust among the American public.

There is also some evidence about another form of civic engagement that ties people to others: serving as volunteer firefighters. These firefighters, whose quarters have been described as "the hub of community life" (Gross 2000, A25) are strongly motivated by a sense of doing good for others (Thompson and Bono 1993, 336–7; Benoit and Perkins 1995, 22). Volunteer firefighters have been replaced by careerists. In 1983 volunteers constituted 80 percent of all firefighters, but by 1998 they were just 74 percent.[26]

vices donations fell from .003 to .0016. See Appendix B for the multivariate analyses for total, secular, religious, health, and human services contributions. All were estimated by two-stage least squares with bootstrapping (1000 iterations).

[26] The data source is Karter (1999, 3). I am grateful to Nancy Schwartz of the National Fire Protection Association for providing me with this information.

Fewer people volunteer because people have less free time, training has become more onerous, two-career families place greater family demands on would-be firefighters, and because of "an unmeasurable but undeniable decline in community spirit" (Grunwald 1999, A6; Gross 2000, A25). The trend in volunteer firefighters as a percentage of the United States population does track trust, but only modestly; however, the volunteer firefighter data don't begin until 1983. If I estimate earlier values for the share of volunteer firefighters in the population, there is a very strong link with trust.[27] So the "decline in community spirit" that is said to be the culprit in the smaller share of volunteer firefighters is none other than falling trust.

OTHER CONSEQUENCES OF DECLINING TRUST

People who have faith in others are more strongly attached to the legal system. As people become less attached to each other, they may feel less of an obligation to maintain civic order and established social norms. As trust has declined, the reported per capita crime rate has increased. Per capita crime – of all sorts – increased from .012 in 1960 to .061 in 1991, before falling back down to .053 in 1996. And while lots of things, especially better reporting procedures, affect trends in crime, trust clearly seems to be one of them. Of course, an alternative thesis is also plausible. Perhaps people look around them and see rising crime. They might reasonably conclude that trusting others is too risky in such a world – as a strategic view of trust would suggest. There is no easy way to sort out the causal connection, though some evidence suggests a reciprocal relationship, with the link from trust to crime rates being much stronger.[28]

---

[27] The correlation rises from .454 to .855. The estimates of values from 1960 to 1982 are through STATA 6.0's impute command, with time as the predictor. This seems reasonable since from 1983 to 1998, the correlation of volunteer firefighters as a percentage of the United States population and time is –.853. Trust now becomes by far the strongest predictor of the share of volunteer firefighters.

[28] The aggregate correlation over time between trust and crime is –.810. In individual surveys, there is less support for the connection between trust and crime. People who have been victims of crimes are no less trusting than others in either the GSS or the 1976 ANES. I am grateful to Francis Fukayama, who provided me with the crime data he obtained from the Program Support Section, Criminal Justice Information Services Division, Federal Bureau of Investigation, United States Department of Justice. Daniel Lederman of the World Bank is working on a cross-national project on crime and social capital. I estimated a two-stage least squares model (with bootstrapping) using the same variables for generalized trust as in Chapter 6 (but adding the reported crime rate). The crime rate was barely significant for trust ($t = -1.566$, $p < .10$), but the effect of trust

Putnam (1993, 180), Knack and Keefer (1997), and LaPorta et al. (1997, 336) have argued that trust also brings prosperity. When people burrow into their own communities, they will not gain the advantages of trading with people who are different from themselves (Woolcock 1998, 171). Prosperity depends upon generalized trust. The logic seems reasonable, but the evidence is not quite so supportive for the United States: Trust is *not* appreciably higher during boom times than when times are bad.[29] The boom years of the Reagan and Clinton administrations were marked by rather low trust, even in comparison with the wrenching stagflation of the last two years of the Carter administration. The aggregate correlation of trust with change in per capita gross domestic product from 1960–96 is .339. The correlations with unemployment and inflation are −.396 and .010, respectively.

There are not sufficient observations on trust to trace trends outside the United States. But there is cross-sectional evidence across many nations and it is more supportive, both directly and indirectly: More trusting societies have higher levels of growth and they also have more open economies (see Chapter 8). There may thus be an indirect connection between trust and prosperity in the United States: If trust leads to greater support for free trade and trade promotes economic growth, trust may help produce greater prosperity in the United States, as well.

We might expect that America has become less tolerant as trust has fallen. Yet this is *not* what has occurred. The tolerance scores discussed in Chapter 6 have actually increased over time. The average American was moderately intolerant in the late 1970s and is now moderately tolerant.[30] Yet, over time, there has been little increase in whites' feeling thermometers toward African-Americans. There has been a very small shift toward more positive scores, but it is not statistically significant. And whites are even slightly less favorable toward blacks now than they were in 1976.[31]

---

on crime is much more powerful ($t = -4.414$, $p < .0001$). The equation for the reported crime rate also includes the change in the Gross Domestic Product ($p < .10$) and the unemployment rate ($p < .05$). While it performs well statistically ($R^2 = .739$, RMSE = .0006), it is theoretically rather thin, so I am reluctant to draw broad conclusions from it.

[29] John Mueller called this to my attention and he is correct. Trust measures are not available for 1975, 1977, 1982, and 1985 in the analysis below.

[30] The average factor score increased from −.135 in 1976 and −.195 in 1977 to .169 in 1996, where positive scores indicate greater tolerance.

[31] The 1964 mean thermometer rating was 60.4; in 1976, it was 67.2; in 1996, it was 63.3.

Fewer Americans now say that African-Americans are different from whites because of "inborn differences" than in 1977 and fewer also say that blacks are different because they don't have as much will. Yet a majority of whites *still* say that African-Americans don't have as much will as whites. And fewer Americans now say that blacks face racial discrimination than admitted this in 1977. Fewer also say that differences are attributable to less education. We may be somewhat more tolerant, but the pace of progress seems rather slow forty years after the first civil rights legislation passed. Had trust not declined, it seems likely that racial attitudes would have become more tolerant.[32]

TRUST AND GOVERNING

Much of the reason I can't establish a more powerful relationship between declining trust and intolerance is that there have been two long-term trends pushing in opposite directions. The first is simply greater acceptance of civil rights. The second is the growth of economic insecurity and particularized trust, while generalized trust has fallen. This leads to ambiguous findings about the decline in trust.

Yet there is clearly one instance in which intolerance prevails. It is in our public life. We may not always express intolerance toward identifiable minorities. But we are increasingly likely to deny that our political opponents are part of our moral community. And this has made political life more contentious. The result has been a stalemate in our legislative institutions. The ability to compromise within the legislature depends upon the level of polarization outside. The more confrontational style of legislative politics these days reflects the waning trust in the larger society (Uslaner 1993). Congress is finding cooperation more and more difficult as members increasingly cast aspersions on each others' motives, especially across party lines.

A less trusting society is a more polarized society. People are apt to deny that their political foes are part of their moral communities. Democrats have prohibited prolife candidates from speaking at their national

---

[32] In 1977, 26 percent of white respondents to the GSS said that blacks were different because of inborn differences, 66 percent because of lack of will, 51 percent because of education, and 41 percent because of discrimination. For 1996, the figures were 10 percent inborn, 52 percent will, 44 percent education, and 35 percent discrimination. Three of the four measures – inborn differences (phi = $-.125$, Q = $-.345$), will (phi = $-.145$, Q = $-.292$), and education (phi = $.129$, Q = $.259$) – had at least moderate correlations with generalized trust.

convention (in 1992). Republicans have fought over ideological diversity on abortion and other issues. The debate over the impeachment of President Clinton in 1998 was not just acrimonious. Each side, both in the Congress and in the public, talked past one another (Uslaner 2000). Members of Congress have lost the trust that underlies the capacity to reach compromises.

The problem of trust has gotten so bad that an outside agency, the Pew Foundation, has tried to restore comity by sponsoring two retreats in Hershey, Pennsylvania to get members of the House of Representatives talking to each other. The 1997 getaway was marked by good spirits all around, but the cheerfulness quickly faded. About a month later, the House Subcommittee on Rules and Organization realized the depth of the problem and held hearings on what might be done to restore civility. The initial hearings were called to a halt when the members had to scurry to the House floor to vote on a motion to censure a House Democratic leader for insulting the Speaker.[33] The 1999 meeting came after each party had inflicted further wounds on the other during the debate on the impeachment of President Clinton. Two weeks before the retreat one of the Democratic party's leaders (Steny Hoyer, D-MD) said that the gathering would be a good opportunity to lecture the Republicans on how to behave more civilly.

The decline in interpersonal trust is also linked to the waning of norms of cooperation in the Congress. As trust has waned, so has the norm of committee reciprocity in the House of Representatives and the increasing use of restrictive rules for legislation (which prohibit members, especially from the minority party, from offering amendments) has strong links to the decline in interpersonal trust (Uslaner 1993, Chapters 4–5). Congress divides its work among its committees, so that the body can take advantage of the expertise members have (or develop) by concentrating their efforts on particular topics. This specialized knowledge gives committee members key advantages in the shaping of legislation (Krehbiel 1991).

When members trust each other, they will acknowledge these advantages and will not fear that other legislators will somehow exploit their privileged positions. They accept a norm of committee reciprocity that expects legislators to respect the expertise of *all* committees (Matthews 1960). When legislation comes to the floor, any amendments offered

---

[33] The leader was Rep. John Lewis (D-GA). I was scheduled to testify at this hearing in April. It was rescheduled for May.

should come from members of the sponsoring committee. If you don't know much about the legislation at hand, you should keep quiet. When everyone who might have an idea gets into the act of legislating, the prospects for reaching an accommodation drop precipitously. As trust in the larger society has plummeted, the percentage of House bills with amendments from outside the sponsoring committee has increased.[34]

Perhaps the most well-known procedure to block legislation in the Congress is the filibuster in the Senate, which has become far more frequent in recent years (Binder and Smith 1996).[35] Increasing use of the filibuster is a sign that members are not willing to accept legislative decisions as binding. Stalemate is preferable to losing or even compromise. The number of attempts to cut off filibusters (cloture petitions) in a year has increased from an average of three from 1960 to 1973 to more than 20 in the 1990s. The level of trust in society is the strongest determinant of the number of cloture motions filed. It is even more important than the level of partisan conflict in the Senate.[36] Taken together, the rise in obstructionist tactics makes cooperation less likely and there is also a direct linkage between the fall in trust and the decline in congressional productivity (Uslaner 1993, Chapter 6).

Declining trust not only leads to obstructionist tactics. It is also responsible for greater stalemate in the legislative process. As trust has declined, so has legislative productivity, whether measured by Mayhew's (1991) list of major laws passed in each Congress or Binder's (1999) newer measure of gridlock (stalemate). By either measure, trust is the most important determination of legislative productivity.[37]

---

[34] See Uslaner (1993, 97–101) for a discussion of the effects of trust on amendments from outside of the committee membership in both the House and the Senate. An updated data set on the House from John Owens of the University of Westminster continues to show that trust (together with *public mood*) has a strong effect on the percentage of amendments offered by legislators not on the originating committees.

[35] The filibuster is extended debate. The rules of the United States Senate do not provide for a time limit on debate for a piece of legislation. Unless Senators can agree unanimously to consider a bill, a minority can effectively defeat a bill by "talking it to death." The Senate can cut off debate and move to a vote only if 60 Senators (an absolute figure, not a percentage of members present) vote to invoke cloture, and thus end a filibuster.

[36] The data on cloture motions was provided by Richard Beth of the Government Division of the Congressional Research Service, Library of Congress.

[37] For Mayhew's measure, see Uslaner (1993, 148–51). Gridlock is another term for stalemate. The origin of the word stems from traffic grids in New York City, which are frequently impassible. Binder's (1999) measure of gridlock controls for the salience of legislation by counting *New York Times* editorials on major issues of public policy and

It becomes more difficult to arrive at compromises when there is a large ideological gulf between the parties. And the ideological gap between the parties has widened in both the House and the Senate as Americans have become less trusting (Uslaner 2000).[38] Here is a prime example of how trust can lead to collective action. In American society, major legislation usually commands overwhelming majorities (Mayhew 1991), perhaps because our antimajoritarian culture doesn't readily tolerate major policy shifts enacted by narrow coalitions. To get to such majorities, political leaders must make compromises. And trust makes compromise possible because it fosters respect for alternative points of view. Without trust, leaders must assemble coalitions piece by piece. Strong ideological divisions make it difficult to form broad coalitions and small party majorities make it difficult to enact even the most basic legislation, such as budgets. We have become a less cooperative society where stalemate is the order of the day.

TRUST'S CONSEQUENCES

The most important consequence of trust, as Putnam (1993, 171) noted, is that it fosters cooperation. When people trust each other, they do not have to renegotiate the terms for negotiation each time they seek to make a collective decision. Yes, we can reach agreements without trust (Levi 1999), but collective action appears to be easier in trusting environments. People with faith in others are more likely to cooperate with others because they do not see their interests as incompatible with those of others, even those they know they disagree with.

Trusters believe that there is a common culture. And they also believe that they have an obligation to ensure that all members of that common

determining how many of the issues cited in the editorials were enacted. The gridlock scores are not publicly available, so I interpolated them from the graph in Binder (1999, 525). While Binder used conditional logit to control for the size of the Congressional agenda (from the *Times* data), I decided instead to include agenda size as a predictor of gridlock, together with the average ideological distance between the two parties in the House and Senate and measures of divided government. I estimated the models by ordinary least squares, three-stage least squares (with and without a separate equation for filibustering), and ARIMA modeling. In every case but one, trust was the most significant predictor. In that one exception (the simultaneous equation model with filibustering included), trust came in second behind the agenda size.

[38] In Uslaner (2000), I operationalize the ideological gap between the parties as the difference in DW-Nominate scores provided by Keith Poole in each chamber. Trust was the most important determinant of the ideological gap.

culture are treated equally and with respect. They are thus likely to support policies that promote civil rights and civil liberties and to shy away from standards of behavior (as well as actions) that would disrupt this social consensus. Beyond these commitments to a more inclusive society, people who have faith in strangers feel an obligation to make society better. They volunteer their time and give money to charity and will seek out opportunities to help people who are different from themselves and who may need assistance more. Trusters "resolve" collective action problems by waving away the fundamental assumption that what is good for you must be bad for me.

Trusters aren't simply "joiners." They are civic activists for "good causes." So it should not be surprising to find trusters no more likely to join most types of organizations than other people. And while people may gain all sorts of enjoyment from organized group life, they are not likely to become more trusting by linking up with people like themselves. The sorts of things that trust produces – helping solve collective action problems, becoming committed to a cause, and the like – are not likely to be learned, especially as an adult, at social gatherings of people who get together for good times.

Yet the good things that trust brings are increasingly in short supply: charitable giving as a share of national wealth, at least some volunteering, and the good humors that make it easier to resolve collective action problems. Much of this decline can be traced to the waning of trust.

Are these results generalizable beyond the United States? In the next chapter I move to a cross-national examination of trust, its causes, and its consequences.

8

Trust and the Democratic Temperament

It's difficult to have a civil society when the country is corrupt and criminalized. . . . When society is under stress, it's not a good time to talk about civil society. You need stability. . . . Now, we are just surviving. We don't have enough energy, time, and money for this. It's hard times, like during the war, and you have to survive on your own.

– Russian pollster Masha Volkenstein, as quoted
in Hoffman (1996, A40)

Some years ago the noted novelist E. M. Forster (1965, 70) gave "Two Cheers for Democracy,"

one because it admits variety and two because it permits criticism. Two cheers are quite enough: there is no occasion to give three. Only Love the Beloved Republic deserves that.

Perhaps there is a reason for a third cheer. Democratic societies are trusting societies.

The big payoff from interpersonal trust, most contemporary observers say, is that it leads to "better" government and to a public that is happier with government performance. Or maybe good government makes people more likely to trust each other. Or perhaps both.

Here I seek to examine, in a broader, cross-national context, the causes and consequences of trust. More specifically, I shall show that the same arguments made about the effects of trust in American society and its polity apply more generally across nations. A host of factors have been cited as potential determinants of trust, including education levels, media usage, a strong legal system, corruption, and the foundation of a civil society – membership in voluntary organizations. And trust is held by many to be the hallmark of democratic societies. If you could bolster education, reduce television viewing, reform the judicial system, combat high-level corruption, get more people involved in voluntary organizations, and tinker with the constitutional system to make it "more democratic," you could get a more trusting society – with all of the benefits that go with it. Wrong. Many of these "causes" have no effect in multivariate analysis. Others are more likely to be effects than determinants. When all is said and done, trust depends upon a supportive political culture and especially on a base of economic equality. Culture has a long shadow of history and cannot be readily changed. Economic equality is more malleable, but it seems to change slowly over time. It does not seem to be much easier to change trust at the aggregate level than it is for individuals.

The big payoff for trust in the United States is a more engaged citizenry, greater toleration, and a more productive government (see Chapter 7). A more trusting citizenry is more cooperative and government seems to run more smoothly. Even though there is little direct connection between trust in people and faith in government, there might be an indirect linkage through improved governmental performance. This linkage was originally formulated by Putnam (1993). Trust, he argues, is what makes democracy work. A more trusting society leads to a cooperative spirit among the public and to a more participatory population. An active population, mostly through voluntary organizations, is more able to make demands on government, to keep it honest and responsive. And an honest and responsive government will bring its citizens greater prosperity.

Putnam's argument about trust and governmental performance is mostly correct. Trust does lead to better government performance and greater prosperity. But it does so without the "middleman" of an active citizenry. As I argued in Chapters 2 and 5, joining civic groups may be all to the good, but of themselves they do not produce trust. Now we see that they do not produce better government either. Instead, the link between governmental performance and trust is direct.

A more cooperative spirit leads people to invest their governments with the power and authority to spend more on those who have less. Trusting societies also redistribute wealth from the haves to the have-nots. And trust in people also leads to a more responsive and efficient government. Trusting societies develop strong legal systems that gain the confidence of citizens. The opposite dynamic – strong legal systems leading to greater trust – does *not* hold. Trusting societies also have less corrupt governments, and are more open to free trade (see Chapter 7 for American public opinion), so the cooperative spirit leads to greater wealth, as well (Putnam 1993, 180; Woolcock 1998).

Trust, then, really is the chicken soup of much of social life. It is not an all-purpose elixir, but it has many important consequences. I shall detail them below, noting that they hold primarily for countries without a legacy of communism. But as I show how trust is important, note what is *not* so critical for government performance: voluntary associations and democratization. It is trust, rather than civic engagement, that brings us so many good consequences. And it is trust, not democratization, that gives us better government. Reformers go from country to country tinkering with constitutions and seeking to instill a participatory spirit in people. Yet there is little evidence that either will make a society work better. It is easy to make a democracy, as Mueller (1999) argues. It is tougher to make a democracy work (Putnam 1993). That is the task of trust.

THREE CHEERS FOR DEMOCRACY?

There is nearly a consensus in theoretical and empirical cross-national discussions of trust that there is a link between democracy and generalized trust (Putnam 1993, 111–15; Offe 1997, 26; Rahn, Brehm, and Carlson 1997, 24; Levi 1998, 96; Stolle 1999b, 9; Rothstein, in press). Democratic institutions are the foundation of a civil society. Democracy promotes the rule of law. When people feel that their government treats them fairly, they will also believe that their fellow citizens are trustworthy. Levi argues that democracies can change preferences by structuring the range of acceptable choices in a society. She does not specify how these changes occur, but seems to argue that democracy empowers people who don't control many resources. When political leaders need to rely upon the mass citizenry for political support, they are not free to adopt policies that enrich themselves (corruption) or the dominant interests in a society (economic stratification).

Democracies also establish strong legal systems. The courts in democratic regimes relieve individual citizens of the burden of monitoring the trustworthiness of other people. When people know that they will be treated fairly, they will develop respect for the legal system (Tyler 1990) and realize that they must behave honestly themselves (Levi 1998).

Corrupt governments set bad examples for the types of behavior that will be tolerated from the citizenry. The most corrupt countries have the least trusting citizens.[1] This is hardly surprising, since "kleptocracies" send clear messages to the people that crime *does* pay.[2] Citizens feel free to flout the legal system, producing firmer crackdowns by authorities and leading to what Putnam (1993, 115) calls "interlocking vicious circles" of corruption and mistrust.

Honest government both establishes a model for ethical behavior and enforces those standards. When governments are either repressive or corrupt, they send signals to citizens that honesty may not be the best policy. There is little debate over whether democracy and trust go together. The big question seems to be whether democracy causes trust (Muller and Seligson 1994) or trust causes democracy (Inglehart 1997, Chapter 6).

I am part of a small coterie that challenges this conventional wisdom (cf. Rosenblum 1998; Mueller 1999). Just as trust in government does not lead to generalized trust (see Chapter 5), neither does democracy. Some democracies have lots of trusting citizens, others have relatively few. Authoritarian states *can* destroy trust, but trust can't be built just by changing institutions. The formerly Communist states of Eastern and Central Europe actually became *less trusting* as they became more democratic.[3] An Indian journalist commented on the sharp cleavages that led to a cycle of unstable coalitions, none of which could form a government: "We have the hardware of democracy, but

---

[1] The correlation between societal corruption and interpersonal trust across 52 countries is -.613. As in Chapter 2, the data base is the countries that have World Values Survey questions on interpersonal trust in either 1981–2 or 1990–3. For countries with surveys in both years, the figure for trust is the average. I eliminated China, since its trust score is suspiciously high. (The correlation is reflected, since higher scores on the corruption index indicate honesty in government.) Later in the chapter, I shall analyze trust data for countries without a legacy of communism. I simply note here that the correlation rises to -.749 when I restrict the analysis to these 34 nations. The data on corruption (for 1998) come from the global organization Transparency International and are found on its web site at http://www.transparency.de/documents/cpi/index.html.

[2] The correlation between the measures of corruption and tax evasion in the LaPorta et al. (1998) Quality of Government data set is .619.

[3] These data come from the eight formerly Communist countries surveyed by the World Study in 1990 and the mid-1990s: Belarus, East Germany, Estonia, Latvia, Lithuania, Poland, Russia, and Slovenia (see note 5) and the Freedom House freedom scores (see note 4). The eight formerly Communist countries became 5 percent *less* trusting, but the average freedom score increased from a "not free" 11 in 1988 to 4.75 in 1998, comparable to Chile, the Dominican Republic, India, the Philippines, and Venezuela.

not the software, and that can't be borrowed or mimicked" (Constable 1999, A19).

Trust across countries, like trust in the United States, depends more on values (culture) and the distribution of resources (economic equality) than on political institutions. There is little evidence that trust depends either on democracy or on the level of group membership in a country. Trust instead depends (in varying specifications) on optimism, economic equality, and the basic values and beliefs among the population. Countries with large Protestant populations are more trusting and more egalitarian. The "Protestant ethic" is an individualistic creed: To succeed in a competitive world, we need to rely upon other people. In collectivist societies, people can rely upon their peer groups and get by with particularized trust. In individualistic societies, generalized trust becomes essential (Tocqueville 1945, 98).

Cross-nationally as in the United States, trust helps to bring about good things – better functioning government and more redistribution from the rich to the poor. They have more open economies and have higher growth rates. Countries with many generalized trusters have more efficient judiciaries and bureaucracies. They also have less corruption and their citizens have more confidence in the legal system (Putnam 1993, 111; LaPorta et al. 1997, 335).

Yet neither honest governments nor legal systems that meet with popular approval create trust. Honest government depends upon a foundation of generalized trust. Trusting people have confidence in their laws because they know that they don't have to rely upon the strong arm of the law as a matter of course (cf. Macaulay 1963, 58, 60). Trust leads to empathy with others, and thus a respect for the law. Statutes simply ratify the moral codes that trusters strongly endorse (see Chapter 7).

Even the linkage between corruption and trust in other people is not the creation of the state. While there is no gainsaying the sizeable correlation between the two, the direction of causality goes from trust to cooperation. Political leaders are not quite so free to rob the public purse in high-trust societies. They can only get away with their con games when many people already don't trust one another.

Trusters also have an expansive view of their moral community – they feel that people who are less fortunate need to have a social safety net. So countries with many trusters have strong states that redistribute resources from the rich to the poor. Trusting publics will also produce more responsive governments and are more likely to adopt policies that will promote economic equality, and thus create more trust.

States don't create trust – neither does confidence in the state. Our faith in government reflects our estimation of how well our leaders are performing in their jobs. We pledge our allegiance to our leaders only when we have a reasonable expectation of "ethical reciprocity" from them (Levi 1998, 86–8). Yet this is precisely *not* what we mean when we place faith in other people, as I have emphasized in Chapters 2 and 4. It initially seems reasonable that people who trust government would also trust other people and vice versa. But a little reflection will show such reasoning to be misplaced. We have come a long way from strategic trust, which I discussed at length in Chapter 2 and then largely dismissed as unrelated to my larger themes. Here I come back to it, showing that trust in government *is* contingent and depends upon what we know about our leaders and how we come to evaluate them. Trust in other people is *not* contingent upon our expectations of others. We demand evidence of trustworthiness from our leaders, perhaps because many have proven to be unworthy of our confidence. We are more willing to make leaps of faith about the goodwill of people we don't know.

Societies with many trusters are more pleasant places to live. Not only are they more equal, but they also have better-performing governments (less red tape and more responsive judiciaries). Their governments pursue policies that lead to even more equality: a larger public sector, more transfers from the rich to the poor, and more spending on education.

TRUST AND EXPERIENCE

Democracy and trust have an uneasy relationship. On the one hand, social trust provides the bonds among an otherwise anonymous citizenry that, in Putnam's (1993) felicitous title, "makes democracy work." You can have democracy without trust – we often do (see below). But effective democracy, a government where people can come together to resolve pressing issues, may well depend upon the social bonds of trust.

On the other hand, democracy presumes distrust of authority, as well. Consent in democratic regimes is always contingent upon leaders' fulfilling their part of a contract. Leaders must keep their promises, perform reasonably well, and treat citizens fairly (Levi 1998, 88). The power of democracy is the ability to "chasten authority, to limit its claims and dangers" (Warren 1996, 47).

A reasonable person might well conclude that most politicians can't be trusted. And this might not be such a bad thing if we used our skepticism wisely. One of the great virtues of democracy, Forster argued, is that it "permits criticism." Levi (1998, 95) goes further: It makes consent possible by exposing venality. In a democracy we can uncover misdeeds and punish those who perpetrate them. So it makes sense to be wary of our leaders: "Distrust may be the major engine for an even more democratic state" (Levi 1998, 96).[4]

Still, not everyone agrees that democracy is either necessary or sufficient to generate trust. Mueller (1996, 118) argues that democracy "can function remarkably well even when people exhibit little in the way of self-discipline, restraint, commitment, knowledge, or, certainly, sacrifice for the general interest. . . . Democracy's genius in practice is that it can work even if people rarely, if ever, rise above the selfishness and ignorance with which they have been so richly endowed by their creator." Well, yes and no. Mueller sees democracy as primarily procedural – the right of people to complain about things that go wrong. And the only precondition for such procedural democracy is the absence of "thugs with guns" (Mueller 1996, 118). Without repressive authorities, people will find democracy an entirely natural system. So no wonder democracies are all over the map on trust. You don't need trust to get to democracy and there is little reason to believe that democratic regimes will build trust over time. Trust goes up and down in many nations over time even as institutional structures remain the same (cf. Inglehart 1997, 207–8).

Democracies *are* more trusting. A wide range of measures of democratization shows that *the more democratic the constitutional structure, the more trusting citizens are*. I show correlations between trust and measures of democracy in Table 8-1. The indicators of democratization I use are the measures of political freedoms, civil liberties, and the overall freedom score developed by Freedom House and reported in Gastil (1991); updated Freedom House measures for 1993–4 and 1998–9;[5] a summary measure of Freedom House scores that assigns each country a democratization measure from the year closest to the trust measure in the wvs; Coppedge and Reinicke's (1991) indicator of polyarchy;

---

[4] The correlation between trust in people and confidence in the legal system in the World Value Survey is modest (tau-c = .069, gamma = .122). And the country-by-country correlations tend to be higher where trust in people is higher.
[5] The web site http://www.freedomhouse.org/rankings.pdf supplied these measures. The Freedom House web site contains scores for both political and civil liberties. They were very highly correlated, so I summed the two (cf. Inglehart 1997, 357).

TABLE 8-1. Correlations between Measures of Democracy and Generalized Trust

Measure	All Countries	Non-Communist	Formerly Communist*
Bollen Democracy Score	.375 (62)	.530 (29)	.114 (21)
Vanhanen Democracy Score	.439 (57)	.578 (37)	.139 (19)
Gastil Civil Liberties Score (1988)**	.501 (58)	.617 (40)	-.029 (17)
Gastil Political Rights Score (1988)**	.361 (58)	.369 (40)	-.100 (17)
Gastil Composite Freedom Score (1988)**	.424 (58)	.497 (40)	-.070 (17)
Freedom House Composite Freedom Score (1993–4)**	.377 (65)	.600 (41)	-.188 (18)
Freedom House Composite Freedom Score (1998–9)**	.357 (69)	.639 (41)	-.402 (21)
Freedom House Composite Freedom Score (Year Closest to Survey)****	.393 (67)	.655 (41)	-.466 (19)
Gurr et al. Democratization Score (1978)	.604 (50)	.530 (29)	.000 (21)***
Gurr et al. Democratization Score (1994)*****	.439 (57)	.578 (37)	.130 (19)
Coppedge and Reinicke Polyarchy Score*	.311 (62)	.328 (40)	-.009 (21)
LaPorta et al. Property Rights Score	.530 (55)	.627 (36)	-.053 (19)

* China is excluded.
** Scores reflected from original coding.
*** Scores reflected from original coding; when survey is from 1990, 1988 Freedom House scores used; when survey is from 1995 or 1996, 1993–4 Freedom House scores are used.
**** Correlation is zero because there is no variation in the coding of democratization.
***** Source: LaPorta et al. (1998).

224

measures of democratization reported in Bollen (1991); Gurr, Jaggers, and Moore (1991); Vanhanen (1997), and updated scores for the Gurr measure from LaPorta et al. (1997). The measures of trust are the most recent available figures from the World Values Study for 63 countries over the course of the three waves of the wvs.[6]

The correlations of measures of trust with indicators of democracy are mostly modest, though a few are robust.[7] The message is simple: Democracies don't necessarily go hand-in-hand with high trust (cf. Inglehart 1999). You can't increase trust by making a country more democratic, but you can destroy trust by making a country undemocratic. Authoritarian governments that set people against each other, such

---

[6] I am grateful to Ronald Inglehart for providing updated data for the third wave (1995–6) of the World Values Survey, where available. These figures are *not* averages (see below for some analyses that use the mean trusting shares for the first and second waves). The nations and the years for which I have trust data are: Argentina (1996), Armenia (1995)*, Australia (1995)*, Austria (1990)*, Azerbaijan (1995)*, Bangladesh (1997)*, Belarus (1996)*, Belgium (1990), Brazil (1996), Bulgaria (1990)*, Canada (1990), Chile (1996), China (1995)*, Colombia (1996), Croatia (1996)*, Czech Republic (1990)*, Denmark (1990), the Dominican Republic (1996), East Germany (1996)*, Estonia (1996)*, Finland (1996), Georgia (1996)*, Ghana (1995), Greece (1990), Hungary (1990)*, Iceland (1990), India (1996), Ireland (1990), Italy (1990), Japan (1995), Latvia (1996), Lithuania (1996)*, Luxembourg (1990), Mexico (1996), Moldova (1996)*, Montenegro (1996)*, Northern Ireland (1990), the Netherlands (1990), Nigeria (1995), Norway (1996), Peru (1996), the Philippines (1996), Poland (1996)*, Portugal (1990), Romania (1990)*, Russia (1995)*, South Africa (1996), South Korea (1996), Serbia (1996), Slovakia (1990)*, Slovenia (1995)*, Spain (1996), Sweden (1996), Switzerland (1996), Taiwan (1995), Turkey (1996), the United Kingdom (1990), the United States (1996), the Ukraine (1996)*, Uruguay (1996), Venezuela (1995), and West Germany (1996). Countries marked with an asterisk (*) either formerly had Communist governments or are still Communist regimes (China). See the discussion in the text below. I generated some aggregate results directly from the wvs and in other cases used the compendium by Inglehart et al. (1998).

[7] The range is from .3 for the Coppedge measure of polyarchy and the Freedom House indicator of political rights in 1988 and the Freedom House measures in 1993–4, 1998–9, and the summary index to .6 for the Gurr et al. measure of democracy in 1978 and the Vanhanen democracy scores. And these differences tell an important tale: There are important differences between countries with democratic traditions and those without such legacies. The Gurr et al. measure places all of the Eastern bloc countries at the lowest end of the democracy scale, which is precisely where they were in 1978 when the index was constructed. Even two decades later, this measure of democratization, with its strong split between democracies and nondemocracies, has a stronger predictive power for interpersonal trust than do more nuanced indicators of civil, political, and property rights. Indeed, the 1978 Gurr et al. measure of democratization has a higher correlation with interpersonal trust than does the 1994 index. The other good predictor of trust, Vanhanen's (1997, 34–5) democratization score, is a composite of the level of party competition and popular participation in elections, not of the constitutional structure of a nation.

as the former Communist regimes in Eastern and Central Europe, can make trust hazardous.[8] When people feel compelled to turn against their friends lest the state turn against them, interpersonal trust may become too risky. In such a world, you really can't be too careful in dealing with people, even if everyone would strongly prefer to treat others as if they were trustworthy. Even with democratic institutions in place, people living in countries with legacies of oppression will neither trust their fellow citizens nor participate in civic life. Instead, they will form close bonds with rather small groups of close associates, as in Banfield's Montegrano, and shut out the rest of society (Krygier 1997, 56).

Democracies may be trusting or mistrusting. In countries with no legacy of Communist rule, the mean proportion of trusters in highly democratic regimes is .411, compared to .217 in the formerly Communist regimes. (I shall also refer to countries with no legacy of Communist rule as "democracies" for the present, fully recognizing that many of these nations have not always respected the rights and freedoms associated with democratic regimes.) Democracies are all over the place in trust, ranging from .03 (Brazil) to .65 (Norway). Formerly Communist regimes also vary in trust, but only from .06 to .34. Half of all democracies have more than 34 percent trusters. The standard deviation for democracies is .151. It is less than half that value (.062) for authoritarian states. Democracies make trust possible. They don't necessarily produce it. Totalitarian governments make trust implausible, though not impossible.

Democracies have higher levels of trust because authoritarian states have lower levels of trust. Democratic constitutions provide little guarantee – or even likelihood – of enhancing trust. Yes, they can maintain order better because people believe that law enforcement is fair. And, yes, democratic governments are almost assuredly more popular (and thus more trusted) than dictatorships. But trust in the legal system or in government more generally is not the same as faith in other people. Even

---

[8] Communist governments still existing elsewhere, as well as other tyrannical regimes, fit the pattern as well; however, I omit China from all discussions below. It has a very high (52) percentage of generalized trusters. Inglehart (1999) attributes this to its Confucian culture, comparing it with Taiwan (where 42 percent of people say most people can be trusted) rather than with other countries with legacies of Communist rule. I see the Chinese figure as a likely outlier that might reflect the hazards of conducting survey research in a country that Freedom House places at the bottom of its rankings on both political and civil liberties.

in high trusting countries such as Sweden, there is only modest support for the claim that people who have faith in the legal system also trust others (Rothstein 2000). There is certainly little evidence that democratization increases trust. The correlation between change in trust in 22 nations from 1981 to the early 1990s (according to the World Values Survey) and variations in Freedom House scores from 1978 to 1988 is effectively zero.[9]

So is a third cheer for democracy misplaced? Maybe not. There is *some* evidence that democracy matters. Across 41 countries the correlation between the number of years of continuous democracy (Inglehart 1997, 172) and trust is .769. And no set of controls or simultaneous equation estimation makes the linkage go away. One could, of course, agree with Inglehart's (1997, 180–8) reasonable argument that *stable* democracy depends upon a trusting public. Regimes that merely give constitutional protections against state interference don't need an underbelly of civic responsibility (Mueller 1996, 118). The democratic march to trust is a long and winding road. It takes 46 years of continuous democracy to move a country from well below the mean on trust to above it. Countries with less than 46 years of continuous democracy are no more likely to have trusting citizens than authoritarian states. If institutions matter, their effects are very slow and difficult to disentangle from other changes occurring in societies.[10]

Nor does there appear to be a special type of institution that builds trust. The only two measures of democracy (apart from the number of years of continuous democracy) that have strong correlations with interpersonal trust are the Vanhanen and Gurr et al. indices. The first is an indicator of political competition (the share of votes of the smallest party) and participation (voter turnout). The second is a mixture of constitutional provisions (restrictions on participation, the extent of executive power, and formal guarantees of civil liberties) and behavior (how executives are recruited and the levels of competition and openness of recruitment). While each of the other measures also has some component of how well constitutional promises are met, they focus more on

---

[9] The correlation is modestly *negative* (−.381). Yet all of the variation seems to come from two countries that had large changes in freedom: Argentina and South Korea, both of which became more democratic and less trusting over the decade. Eliminating these cases drops the correlation to −.076.

[10] The correlation is .056, $N = 22$, $p < .237$, one-tailed test.

the structural components of democracy. Yet how well democratic institutions function depends more on how long a country has been a democracy rather than on how trusting its citizens are.[11]

Democratic institutions, such as they are, do little in the short-to-intermediate term to build trust. The correlations between democratization and social trust in formerly Communist states are minuscule. Some are even negative. Of the eight Eastern bloc countries for which we have measurements on trust in 1990 and 1995–6, only one nation had an increase in faith in others (Latvia, 6 percent), while seven had decreases, four of which were substantial.[12] The constitutions of Eastern and Central European nations have become increasingly democratic over time.[13] As democratization proceeded apace, trust lagged behind and the correlation between trust and democratization became increasingly (and significantly) negative.[14]

Trust is neither a prerequisite for nor a consequence of democracy. The democratic revolution that swept Eastern and Central Europe a decade ago – and quickly spread through many of the world's remaining autocracies – did not depend upon social trust. Eastern bloc countries with more trusting citizenries did not become democratic sooner than nations whose populations had less faith in others. Formerly Communist countries with higher levels of trust didn't create polities with more political or property rights. There is even a perverse *positive* relationship between trust and corruption in these nations as late as

[11] The partial correlations of the early Gurr et al. index and the Vanhanen measure of democratization with trust, controlling for the years of continuous democracy, are –.036 and .094, respectively. The partials with the years of continuous democracy controlling for trust are .673 and .616.

[12] The rise in Latvia was 24 percent. The drops are: Estonia (6 percent, 21.4 percent of 1990 base), Lithuania (9 percent, 29 percent of the base), Russia (14 percent, 37 percent of the base), and Poland (17 percent, 49 percent of the base). Belarus, East Germany, and Slovenia each had a drop of 1 percent (4, 4, and 6 percent of the 1990 bases). The 1996 measure on Hungary was not yet available, but there is a 1981 survey and it has more of the same bad news: Trust fell 8 percent from 1981 to 1990, or a third of the base.

[13] The mean value on the freedom index ranges from 2 (completely free) to 14 (not at all free) and it moved from 12.167 in 1978 to 11.056 a decade later to 7.222 in 1993–4 and to 6.047 in 1998–9. By 1998–9, 44 percent of the nations of Eastern and Central Europe had scores of three or lower. Just 50 percent of countries with no legacy of communism had scores of three or less. Belgium, Italy, Japan, Northern Ireland, South Africa, Spain, Uruguay, the United Kingdom, and the former West Germany each had scores of three, as did the Czech Republic, the former East Germany, Estonia, Hungary, Latvia, Lithuania, Poland, and Slovenia.

[14] The correlation is –.466 in 1998–9, $p < .02$, one-tailed; $p < .04$, two tailed.

1998.[15] There is no simple explanation for these results, though it may well be that Marxist regimes that permitted more economic inequality placed less emphasis on ideology and more on the market. Markets depend upon trust.

Thus democracy only effects trust in long-standing democracies. The correlations between levels of democracy and generalized trust are *almost always* higher for countries with no legacy of Communist rule than for all countries (see Table 8-1). The major exception is for the earlier Gurr et al. index, where all Communist countries had identical scores at the bottom of the democratization scale. Democratization has no appreciable effect on trust for countries in Eastern and Central Europe that formerly were authoritarian regimes. In some cases the correlation between trust and democratization is even negative (though never significant).

Yes, many democracies in the sample have experienced authoritarian rule from time to time (and more than from time to time): Ghana, Nigeria, India, Spain, Portugal, Greece, Turkey, Peru, and Bangladesh are notable examples. And many "democracies" in form have not been quite so "free": South Africa, South Korea, Mexico, Taiwan, and the Dominican Republic (among others) fit this pattern.

Democratization is correlated with trust for countries without a legacy of communism (see Table 8-1). Yet, even here, the correlations are often modest and largely reflect the differences between countries with long-standing democratic traditions and countries that have not been democratic quite so long. And all of these effects, except for the years of continuous democracy, vanish in multivariate analyses. The long lag between democratization and trust in Inglehart's continuous democracy measure show how difficult it is, if it can be done at all, to generate new values from structural changes.

TRUST ACROSS CULTURES

A principal reason why democratization does not lead to greater trust is that generalized faith in others doesn't move much at all over time. There

---

[15] The correlation is .274. The measures of political and property rights come from LaPorta et al. (1997). The correlation with corruption is reflected since higher scores on the corruption perceptions index indicate more honesty. The trust measure used is *not* an average, but rather the most recent available figure for social trust. I am grateful to Ronald Inglehart for providing some available data from the third wave of the World Values Survey.

are powerful correlations for trust over time, ranging from .834 (1981–95) to .930 (1990–5). In each time period, 90 percent of the countries experienced changes of less than 10 percent. Generalized trust simply doesn't change much over time. And half of the countries that experienced greater than a 5 percent change from 1990 to 1995 were democratizing nations that *became less trusting*.[16]

Why, then, are some nations more trusting than others? As in the United States, the most important determinant of trust is the level of economic inequality. Cultural factors matter as well, as reflected in a country's dominant religious tradition.

The more equitable the distribution of wealth in a country, the more trusting its people will be. For countries without a legacy of communism, the simple correlation of generalized trust and the Gini index is −.684 (see Figure 8-1).[17] Economic inequality is strongly related to trust, and this connection does *not* vanish in multivariate tests. It *does* go away in the formerly Communist nations of Eastern and Central Europe (where the correlation falls to −.239).[18] The dynamic of economic inequality and trust clearly works differently in democracies and authoritarian societies.

I estimate two sets of models. The first has fewer cases (22), but it allows me to test the link between trust and optimism. I have argued in Chapter 2, supported by data analysis from surveys (Chapter 4) and over time (Chapter 6), that trust depends upon an upbeat worldview. The best cross-national measure of optimism available is the aggregate measure from the wvs on whether people "can count on success in life." Countries with more optimistic populations should also have more trusting citizenries.[19] The "count on success"measure is, however, only

---

[16] Across 22 countries between 1981 and in 1990, the simple correlation is .907. The 1990–5 comparison is for 26 countries and the 1981–95 comparison for 12. The democratizing countries that experienced more than 10 percent shifts are Estonia, Latvia, Lithuania, Poland, Russia, and South Africa. Two countries are omitted from this calculation: China (see note 1) and the United States, which had an unusually high percentage of trusters in the wvs compared to other surveys discussed in Chapter 3.

[17] The Gini index comes from Deininger and Squire (1996) and the data base available at http://www.worldbank.org. I used the Gini index with the best available data in the Deininger-Squire data base and matched the Gini index to the year in which trust was measured for each case.

[18] With China included, it turns positive ($r = .255$).

[19] Again, this only holds in countries with no legacy of communism. In those societies, the simple aggregate correlation between trust and success is .646. For countries in Eastern and Central Europe, there is a *negative* correlation between the two measures ($r = −.177$).

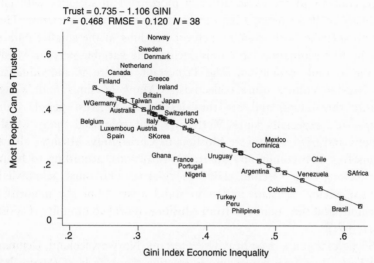

Trust = 0.735 – 1.106 GINI
r^2 = 0.468 RMSE = 0.120 N = 38

FIGURE 8-I. Trust and Economic Inequality for Countries without Communist Legacies.

available for 26 countries without a legacy of communism. To estimate a broader model, I must drop the measure of optimism and focus on other values.

Beyond economic inequality and optimism, I posit a cultural basis for generalized trust. I expect that Protestant societies should be more trusting and Muslim societies less trusting. Inglehart (1999, 92–3) argues that Protestant societies are more trusting because Protestant churches have been more decentralized than Catholic churches. Decentralization means local control, especially compared to the hierarchical Catholic church. Individual congregants thus could take on more responsibility and power within the church (Lipset 1990, Chapter 5; Putnam 1993, 175).[20] The Protestant ethic is an individualistic philosophy, and, as I argued in Chapter 2, generalized trust becomes more important in individualistic cultures (Weber 1958, 105; Triandis 1995, 126).

[20] Inglehart (1999) argues that religious identification must be considered a historical cultural influence rather than a contemporary indicator of the depth of faith since church attendance has fallen in many of the Protestant countries. The correlation between the frequency of church attendance and the share of Protestants in a country is –.242. The measures of percent Protestant (and later percent Muslim) come from LaPorta et al. (1998).

In contrast to my expectation of more trust in societies with large numbers of Protestants, I expect less trust in Muslim societies. There are no societies with even 15 percent Muslims in the smaller data set for the first estimation, so I only include the variable percent Muslim in the second estimation. The Protestant culture is individualistic, the Muslim culture more collectivist.[21] Many Muslims find Western culture threatening and are thus less likely to trust people unlike themselves, especially since Westerners had colonized many Muslim nations and tried to convert Muslims to Christianity. Muslims also see themselves as a community apart: Non-Muslims, according to Islamic law, belong to a "second class" of citizens, who must acknowledge the supremacy of Islam and who stand apart from the majority of Muslims, and thus removed from Muslims' moral community (Esposito 1991, 291).

Societies that are most heavily Protestant (Norway, Iceland, Denmark, and Finland) are 28 percent more trusting than the least (Spain, Italy, Belgium). And the country with the most Muslims (Bangladesh) is 16 percent less trusting than nations with no Muslims (distributed throughout Latin America, Asia, and Europe). To be sure, there are few countries with large shares of Muslims in the wvs surveys – the countries included are hardly representative.[22] Nevertheless, the results below do conform to theoretical expectations; they warrant further investigation as the number of wvs countries expands.

In the first estimation, I *average* the aggregate proportion of trusters in the 1981 and 1990–3 wvs samples in each country, using only countries without a legacy of communism.[23] In the second I use the *most*

---

[21] The correlation between the Protestant share of a nation's population and the Triandis ranking for individualism is .497 for democracies. The correlation with the percentage Muslim is –.472. There are not many Muslim nations in the data base and the result is largely due to the extreme score on the individualism scale of the only country dominated by Islam in the data base (Bangladesh). Without Bangladesh, the correlation falls to –.198. The correlation between trust and percent Muslim is *not* appreciably reduced when I eliminate Bangladesh. Because of missing data on the Gini index, Bangladesh is not included in the model in Tables 8-2 or 8-3, anyway.

[22] There are few public surveys in Muslim nations, perhaps reflecting a distrust of others' motives in seeking to find out what's on people's minds.

[23] For countries that have only a 1990 measurement, I use that survey. The countries in this analysis are as follows: Argentina, Austria*, Belgium, Brazil*, Canada, Chile*, Denmark, Finland, France, India*, Ireland, Italy, Japan, Luxembourg*, Mexico, the Netherlands, Norway, Portugal*, Spain, Sweden, Turkey*, the United Kingdom, and the United States. Nations marked with an asterisk (*) only have 1990 surveys available. I constructed Gini indices from the Deininger-Squire data set for all available years

recent estimate of trust, using either the 1990–3 or the 1995–6 wave. Knack (1999) argues that the causal arrow runs from trust to inequality, rather than from inequality to trust, as I argue. To test this claim, I estimate simultaneous-equation models to see whether trust is both the cause and effect of economic inequality.[24]

The first model for economic inequality includes trust and measures of economic growth, redistribution by the government, and individualism. (Individualistic societies should be more egalitarian.) These variables did not fare so well in the second estimation. Instead, I include the population growth rate, the percent Muslim, and a measure of corruption (the log of the black market currency value). Countries with more Muslims may be less trusting, but they are more egalitarian (cf. Esposito and Voll 1996, 25).[25] And the final variable in the model indicates that the unofficial economy perpetuates inequality. The key point of this exercise is not to explain income inequality across countries, but rather to determine whether more trust also leads to a more equitable distribution of income, or whether the causal connection goes only from equality to trust. I report the estimations in Tables 8-2 and 8-3.[26]

from 1981 to 1990, using the most accurate data sources in their data set. For countries that only have 1990 measures of trust, I used the 1990 Gini index (or the year closest to it).

[24] The method is again two-stage least squares, with bootstrapping (using 1,000 samples). The model for economic inequality includes trust and the growth rate in Gross Domestic Product (LaPorta et al. 1998). I use LaPorta et al.'s (1998) measure of transfers as a percentage of Gross Domestic Product from 1974–94. I also expect that countries with more entrepreneurial political cultures will be *more* equal than collectivist societies. Hofstede (1984) and Triandis (1989) have constructed cross-national measure of individualism versus collectivism. The data for the Triandis individualism scores come from Diener et al. (1995).

[25] As Protestantism has stressed individual achievement, Islam has placed greater emphasis on collective goals, especially on one's economic responsibility to the larger community (as reflected in the prohibition on charging interest on loans). So it should not be surprising to find a powerful coefficient on percent Muslim for economic equality. Were the sample of Muslim nations more representative, the results might be even more powerful. Beyond Islam, two other variables shape economic equality. High population growth rates lead to more inequality: the poor getting poorer. The data on population growth rate come from LaPorta et al. (1998). The black market currency value is the premium of a nation's currency on the black market compared to its official rate. The higher the value of the (log) of the black market currency value, the more important the unofficial economy is to a country's well-being.

[26] The equations in Table 8-5 are rather robust. The bias measures from bootstrapping are quite small. Even the value for trust in people in the equation for the Gini index is modest, given the size (and insignificance) of the unstandardized regression coefficient. The root mean squared error values (RMSE) are all rather small, indicating that each equation has a good fit to the data.

TABLE 8-2. *Two-Stage Least Squares Estimation of Trust and Economic Inequality for Countries with No Communist Legacy: Model I*

	Gini Index Equation Including Trust				Gini Index Equation Excluding Trust			
	Coefficient	Standard Error	t Ratio	Bias	Coefficient	Standard Error	t Ratio	Bias
Equation for Trust	$R^2 = .834$ RMSE = .071							
Gini Index of Inequality	-.005**	.002	-2.251	-.0003				
Count on Success in Life (wvs)	.195**	.086	1.870	.005				
Percent Protestant	.003****	.001	5.215	.001				
Constant	.152	.179	.847	.001				
Equation for Gini Index	$R^2 = .642$ RMSE = 6.329				$R^2 = .726$ RMSE = 5.385			
Trust in People	18.367	17.949	1.023	-.724				
GDP Growth Rate	-5.184****	1.216	-4.263	-.007	-4.584****	.907	-5.057	.083
Individualism Score (Hofstede)	-2.196**	1.197	-1.834	-.025	-1.304**	.698	-1.868	-.069
Transfers as % GDP 1974–94	+.465**	.218	-2.131	.007	-.401**	.178	-2.254	.009
Constant	60.511****	5.205	11.625		59.366****	4.326	13.724	

**** $p < .0001$ *** $p < .01$ ** $p < .05$ * $p < .10$.

$N = 22$.

TABLE 8-3. *Two-Stage Least Squares Estimation of Trust and Economic Inequality for Countries with No Communist Legacy: Model II*

	Gini Index Equation Including Trust				Gini Index Equation Excluding Trust			
	Coefficient	Standard Error	t Ratio	Bias	Coefficient	Standard Error	t Ratio	Bias
Equation for Trust	$R^2 = .733$	RMSE $= .084$						
Gini Index of Inequality	-.908****	.192	-4.735	.004				
Percent Muslim	-.004**	.002	-2.062	-.002				
Percent Protestant	.003****	.001	4.963	.00002				
Constant	.626****	.077	8.125					
Equation for Gini index	$R^2 = .619$	RMSE $= .066$			$R^2 = .642$	RMSE $= .063$		
Trust in People	.041	.166	.245	.062				
Log Black Market Currency Value	.516***	.148	3.491	.103	.490****	.100	4.914	.372
Percent Muslim	-.013****	.003	-4.443	.00003	-.012****	.002	-5.733	.0002
Population Growth Rate	.072***	.025	2.951	.006	.069****	.020	3.452	-.003
Constant	.271****	.076	3.569		.289****	.020	14.542	

**** $p < .0001$ *** $p < .01$ ** $p < .05$ * $p < .10$.

$N = 33$.

In both models, economic inequality is a powerful predictor of trust. Yet trust has no effect on economic inequality. The direction of causality goes only one way. In the first model, inequality lags behind the percent Protestant as a predictor of trust. But in the second model, with more cases, it is by far the strongest determinant of trust. There is also support for the idea that optimism matters in the first model. There are more trusters in countries where many people expect to achieve success in life. And there are fewer trusters (Model II, Table 8-3) in Muslim countries. In countries without a legacy of communism, trust depends upon a mixture of economic inequality, optimism, and culture. The statistical models perform admirably, accounting for between three quarters and 83 percent of the cross-national variation in trust.

Inequality does not depend upon trust. Instead, it reflects some cultural factors – Muslim societies and individualistic cultures are more equal – as well as economic conditions (the growth rate of the economy and the population), government policy (transfers), and corruption. Inequality is more of a cause of trust than a consequence. Yet governments seem to have the wherewithal to reduce inequality through redistributive spending. And this suggests that by boosting equality, they can at least indirectly increase trust. And this is fortunate, since there is little we can do to change culture. Interpersonal trust has been *rising* in Sweden, from moderately high to very high levels (Rothstein in press). And economic inequality has been falling.[27] The longer-term cultural variables don't change much over time.

There is evidence that the causal connection that starts with inequality, goes through optimism, and winds up with trust holds cross-nationally. It is not quite as strong as in the United States, which might be expected since optimism may be more ingrained into American culture than it is elsewhere. Cross-nationally, expectations for success do not track levels of inequality across cultures. But they are strongly related to the overall wealth of a society as measured by the log of the Gross National Product and a measure of the "total quality of life" offered by Diener.[28] I present graphs of these two relationships in Figures 8-2 and 8-3. In addition to these measures, expectations of success also vary with

[27] According to data in the Deininger-Squire data base.
[28] The wealth of a society is measured by the log of its Gross National Product. The total quality of life index includes: basic physical needs fulfillment; physicians per capita; the suicide rate; the literacy rate; college and university attendance; gross human rights violations; the Gini index; deforestation; major environmental treaties; the homicide rate; the monetary savings rate; purchasing parity power; per capita income; and subjective well-being (represented by survey responses to happiness and life satisfaction). See

FIGURE 8-2

Counting on success and log of gross national product in countries with no communist legacy

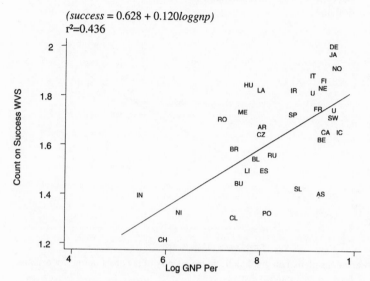

$(success = 0.628 + 0.120loggnp)$
$r^2=0.436$

Note: Observations plotted on graph indicate the country of the observation (for example, COL is the observation for Columbia)

the infant mortality rate, how many years of school the average person has had, and life expectancy.[29]

Trust is essentially cultural, but, like culture itself, is shaped by our experiences. Ultimately culture, economics, and politics are all intertwined, so it is well near impossible to establish a simple causal ordering. What does stand out from the results in this chapter is that culture (and likely economics and politics) shapes institutions more than it is (they are) formed by formal structures.

WHAT DOESN'T MATTER

Skeptical readers might think that the models for trust may appear to leave out a lot. Inglehart (1999), for example, argues that rich nations

Diener (1995, 113). Counting on success is a three-point scale with higher values indicating greater optimism. The correlations of counting on success with trust are −.323 for 24 democratic countries, −.249 for all 35 countries, with the log of GNP .660 (N = 23), and with the quality of life index .683 (N = 23).

[29] The infant mortality and education rates are both logged and come from LaPorta et al. (1998); the average life expectancy comes from Barro and Lee (1994) and is my averaging of the male and female rates. The correlations with counting on success are −.662 for infant mortality, .533 for education, and .563 for life expectancy.

FIGURE 8-3
Counting on success and total quality of life in countries with no communist legacy
(*success* = 1.478 + 0.150*totalqol*)
r²=0.467

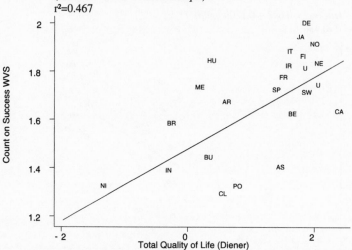

Note: Observations plotted on graph indicate the country of the observation (for example,
COL is the observation for Columbia)

are trusting, poor countries more distrustful. Putnam's (1993) logic goes
the other way around: Trust brings economic growth and prosperity. We
can argue it either way, but there ought to be a connection between trust
and wealth. Beyond simple measures of riches, there are several other
reasonable correlates of trust: education levels; poverty rates; infant mortality; life expectancy; the fertility rate; ethnic diversity; postmaterial
values; media exposure; and civic engagement.[30] Are these factors also
associated with trust across democracies?

Perhaps the most important possible determinant of trust that I have
left out so far is civic engagement. Trust, Putnam (1993, 180) argues,
may lead to better government performance, but faith in others rests
upon the foundation of an engaged citizenry. To increase trust, we must
get people involved in their communities and polities.

Trusting societies *are* participatory societies, though trust is not sufficient to generate participation. More critically, trusting societies have
"better" government, as Putnam (1993) argued. Governmental institutions in trusting countries perform better. They are simply more efficient.
Corruption is less rampant in trusting societies. And, perhaps most critically, even though trust does not lead to social equality, it is a pathway

[30] I owe this suggestion to my colleague Ted Robert Gurr.

to policies that can reduce income disparities between the rich and the poor and, thus, boost trust in turn.

At least in democracies, membership in all organizations and secular groups are correlated with trust. So is turnout in elections. In multivariate analyses, trust is neither the cause nor the effect of civic engagement.[31] Group membership is highest in wealthy individualistic cultures (cf. Triandis et al. 1988), and trust has nothing significant to add beyond these factors.[32] Mueller (1996, 117–18) is certainly correct when he says that "democracy is at base a fairly simple thing – even a natural one. If people feel something is wrong, they will complain about it." You don't need trust to be willing to petition the government. Indeed, the simple correlation between faith in others and willingness to petition is negative.[33] All you need is something to complain about, a feeling that the authorities are not responsive enough, and no thugs with guns. You don't need trust.

Another likely source of trust is ethnic homogeneity. Knack and Keefer (1997, 1278–9) argue that ethnically diverse societies are more likely to develop sharp cleavages which, in turn, destroy trust. I showed in Chapter 4 that parents who wanted their children to hold values that emphasize the welfare of others are more likely to trust other people. Inglehart (1999) extends this logic: People whose own values are less materialistic (or *postmaterialistic*) should also be more trusting.[34] He finds support for this argument only in the 15 richest nations. Putnam (1995b) tracks changes in trust in the United States to increased viewing of television and a drop in newspaper readership. Newspapers tie us to

[31] The correlations are .625, .599, and .736, respectively, for group membership, membership in secular organizations, and turnout.
[32] The group membership variables and petitioning come from the wvs, while the turnout figures come from Vanhanen (1997, 34–42). These and subsequent analyses in this chapter are based upon two-stage least squares estimations.
[33] The correlation is –.389. Group membership and electoral turnout don't depend upon trust, but are strongly related to the number of years of continuous democracy. Group membership has an irregular pattern until a country has been democratic for 75 years and then it leaps dramatically. Electoral turnout increases more straightforwardly as the number of years of continuous democracy gets larger. Civic engagement grows as people become accustomed to taking part in politics, not because they trust each other. Indeed, willingness to sign petitions points to a dissatisfaction with the political system rather than to the belief that politicians and other citizens are trustworthy and responsive, if only they could know what's on your mind.
[34] Postmaterial values include putting more emphasis on freedom of speech and having more say on the job (and in government), rather than maintaining order and fighting price rises (Inglehart 1997, Chapter 4).

other people, while television keeps us inside our homes, away from civic engagement. We might also expect that countries that rank high on corruption will also have less trust (LaPorta et al. 1997, 335). If others are untrustworthy, why should I play the fool, a reasonable person might ask? All of these arguments are reasonable and none of them holds. Various measures of income, education, and well-being all fall to insignificance in multivariate analyses.[35]

All of the measures of income and well-being fall to the greater explanatory power of economic inequality. Postmaterialist values are only modestly correlated with trust. All forms of media exposure, including television viewing, are *positively* related to trust. Television viewing supposedly destroys trust (Gerbner et al. 1980; Putnam 1995b). Yet, in the aggregate analysis, it seems to *increase* trust. But all of these relationships vanish, too, in multivariate tests.[36]

When I tell people about the connection between trust and inequality and why it explains the high levels of faith in others in Scandinavian countries and in the American states of Minnesota and the Dakotas (cf. Rice and Feldman 1997), at least one skeptic always points to ethnic homogeneity as an alternative thesis. It is easy to trust other people in a homogeneous society. Of course, most people can be trusted. They look and think just as you do. And, yes, the Scandinavian countries *are* more

[35] At bivariate levels, most of these variables matter at least in countries with no legacy of Communist rule. Two measures of schooling – the total number of school years from the Barro and Lee (1994) data set and the log of school attainment from 1960 to 1985 from LaPorta et al. (1998) – show correlations about .60 with trust for countries with no Communist legacy. A logged measure of infant mortality (also from LaPorta et al. [1998]) shows an even more powerful simple correlation for the same group of countries ($r = -.711$). The same story holds across a wide variety of measures of income and life quality (Diener 1995). The measures come from a variety of sources (and web sites): LaPorta et al. (1998); Diener et al. (1995); the World Bank, the United Nations, the Barro-Lee (1994) data set (located at http://www.nber.org /pub/ barro.lee /ZIP/ BARLEE.ZIP); the Easterly-Levine data set from http://www.worldbank. org /growth /ddeale.htm; the Johnson, Kaufmann and Zoido-Lobatón data set (1997) from http://www.worldbank.org. The log of per capita GNP (averaged from 1970 to 1995, from LaPorta et al. [1998]) correlates at .625 with trust for countries with no legacy of communism; the Diener et al. measures of total quality of life and advanced quality of life correlate at .683 and .732, respectively, with trust. For various measures of economic well-being, the correlations fall to around .45.

[36] The measures are newspaper readership per 1,000 population and the number of television and radio receivers per 1,000 population (*The Economist* 1990, 126–7). Newspaper readership in democracies is associated with higher faith in others ($r = .686$). But television viewing, which supposedly destroys trust, perversely increases social trust ($r = .597$), as does listening to the radio ($r = .548$). The correlations for media use all vanish when I control for income and especially education.

homogeneous.[37] They are also more egalitarian and especially more heavily Protestant.[38] Interpersonal trust in Sweden has been *increasing*, not declining (Rothstein in press), even as the society is becoming *less* demographically homogeneous.[39] Overall, ethnic diversity does not shape trust – or, even indirectly, economic inequality.[40]

Scandinavian societies are trusting because they are more equal and more Protestant, not just because they are all blonde with blue eyes. A society doesn't need to be predominantly Protestant to be trusting. Even a small share such as 16 percent is enough to boost generalized faith significantly (to 44 percent). Societies with a majority of Protestants also, on average, have majorities of trusters. This analysis resolves the puzzle of why ethnic diversity doesn't seem to matter.

The story so far is reassuringly similar to the one I outlined for American politics. Trust reflects both an optimistic worldview *and* the real world circumstances that make optimism rational, a more egalitarian distribution of income. The Gini index in turn is tied to both an individualistic culture and, more critically, public policies that promote economic growth and redistribution of income. And perceptions of the ability to become successful *are* also based upon reality. Such views are not strongly tied to the Gini index, but they are linked with the infant mortality rate and per capita income for countries with no legacy of communism.[41]

Political culture and economics are thus complementary, rather than alternative explanations. Trust depends upon an optimistic worldview and a more egalitarian distribution of income. Its strongest roots are in Protestant cultures, which stress both entrepreneurship and the equality

[37] The Scandinavian countries rank 7th (Denmark), 17th (Sweden), 20th (Norway), and 23rd (Finland) among 45 countries on the Easterly-Levine measure of ethnic fractionalization (see note 25). The mean score for the Scandinavian nations is .067, compared to .220 for other countries with no legacy of communism (which only reaches significance at $p < .12$, one-tailed test).
[38] The average Gini index in Scandinavian countries is .383 compared to .313 for other countries with no legacy of communism ($p < .10$). But the five Scandinavian countries have an average of 88.63 percent Protestants, compared to 18.73 percent in other countries ($p < .0001$).
[39] Bo Rothstein, personal communication.
[40] Data on ethnic diversity come from Ted Gurr's Minorities at Risk Phase I Dataset (Lee 1993) and the Easterly-Levine (1997) measure of ethnic fractionalization (from LaPorta et al. 1998). The correlations with trust are –.242 and –.108, respectively.
[41] The correlation of trust with the Gini index is –.355. The correlations of logged infant mortality rate and logged GNP per capita (both from LaPorta et al. 1998) are –.696 and .683.

of all parishioners (Lipset 1990, Chapter 5). There is something of an
irony in these findings. Protestant denominations have not been notably
active in pressing for economic equality, while Catholics have often been
at the forefront of movements for economic justice, both in pronounce-
ments from Rome and in movements such as Catholic Workers and lib-
eration theology. Yet the ethic of social egalitarianism among Protestant
denominations gave rise to the welfare state in Europe, which led to both
wealthier and more equitable societies than we find in Catholic countries
(Inglehart 1997, 95). Individualistic cultures lead to more economic
equality and hence to greater interpersonal trust.

THE CROSS-NATIONAL CONSEQUENCES OF TRUST

The big payoffs from trust in the United States are ties to people who
are different from yourself – through charitable contributions and
volunteering – and more cooperation in political life. There are no comparable cross-national data, so I cannot make direct comparisons.[42] But
there are three realms where there are clear cross-national effects of trust.
Trusting countries have better governments, better economies, and
arguably better public policies.

Putnam (1993, 176) is correct when he argues that trust in people
leads to better government performance. Trusting countries are less
corrupt than countries with many mistrusters. They also have better-
performing bureaucracies and more "efficient" judicial systems, as well
as more people who trust the legal system (cf. LaPorta et al. 1997,
335–6).[43] *In each case, the causal connection goes from trust to better
government and not the other way around.*

Trusting societies are less corrupt and have better government
performance. Trust has powerful effects on corruption (cf. LaPorta et al.
1997). Theoretically, if you could make Chile as trusting as Denmark, it

---

[42] The wvs data on volunteering are not directly comparable to the United States data,
particularly the aggregate figures.
[43] The data set is described in LaPorta et al. (1997, 1998). Each of the dependent variables except for confidence in the legal system (from the wvs), openness of the economy
(Barro-Lee data set), and economic performance (Fedderke and Klitgaard 1998) in this
section comes from the LaPorta et al. data set. The independent variables in the economic performance equation also come from Fedderke and Klitgaard (1998). I found
that more trusting societies have higher rates of transfers and subsidies as a percentage
of Gross Domestic Product from 1974 to 1994 ($r = .509$, $N = 40$; $r = .598$, $N = 35$ for
democracies). They also devote a greater part of their Gross Domestic Product to
government programs ($r = .630$, $N = 43$; $r = .735$, $N = 36$ for democracies); see below
for a more detailed discussion and for multivariate analyses.

would also be as clean as this least corrupt country in the world.[44] The effect of trust on corruption is almost one-and-a-half times as large as the next most important predictor, the average number of school years completed. We might suspect that corruption has a greater impact on trust than faith in others has on robbing the public purse. But it doesn't. Kleptocracies thrive in low-trust societies. They can't get off the ground when most people trust each other.

Bureaucrats are more responsive – and less likely to keep public policy tied up in red tape (LaPorta et al. 1998) – when social trust is high (cf. LaPorta et al. 1997). And once more, a responsive bureaucracy does not lead citizens to trust each other (or, ironically, in the legislative branch of government either).

Trust also leads to better judicial systems. An efficient judicial system (Mauro 1995) depends upon an underlying foundation of social trust. And, once again, good judges don't make good citizens. Countries with efficient judicial systems don't become more trusting.[45] The link from trust to judicial efficacy is strong and powerful, whereas the link in the opposite direction is insignificant with an incorrect sign.

More telling is confidence in the legal system, which Rothstein (in press) regards as the key mechanism for translating support for the government into trust in people (see Chapter 2). Yes, there is a link between confidence in the legal system and trust in people. There is a moderate correlation between them for countries without a legacy of communism and a powerful link from trust to approval of the legal system in a simultaneous-equation model. Yet the direction of causality seems to go only one way, from trust to faith in the law. The link from confidence in the legal system to trust is insignificant with an incorrect sign. Since people who trust others have deeper commitments to the values underlying the law (see Chapter 7 and Uslaner 1999b), it is hardly surprising that they have greater faith in the legal system. There is clear evidence that people did not see the legal authorities as brokers of trust in formerly Communist states: The aggregate correlation between confidence in the legal system and generalized trust is moderate and *negative*.[46]

---

[44] The corruption index comes from Transparency International and is the 1998 ranking.

[45] In countries without a legacy of communism, the correlation between confidence in the legal system and interpersonal trust in the 1990–1 World Values Survey is .372. With Communist countries other than China included, it rises to .406.

[46] In countries without a legacy of communism, the correlation between confidence in the legal system and interpersonal trust in the wvs is .372. For the 13 former Communist countries, the correlation is –.470.

A better measure than confidence in the legal system is perceptions that the legal system is fair. While there is no direct measure of public opinion, the Institute for Management Development in Lausanne, Switzerland surveys business executives on their "confidence in the fair administration of justice in society" (published in the Institute's *World Competitiveness Yearbook* and reported in Treisman 1999, 18). The fairness of the justice system has a higher simple correlation with trust than confidence in the legal system. But the story is very much the same: When you have a trusting society, people see the justice system as fair. But an evenhanded judicial system will *not* produce trust.[47]

Trusting societies may breed more than confidence in the law. They may also lead to compliance with the law. LaPorta et al. (1997, 335–6) report that countries ranking high on trust also have lower rates of tax evasion. Rates of tax evasion are strongly correlated with trust, even when I include formerly Communist countries. But if the model for tax evasion also includes confidence in the legal system, trust is no longer significant.[48] Since trust is a powerful predictor of confidence in the legal system, there is at least an indirect connection from trust to tax compliance.

Societies with more trusters also have a lower theft rate, especially when we include the formerly Communist countries in the analysis. Here the direction of causality is somewhat more difficult to establish (as in the time-series results for the United States). Including the formerly Communist countries in the analysis shows a powerful reciprocal relationship between theft and trust: The more theft, the less trust; the less trust, the more theft. The theft rate is markedly higher in formerly Communist countries, while the share of trusting people is smaller.[49] When I eliminate formerly Communist countries, trusting countries still have fewer thefts, but there is only a weak link from thievery to mistrust. Trust, but not confidence in the legal system or the effectiveness of the judiciary, determines the rate of theft in both democracies and formerly Communist countries. The long arm of the law is thus not

[47] The simple correlation with trust (for all countries, including those with a legacy of communism) is .712, considerably higher than the correlation of .439 for confidence in the legal system (.439). I am grateful to Daniel Treisman for providing me with the data on this and other variables.

[48] The simple correlations are .534 for the 32 countries with no Communist legacy and .569 for 36 countries. The multivariate estimation is a two-stage least squares including models for trust, confidence in the legal system, and tax evasion.

[49] Thirteen of the 18 formerly Communist countries have theft rates above the median.

sufficient to deter crime. You are better off living in trusting Sweden than in a country with a reputation for swift and sure punishment, Singapore.[50] Trust is hardly a cure-all for crime, however. It is *not* a significant predictor of assaults or homicides once I control for economic conditions in a country.

Just as democracy does not breed trust, neither does good government (but see Stolle [1999b] for an alternative view). While trust does not make democracy either, it does make democracy work (better).

In more than one way, trust makes democracies rich. The first link is indirect. Because trust reflects sentiments toward people who are different from ourselves, it makes it easier for societies to reach out and deal with other countries. Trusters favor free trade. And trusting societies are more willing to reach out to outsiders: High trust goes hand-in-hand with open economies and fewer restrictions on trade, which in turn leads to greater prosperity (cf. Woolcock 1998, 158).

Even more critically, trust leads directly to economic prosperity. Trusting countries have greater economic growth – trust is the *strongest predictor of growth*.[51] A growing economy does not, however, lead to more trust. Once again, the link goes just one way.

Trust depends upon economic equality and it leads to even more equality. Trusting societies have bigger governments that redistribute wealth from the rich to the poor, spend more on education, and pursue policies that will stimulate economic growth. Thus while there is no direct connection from trust to economic equality, trusting societies in democratic regimes pursue programs that indirectly will boost faith in others. Trusting nations spend more of their total income on governmental programs in general and on education in particular. They also have a larger share of their total population employed by the government. In particular, trusting societies are more likely to devote a higher share of their national wealth to transfer programs that assist the poor. Finally, trusting societies have more open economies, and trade promotes economic growth.[52]

---

[50] Sweden ranked last of 42 countries in the theft rate, compared to Singapore's rank of 27. On assault, Sweden was 37th of 38, while Singapore was 14th. On homicide, it is better to live in Singapore (ranked 35th of 47) compared to Sweden (ranked sixth).

[51] The measure is the mean yearly growth in Gross Domestic Product from Fedderke and Klitgaard (1998).

[52] All of the dependent variables except openness come from LaPorta et al. (1998). Trust is significant at $p < .01$ for the share of the population employed in the public sector and at $p < .05$ in the other equations.

Governments that redistribute income, spend money on education, transfer wealth from the rich to the poor, have large public sectors, and maintain open economies do *not* generate trust. Trust seems to come first. Well, almost. Economic equality is a strong determinant of trust. And trust leads to policies that create wealth and reduce inequalities.

Here we find what Putnam would call a "virtuous circle." The equal become more equal. Yet there is also a vicious circle: Misanthropy and inequality feed on themselves. Yes, you can increase trust indirectly by pursuing policies that reduce economic inequality: Each of the public policies I have considered leads to more economic equality, though the correlations are moderate except for one, the openness of the economy.[53] And, yes, you can adopt these policies without a trusting citizenry. But a public that is public-spirited gives some countries advantages over others in reducing inequality and boosting trust. My consideration of American politics and the findings in this chapter about responsive government also suggests that it is easier to make the hard political decisions when there is trust in the land (cf. Rothstein 2000).

Trust in people may lead to trust in government. People have confidence in their leaders when government is working well. Their judgments about government performance reflect their evaluations of specific personalities, institutions, and policies. But each of these actors must work in, and perhaps contribute to, an atmosphere of compromise or confrontation. And political leaders are ultimately responsible and responsive to the public and its hopes and fears. Government cannot produce trust in people. People can provide government officials with the latitude to work on major social problems, and thereby make it easier for government to function more effectively. Yet a government that works well is not always a popular government. What the government does also matters. A regime that pursues unpopular policies may even become *less* popular if it manages to adopt a big agenda.

Whatever government does, a trusting environment makes it possible for government to act. Mueller (1996, 106) argues that we oversell the benefits of democratic government: "Democracy is . . . an extremely disorderly muddle in which contending ideas and forces do unkempt, if peaceful, battle and in which ideas often are reduced to slogans, data to distorted fragments, evidence to gestures, and arguments to poses."

---

[53] The correlations are in the range of .4 to .5, except for the openness of the economy (where the correlation approaches .7).

FIGURE 8-4
Belief in one true religion and trust in people

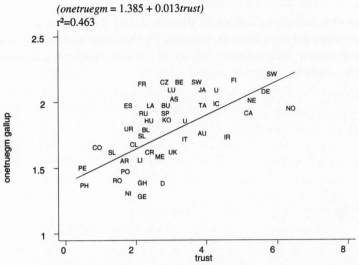

(onetruegm = 1.385 + 0.013trust)
$r^2=0.463$

Note: Observations plotted on graph indicate the country of the observation (for example,
    COL is the observation for Columbia)

Yes, but. If Inglehart (1997, 180–8) is correct, then democracies that are
stable and that work well rest upon cultural foundations, especially
social trust.

As I have shown in Chapters 4 and 7, trust rests upon egalitarian sentiments and leads to greater tolerance. There is some cross-national evidence for this, as well. Countries where many people believe that there
is only one true religion have less trusting citizenries. I show the relationship in Figure 8-4 (and the relationship is *not* confined to countries
without a legacy of communism). The direction of causality is not clear
here, since this question can reflect both acceptance of out-groups (see
Chapter 4) and tolerance more generally (see Chapter 7). The relationship is very strong, either as cause or effect. I showed in Chapter 7 that
trusters are more supportive of women's rights in the United States. There
is cross-national support for this, as well. The Gallup Millennium Survey
in 2000 asked a cross-national sample whether they agreed that families
will be hurt when women work. Although the sample of countries where
I can match the trust question with women's roles is small (15), the
impact of trust on support for a woman's right to work is powerful
and stable – even slightly more powerful than the level of women's

education.[54] Trust makes democracy work because it reflects a tolerant society.

Democratic structures cannot be dismissed, but overall they are generally less powerful determinants of inequality than trust and usually sink to insignificance in multivariate analyses. In the end, democracy is worth two cheers. Save the third for trust.

[54] The data on women's rights come from the International Social Survey Programme's 1998 religion survey (which also includes the generalized trust question, although measured differently). The data are available for download at ftp://unix1.za.uni-koeln.de/za-koeln/uher/relig98/. Trust, the level of women's education, and a measure of left-right party identification of a nation's electorate are all significant predictors of attitudes toward women's working (other demographic and economic indicators are not significant) at $p < .01$ or less. When I multiply the regression coefficients by the range of the predictors, the regression effects for trust, women's education levels, and left-right party identification are .708, .689, and .476 (all reflected to indicate support for women's right to work). To ensure that the estimates are reliable, I bootstrapped the estimates and found support for the stability of all three coefficients. There is also a moderate correlation between a dichotomized measure of trust and support for women's working at the individual level (tau-c = .143, gamma = .230, $N = 37,420$). Trust was a significant predictor of women's rights (at $p < .0001$) in an individual-level ordered probit that also includes gender, age, education, how often one prays, how active one is in her place of worship, and whether one describes herself as religious, as well as a set of country dummy variables. The question on one true religion comes from the Gallup Millennium Survey. I am grateful to Meril James, Secretary General of Gallup International, for providing these data.

Epilogue

Trust and the Civic Community

Thanks to recent cautionary tales, it's easy to wonder if everyone is out to get us. Treachery just isn't what it used to be in the good old days of gentlemen's duels. From an F.B.I. counterintelligence expert [exposed as a Russian spy] to a ... busboy [who obtained the Internet passwords of 217 of the world's richest people and ran a series of scams that garnered him millions of dollars], cutting-edge duplicity fuels the rising public suspicion that no one is to be trusted.

        – Bader (2001, WK4)

Trust, once more, is the chicken soup of social life. But like chicken soup, its curative powers have been oversold. Both trust and chicken soup do lots of good things, but they don't cure all of our ills or solve all of the problems we face in daily life. Neither chicken soup nor trust will make us better golfers or bowlers or even make us more likely to join a bowling league. Both chicken soup and trust can make us feel better, and trust trumps chicken soup because it can also make us feel better about others. It can lead us to civic engagement with people who are different from ourselves and it can foster doing good deeds for those who are less fortunate. It can also make us more willing to look for common ground when we disagree with others about how to solve societal problems.

We are often wary of people who think differently from ourselves. And we are likely to think that people who *look* different from us may hold different values, as well. We worry that people with different values might somehow take advantage of us if we let them have their way. Perhaps they would press for public policies that would grant themselves special privileges at our expense. So one way we cope with the fear of being exploited is only to trust people we know. But since even the most sociable person cannot know very many people, we might restrict our trust to people we know (or believe that we know) think as we do. Yet barricading ourselves into communities of our own kind is costly. We won't fare nearly as well as we could when we forsake the gains of trade (Woolcock 1998, 158).

To prosper, we must take risks. And these risks involve trusting other people. When we trust others, we push aside areas where we disagree and look for common ground. You and I may disagree about politics. We may come from different backgrounds, even have different religious beliefs (or none at all). Yet we accept two fundamental arguments. First, at some critical level, most people share a common set of moral values. This assumption seems innocuous enough until we realize that trusting "most people" involves making inferences about people *we don't know* (and will never meet). Such trust involves a leap of faith, as well as a heavy dose of optimism that other people are, in fact, trustworthy. The "safe" path is to assume the contrary – that people are guilty until proven innocent.

The benefits of generalized trust point to its moralistic roots. We are unlikely to accept the argument that most people can be trusted if we rely upon our experience. We don't know "most people" and there is little reason to believe that "most people" are like the people we know. No variety of socializing leads people to become more trusting. The only types of civic engagement that can produce trust clearly have moral roots (volunteering and giving to charity).

It is hard to figure out how socializing with people you know will make you more tolerant of people who are different from you, or more supportive of greater immigration, fewer trade barriers, and civil rights. It is difficult to make a connection between knowledge-based trust and better government institutions. It is even less plausible to make a link between trust in people you know and taking their money and giving it to poorer people that neither you nor they know. You can make a better argument that strategic trust might make it easier to pass laws. The literature on norms in Congress is filled with accounts of stories of how trust among members helps get legislation passed (Matthews 1960, 97–9; Loomis 1988, 28; Uslaner 1993, Chapter 2). The connection between generalized trust and legislative success makes more sense if there is a moral foundation to faith in others.

Second, sometimes the normal democratic patterns of decision making don't work well. Perhaps there is no alternative that a majority prefers to all others, or perhaps feelings can get so intense that simple majority rule threatens to tear the social fabric apart. Then, we might all be better off if we reach some compromise than if either of us tries to impose our will upon the other. This second assumption follows from the first. If we have nothing in common, then looking for common ground is fruitless.

People who trust others don't see differences in values as a call to arms. They are tolerant of people unlike themselves. They see the potential for mutual gains by working together. Yes, you can cooperate with others without trusting them (Levi 1999). But it is more difficult to do so. Each time you want to reach agreement on some collective action problem, you need to start from scratch to establish the ground rules for cooperation. Without generalized trust, you need to build strategic trust time and time again.

Generalized trust makes life easier by making assumptions about the world – that most people share your common values and that they will not try to exploit you. Clearly, only optimists will accept these postulates without evidence. And this, of course, is why trust depends upon an optimistic view of the world.

Making the inferential leap that most people can be trusted can have great payoffs. Trusting societies are more civil. It is easier to reach collective decisions when most people trust others. Government functions better in an atmosphere of trust. People are more willing to help those less fortunate when they have faith in strangers. And societies who trust people different from themselves are more willing to trade with them – and then to gain the benefits of commerce, higher economic growth, and greater prosperity.

If trust brings so many benefits, why doesn't everyone have faith in others? Mostly because trust isn't easy. Often we are simply wary of others, especially if we live in collectivist societies that place a high value on in-group identification. Trust is both higher and more critical in individualistic societies.[1] Without strong bonds linking groups to one another, people must rely on each other. Trust looms large in American culture. We speak of settlers on the prairies helping roll each other's logs (leading to logrolling, or vote trading, in legislatures). American heroes

---

[1] The highest trusting societies in Chapter 7 are in Scandinavia. One might think that they are collectivist since they have strong welfare states. Yet, on both the Hofstede (1980) and Triandis (1989) indices of individualism-collectivism, they are close to the individualist pole (though Norway's score on each is somewhat more moderate).

include Johnny Appleseed, the solitary woodsman who traverses the country doing good deeds, or the Lone Ranger and Tonto, who ride the range looking for people in trouble.[2] Indeed, the American motto is a paeon to both individualism and generalized trust: "One out of many."[3]

TRUST AND CULTURE

In many ways, trust is cultural. Individualistic societies are more trusting than collectivist ones.[4] And that explains why trust is an enduring value. Trust *does* vary over time, but it is rather stable across individuals (see Chapter 3) and especially across countries (see Chapter 8). The mean change in trust is only .028 over the course of a decade. Trust not only carries over from one generation to another (Renshon 1975; and see Chapter 4), but also within ethnic groups moving from one nation to another (Rice and Feldman 1997).

Yet we should not make too much of stability. In nine of the wvs countries (41 percent), trust either rose or (in just one case) fell by 5 percent or more.[5] And we know that many people – about one quarter of the 1972–74–76 ANES panel, slightly less than 30 percent of the Niemi-Jennings adult sample from 1965–82, and about 37 percent of the Niemi-Jennings youth sample from 1965–82 – change their response to the trust question over time.

Critics of political culture mock the assumption that core values are enduring while social structures and economic performance are not (Jackman and Miller 1996). While many of their arguments are caricatures of the cultural thesis, the critics do make a key point: Cultural values are not static. They change in response to major patterns of turbulence in the society, such as the civil rights movement and the Vietnam War in the United States in the mid-1970s (see Chapter 5).

More generally, political culture is rooted in history. Yes, moralistic trust does not in general reflect your life's experience. We can wave away unfortunate events, but at some point there is a reality check. Banfield's

---

[2] See Chapter 5 for a discussion of these American folk heroes.
[3] This is the official motto of the United States, embossed on its currency in Latin, "*E pluribus unum.*"
[4] The correlation between trust and the Hofstede measure of individualism is .617 ($N = 36$). For the Triandis measure, the correlation is .570 ($N = 35$). Both sets of correlations are for countries without legacies of Communist rule.
[5] The mean absolute change in trust is .048.

(1958) Montegranans and Perlez's (1996) Albanians face cruel worlds worthy of Hobbes's worst nightmares.[6] Trusting strangers in such an environment makes little sense. And so we see far less interpersonal trust in societies where daily life is filled with despair. Where things are good – especially when we believe that they are going to get better, even if they are not so great now – it is far less risky to trust strangers. An expanding pie means that there will be enough to go around. But when you have little and there is no prospect that things will get better in the future, you will see people who are different from you as potential enemies. Just as it would be foolish to walk around trusting strangers in Montegrano, it would also be silly to turn your back on others in Oslo at every blip in the business cycle. Trust does not change dramatically with short-term economic trends. It shouldn't, because what will go down will come back up. Trust becomes irrational when there is no reason to believe that the downside will be followed by an upside.

What distinguishes Southern Italy and Albania from Scandinavia is not just riches, but how income is distributed. If everyone is poor, we're all in the same boat together and there is no reason to believe that others *have* exploited you to get where they are (which is where you are). Inequality, on the other hand, gives you evidence that some people may well be out to get you – hence that trust may not be a good risk.

As inequality grows, the perception that people have a common stake in society's well-being withers. Fundamentalism, anti-immigration sentiment, and opposition to free trade all peak during periods of economic unease in the United States. Each is an assault on the tolerance and openness that lie at the foundation of generalized trust. On the other hand, in some countries there is clear evidence of both increasing trust and growing equality. Trust in Italy rose from 24 percent in the 1960 *Civic Culture* study (Almond and Verba 1963) to 35 percent in 1990, while income inequality fell from .410 in 1974 to .322 in 1990 (Deininger and Squire 1996). Trust rose even more strongly in Mexico, from 8.2 percent to 28 percent in 1996, while economic inequality moved downward, though not so sharply, from .550 to .503 (in 1992).

It makes no sense to argue that trust is exclusively a cultural value or only an instrumental response to one's environment. It is both. Trust doesn't move quickly – providing plenty of evidence for the cultural

[6] See Chapter 2, note 10, and Chapter 4.

thesis. But it is not etched in stone, and it does, at least collectively, respond to changes in the real world.

BUILDING TRUST

This doesn't mean that it is easy to engineer trust. Democratic countries are more trusting, but you can't go around redrawing constitutions (or even courts) and expect to create trust. Imagine a corrupt autocracy that wakes up and discovers civil liberties. Under the old regime, the honest protestors went to prison and the thieves went free. Now, neither group gets hauled before the courts. Are we surprised that trust doesn't rise?

It's not easy to build trust through government policies either. According to one of the results in Chapter 8, you can reduce inequality by increasing transfer payments from the rich to the poor, and by reducing inequality you can increase trust. But you can't simply go in and order countries to increase transfers from the rich to the poor. Countries with low levels of trust are also less likely to redistribute income. Inequality breeds fear and resentment of out-groups. In brief, it gives rise to xenophobia, the opposite of moralistic trust.

It must be easier to build political coalitions for redistribution than it is to change long-term political culture. Somewhere we must be able to break the cycle. And perhaps Italy, where much of the current concern for trust began (with Putnam's classic 1993 study), may offer us at least part of the answer: It was a classic low-trusting society with a moderately high degree of economic inequality in 1960. Trust rose to a moderate level and economic inequality fell to the same level as Sweden by 1990. And Italy ranked just behind Hungary, Sweden, Belgium, and France in the rate of transfer payments.

The United States, on the other hand, saw trust fall from 58 percent in the *Civic Culture* study in 1960 to about the same level (36 percent) as Italy in 1996.[7] Inequality rose to considerably above Italy's level by the 1990s and went far higher by mid-decade.[8] And the United States remains below the mean (even for countries with no legacy of Communist rule) of transfer payments. We know that government in the United States is far more contentious and perhaps less productive than

---

[7] Other surveys show trust at lower levels earlier in the 1990s; see Chapter 1.

[8] The United States Department of Commerce (1996) Gini indices suggest somewhat higher values for the United States than do Deininger and Squire (1996). The former figure is .396 for 1990, compared to .378 for the latter.

it was four decades ago. Has the rise in trust in Italy led to "better government"?

The message to countries that are both poor and mistrustful is simple. If trust matters and can help a country grow richer and have better government, then it pays to be wary of policies designed to get rich quickly. Making markets at any cost will exacerbate inequality. Such a strategy may lead to quick growth, but sustained growth depends upon open markets and a cooperative spirit. As Reich (1999, B4) has argued:

Vast inequalities of wealth and income can strain the social fabric of a nation. They make collective decisions more difficult ... because citizens in sharply different economic positions are likely to be affected by these sorts of decisions in very different ways. . . . Were inequality to grow too wide, we would risk an erosion of Americans' sense of common purpose and identity. . . . A polarized society is also less stable than one with a large and strong middle. Such a society offers fertile ground for demagogues eager to exploit the politics of resentment.

If you want to develop the cooperative spirit that will help overcome collective action problems, *don't get rich, get equal.*

Appendix A

For the equations below, variables significant at $p < .10$ are <u>underlined</u>, variables significant at $p < .05$ are **in bold**, variables significant at $p < .001$ or better are *in italics*, and insignificant variables are in regular typeface.

GOING TO BARS: being *young, single or divorced, male, not very religious, and socializing with friends.*

PLAYING BINGO (from the 1972 ANES): *gender* and *membership in social organizations* are the strongest determinants of bingo playing. Also in the model are **membership in fraternal organizations, believing that luck rather than skill determines whether you win in games of chance,** <u>feeling bored</u>, and satisfaction with your time to relax. The equation for trust included *whether it is safe to walk the streets in the neighborhood, whether you believe that you can make your plans work out, whether public officials care about me,* **trust in government, believing that you can run your life as you wish, whether good Americans must believe in God,** <u>particularized trust (out-group thermometers – in-group thermometers)</u>, <u>a dummy variable for being black</u>, <u>whether the bad is balanced by the good</u>, age, and belief in life after death. In the simple probit, trust is negatively related to playing bingo and is significant at $p < .0001$.

PLAYING PINOCHLE (1972 ANES): A two-stage least squares estimation shows that playing pinochle neither produces nor consumes trust. Predictors of trust include whether *public officials care what happens to you, whether it is safe to walk on the street in your neighborhood,* **how much influence you have over your life, can**

257

one run one's own life, whether your plans work out, trust in government, whether good Americans must believe in God, race, belief
in life after death, and age. Predictors of playing pinochle include
whether one plays for money or fun, being married, satisfaction
with your spare time, race, gender, family income, union membership, membership in social group, and a dummy variable for
Catholicism ($N = 519$, RMSE = .399 for pinochle, and .445 for
trust).

PLAYING BRIDGE (from the 1972 ANES): In the two-stage least squares
estimation for trust, the predictors include *playing bridge, trust in
government, the belief that you can run your own life*, age, safe to
walk the street in your neighborhood, whether a good American
must believe in God, public officials don't care about me, belief in
life after death, particularized trust, race, whether bad is balanced
by good, and whether you can make plans work. For bridge the
predictors are *college education*, trust, number of children the
respondent has, family income, gender, how long one has lived in
the community, age, and a dummy variable for Protestantism.

TRUST MODEL IN TABLE 5-3: The other variables are *race, trust in out-
groups, whether one ought to get involved in helping people*,
education, expectation that the standard of living will be better in
twenty years, interpretation of the Bible as the literal word of God,
a dummy variable for having a job, family income, belief that this
year's economy is better than last year's, trust in in-groups, interest in politics, marital status, number of children, and age. The
1996 ANES also has measures of level of activity in organizations,
but few people admitted more than a passing role in any of the
types of groups.

SOCIAL CAPITAL BENCHMARK SURVEY MODELS FOR RELIGIOUS AND
SECULAR CHARITABLE DONATIONS:

RELIGIOUS DONATIONS EQUATION: *Service attendance, participation in church-synagogue other than attending services, gender
(male), family income, trust in coreligionists*, age, education, own
your home, number of people you can confide in, generalized trust,
Catholic.

SECULAR DONATIONS EQUATION: *Education, income, participating in church-synagogue other than attending services, number of
people you can confide in*, generalized trust, age, own your home,
Catholic, gender, trust in coreligionists.

NEW YORK TIMES MILLENNIUM SURVEY ANALYSIS OF GENERALIZED
TRUST AND KNOWLEDGE-BASED FAIRNESS AND HELPFULNESS:
GENERALIZED TRUST EQUATION: *Age, public officials don't
care about me,* will life for next generation be better, dummy for
Southern residence, number of children, satisfaction with family
life, people you know are fair, education level, expectations for the
future of the United States, family income, Hispanic, people you
know are helpful.

GENERALIZED HELPFULNESS EQUATION: *expectations for future
of the United States,* generalized trust, number of children, public
officials don't care, being employed, concerned more about yourself than others, people you know are helpful, people you know
are fair.

PEOPLE YOU KNOW ARE HELPFUL EQUATION: *how often attend
church,* more concerned about self than others, number of children,
generalized fairness, generalized trust, generalized helpfulness, satisfied with family life.

GENERALIZED FAIRNESS EQUATION: people you know are fair,
generalized trust, married, number of children, people you know
are helpful, government officials don't care, education.

PEOPLE YOU KNOW ARE FAIR EQUATION: generalized fairness,
more concerned with self than others, frequency of church attendance, family income, people you know are helpful, generalized
trust, expectations for future of the United States, married, able to
meet personal goals.

PEW PHILADELPHIA SURVEY OF GENERALIZED AND KNOWLEDGE-BASED
TRUST:
GENERALIZED TRUST EQUATION: *Feel safe walking in neighborhood,* education, like neighborhood, can have an impact on community, parents warned not to trust others, age, Hispanic, trust
federal government, particularized trust factor, black, can turn to
people for support, volunteered for secular organizations.

FRIENDS AND FAMILY (PARTICULARIZED) TRUST FACTOR: *Black,
feel safe at home,* education, can turn to people for support, secular
volunteering, number of children, union member, how long live in
neighborhood, have people you can rely on, own home, generalized trust, Hispanic, parents warned not to trust others, talk to
neighbors.

Appendix B

For the equations below, variables significant at $p < .10$ are <u>underlined</u>, variables significant at $p < .05$ are **in bold**, variables significant at $p < .001$ or better are *in italics*, and insignificant variables are in regular typeface.

WILLINGNESS TO SERVE ON JURY (from 1992 ANES): The ranges reflect the probit results reported in Uslaner (1998a) and the reanalyses I conducted based upon a simultaneous equation estimation with trust as endogenous. Other variables in the model are: *discussing politics*, **trust in government, high school and college education, being divorced, the number of hours worked each week, being self-employed,** <u>talking to others about election campaigns, being married</u>, and the number of hours one's spouse works each week.

IMPORTANCE OF CLASSICS (from 1993 GSS, estimated by ordered probit): Other variables included *education*, *ideology*, **a dummy variable for the South, relative financial status,** <u>party identification</u>, <u>gender</u>, <u>subjective social class</u>, fundamentalism, size of community, frequency of attendance at religious services, age, and dummy variables for being black, Catholic, or Jewish.

ETHNIC REPRESENTATION (1994 GSS): In a two-stage least squares estimation with trust endogenous, the other predictors of ethnic representation are **expectations that the national economy would improve,** <u>fundamentalism</u>, age, and whether the government pays sufficient attention to blacks.

MORAL STANDARDS (1981 World Values Study in the United States): The measures of moral standards are all ten-point scales ranging from least to most acceptable. I estimated a seemingly unrelated system of equations for these standards of moral behavior together with other measures (joyriding, lying, cheating on taxes, and avoiding fares on public transportation). The other predictors include measures of *how much people believe that they obey the secular components of the Ten Commandments, whether there are clear standards of good and evil, how important marital faithfulness is, race, age,* **being married, belief in hell,** belonging to a union household, and education. (These are average significance levels over the eight equations.) The measure of reciprocity is the expectation that other people obey the secular commandments. These results are described in greater detail in Uslaner (1999a) and in a comparative context in Uslaner (1999b).

OBEY UNJUST LAW (1996 GSS): The bivariate correlations are tau-c = .128, gamma = .264, *p* < .001. Trust is also significant in a multivariate analysis that also includes *high school and college education, gender, how important it is that children obey parents, confidence in the legislative branch of government,* **how often one attends religious services, whether one grew up as a religious fundamentalist, and how important it is that children be well-liked.** Religiosity (especially fundamentalism) and the desire that your children be obedient and popular make people more likely to demand that we always obey laws, while confidence in government, as well as trust in people (and higher education), leads people to judge each law on its merits.

PROTEST DEMONSTRATIONS SHOULD BE PERMITTED (1996): Other variables include *whether people should always obey unjust laws, age, gender, education,* **confidence in the executive branch of the government, race, how important it is that children obey their parents, wanting children to think for themselves,** and frequency of attendance at religious services.

NOT CALLING IN SICK (1968 Panel Study of Income Dynamics): The estimation came from a two-stage least squares analysis with trust endogenous. Other predictors include *how long the respondent has been employed in the same position, how important one's own decisions are on the job, age, family income, how much the respondent likes challenges in one's job, union membership (negative coefficient), the number of days unemployed, satisfaction with yourself,* **being single (negative coefficient), being married, education (negative coefficient), having no spare time,** and gender. The PSID employed a trichotomous measure of trust: trusting few, some, and most people.

LOCK DOORS (from 1978 Quality of Life Survey of the Survey Research Center): Positive values indicate that it is unimportant to keep the doors locked. Other variables in the ordered probit are *living in an urban area (negative coefficient), age, how clean the interviewer views the interior of the house, whether the respondent was born in a rural area, how much you like your neighborhood, living in an integrated neighborhood (negative coefficient),* how often you were attacked or robbed in the past five years, family income, gender, born in a big city, owning your own house, a dummy variable for being black (negative coefficient), wanting to stay in your neighborhood, whether anything frightens you (negative coefficient), and education. Just .5 percent of all respondents said that they were robbed or attacked three or more times in the past five years.

PROTECTING YOURSELF WITH A GUN (1976 ANES): Other variables in the model are: *dummy variables for living in the South and border states, gender,* whether you or a family member have witnessed a crime, whether someone has broken into your home or the home of a family member, out-group trust, growing up in a big city, whether you or a family member has been the victim of a physical attack, and in-group trust. There is virtually no correlation with owning a gun in the GSS samples – with trusters being slightly more likely to own guns (phi = .032, Yule's Q = .065); however, being willing to protect yourself with a gun is a less trusting action than simply owning a gun.

PARTICIPATING IN A PROTEST MARCH (2000 Social Capital Benchmark Survey): Trust is significant at $p < .05$. Also in the model are *age (-), trust in coreligionists, participation in activities other than services at houses of worship,* education, political knowledge, gender, and income.

FILIBUSTERING: Also in the model are the **percent of Senate votes that pitted a majority of one party against another** (Ornstein, Mann, and Malbin, Comps. 1998, 210), Stimson's (1998) measure of **public mood** (more filibusters when the public ideology is more liberal, indicating that conservatives, who are most likely to use the filibuster, will be most likely to resort to this tactic when they are out of step with the public mood), and a dummy variable for the congressional session (since obstructionism is more likely in the

second session, an astute observation that Richard Beth made in a
private conversation). The data for public mood are available at
http://www.unc. edu/~jstimson/ann5296.prn.

UNITED WAY CHARITABLE CONTRIBUTIONS: Other variables in the
multivariate model for charitable contributions are *the rate of
change in the Consumer Price Index*, **the rate of change of the
Gross Domestic Product, the Gini index of inequality**, and a
dummy variable dividing the sample into pre- and post-1981 years.
The dummy variable reflects changes in tax laws in 1981 (see
Uslaner 1993, 96–7), but it has the wrong sign. Generally, people
give more to charity when the rate of inflation is low and when
income inequality is lowest, but when the rate of Gross Domestic
Product growth is also lowest (adjusted R^2 = .930, N = 26).
Contributions are highest when people can most afford to give
them, rather than when the need is greatest.

CONGREGATIONAL CHARITABLE CONTRIBUTIONS AND "BENEVO-
LENCES": I estimated the models by two-stage least squares, with
the predictors for trust the same as I use in Chapter 7. The measure
of church attendance comes from the biennial surveys of the American National Election Study. To get annual measures, I imputed
values based upon time trend using the impute procedure in STATA
6.0. The equations for congregational and benevolences also
include the 1981 dummy used in the United Way equation. The
unstandardized regression coefficients for trust are about equal for
congregational gifts (.622) and benevolences (.580), but the *t* ratio
is much higher for benevolences (2.751, significant at $p < .005$ compared to 1,648, $p < .05$). **Church attendance** had a much higher
impact on congregational finances (b = 1.012, t = 2.842, compared
to b = .384, t = 1.927). And the *1981 dummy* had a big impact
on benevolences (b = –.061, t = –3.244, compared to b = –.024,
t = –.711).

GIVING USA TOTAL CHARITABLE CONTRIBUTIONS: Two-stage least
squares estimation with *inflation*, **trust**, 1981 dummy, and change
in Gross National Product. All *Giving USA* estimations treated
trust as endogenous, with the Gini index, the public mood, and the
election year dummies significant at various levels, as well as each
type of charitable contribution, none of which were significant. I
also estimated single-equation ARIMA models and the significance
levels and coefficients were similar to those from the two-stage least
squares.

GIVING USA SECULAR CHARITABLE CONTRIBUTIONS: Two-stage least squares model with **trust, the 1981 dummy, inflation,** and change in Gross National Product.

GIVING USA RELIGIOUS CHARITABLE CONTRIBUTIONS: Two-stage least squares model with *inflation*, trust, and change in Gross Domestic Product.

GIVING USA HEALTH CHARITABLE CONTRIBUTIONS: Two-stage least squares model with **1981 dummy**, trust, change in Gross Domestic Product, and inflation.

GIVING USA HUMAN SERVICES CHARITABLE CONTRIBUTIONS: Two-stage least squares model with *trust*, *inflation*, change in Gross National Product, and 1981 dummy.

.

Appendix C

For the equations below, variables significant at $p < .10$ are <u>underlined</u>, variables significant at $p < .05$ are in **bold**, variables significant at $p < .001$ or better are in *italics*, and insignificant variables are in regular typeface.

CORRUPTION EQUATION: The equation also includes *the average number of school years citizens have attained* (Barro and Lee 1994) and the **1998 Freedom House democratization score**.

JUDICIAL EFFICIENCY EQUATION: Other variables are *the average number of school years* and the **summary Freedom House democratization index**.

CONFIDENCE IN LEGAL SYSTEM EQUATION: A two-stage least squares estimation with trust also endogenous. The equation for trust also includes the *Gini index of inequality* and the *percentage of a country's population that is Protestant* (see below for an explication of the logic of these predictors). The other predictors in the model for confidence in the legal system are the *1988 Freedom House measure of civil liberties* (Gastil 1991) and **assassinations in a country per million people per year from 1970–85** (Sachs and Warner 1997). So countries with higher interpersonal trust, greater civil liberties, and fewer assassinations have more confidence in the law. The impact of civil liberties is the strongest, though the t-ratios for civil liberties and trust are about equal.

FAIRNESS IN THE LEGAL SYSTEM EQUATION: A two-stage least squares estimation with trust endogenous. The equation for trust also includes the **Gini index of inequality** and **percent Protestant**. The equation for fairness of the justice system includes *trust, how extensive is the system of property rights* (from LaPorta et al. 1997), and **assassinations in a country per million people per year from 1970–85** (Sachs and Warner 1997).

THEFT RATE EQUATION: The theft rate in 1990 comes from Daniel Lederman of the World Bank (personal communication, May 1999). Estimated by two-stage least squares with trust endogenous. The trust equation including formerly Communist states ($N = 29$) includes *theft rate*, **percent Protestant**, the Gini index of inequality, and the **percent Muslim**. The theft equation includes *trust* and the **Freedom House measure of civil liberties in 1988**. For countries without a legacy of communism ($N = 19$), **trust** is significant at $p < .05$ for theft, and <u>theft</u> is significant at $p < .10$ for trust.

OPENNESS OF THE ECONOMY EQUATION: The measure comes from Barro and Lee (1994). Other predictors include *transfer payments as a percentage of GDP* and *the country's area* (smaller countries have more open economies). The area measure is also reported in Barro and Lee (1994).

GROWTH IN GROSS DOMESTIC PRODUCT EQUATION (see note 50): Estimated by two-stage least squares, with *the percentage Protestant*, the Gini index of inequality, and the growth in GDP rate in the trust equation. In the GDP growth equation are **trust, the change in years of education for population 15 and over from 1970 to 1990, and growth of trade from 1980 to 1990**.

PERCENT GDP SPENT ON GOVERNMENT EQUATION: Other variables are *the percentage of the population not living on farms* (Vanhanen 1997) and **how much the economy relies upon government rather than the free market** (Barro and Lee 1994).

EDUCATION SPENDING EQUATION: Other variables included are the **log of GNP per capita** (LaPorta et al. 1998) and the <u>adult literacy rate</u> (Vanhanen 1997).

PERCENT OF POPULATION EMPLOYED IN PUBLIC SECTOR EQUATION: Other variables in the equation are *the percentage of people not living on farms* and **how much the economy relies upon the government rather than on the free market**.

TRANSFERS AND SUBSIDIES AS A PERCENTAGE OF GDP (AVERAGE FROM
1975–95) EQUATION: This equation also includes the log of
GNP per capita, <u>bureaucratic delays</u>, and tax compliance (from
the *Global Competitiveness Report 1996*, as reported in LaPorta
et al. 1998).

References

Adorno, T. W., Else Frenkel-Brunswik, Daniel J. Levinson, and R. Nevitt Sanford. 1964. *The Authoritarian Personality*. Part One. New York: John Wiley and Sons. Originally published 1950.

Alesina, Alberto and Eliana LaFerrara. 2000. "The Determinants of Trust." National Bureau of Economic Research Working Paper 7621.

Almond, Gabriel and Sidney Verba. 1963. *The Civic Culture*. Princeton: Princeton University Press.

Amato, Paul R. 1990. "Personality and Social Network Involvement as Predictors of Helping Behavior in Everyday Life," *Social Psychology Quarterly* 53:31–43.

Andreoni, James. 1989. "Giving With Impure Altruism: Applications to Charity and Ricardian Ambivalence," *Journal of Political Economy* 97:1447–58.

Bachrach, Michael and Diego Gambetta. 2000. "Trust in Signs." In Karen S. Cook, ed., *Trust in Society*. New York: Russell Sage Foundation.

Bader, Jenny Lyn. 2001. "Paranoid Lately? You May Have Good Reason," *New York Times* (March 25):WK4.

Baer, Stephen. 1998. "Vote of Support for Employees," *Washington Post* (March 10):A15.

Baier, Annette. 1986. "Trust and Antitrust," *Ethics* 96:231–60.

Bakal, Carl. 1979. *Charity U.S.A.* New York: Times Books.

Baker, Judith. 1987. "Trust and Rationality," *Pacific Philosophical Quarterly* 68:1–13.

Banfield, Edward. 1958. *The Moral Basis of a Backward Society*. New York: Free Press.

Barber, Bernard. 1983. *The Logic and Limits of Trust*. New Brunswick, NJ: Rutgers University Press.

Baron, Jonathan. 1998. "Trust: Beliefs and Morality." In Avner Ben-Ner and Louis Putterman, eds., *Economics, Values, and Organization*. New York: Cambridge University Press.

Barone, Michael. 1990. *Our Country: The Shaping of America from Roosevelt to Reagan*. New York: Free Press.

Barone, Michael and Grant Ujifusa with Richard E. Cohen. 1997. *The Almanac of American Politics 1998*. Washington: National Journal.

Barro, Robert, and Jong-Wha Lee. 1994. "Data Set for a Panel of 138 Countries." Mimeo, Harvard University.

Bendor, Jonathan and Piotr Swistak. 1997. "The Evolutionary Stability of Cooperation," *American Political Science Review* 91:290–307.

Bennett, Stephen E., Richard S. Flickinger, and Staci L. Rhine. 2000. "Political Talk Over Here, Over There, Over Time," *British Journal of Political Science* 30:99–120.

Benoit, John and Kenneth Perkins. 1995. *Volunteer Firefighters*. Unpublished manuscript, Dalhousie University, Halifax, Nova Scotia.

Berger, Mark and John Brehm. 1997. "Watergate and the Erosion of Social Capital." Presented at the Annual Meeting of the Midwest Political Science Association, April, Chicago.

Berman, Sheri. 1997. "Civil Society and Political Institutionalization," *American Behavioral Scientist* 40:562–74.

Bianco, William T. 1994. *Trust: Representatives and Constituents*. Ann Arbor: University of Michigan Press.

Binder, Sarah A. 1999. "The Dynamics of American Gridlock, 1947–96," *American Political Science Review* 93:519–34.

Binder, Sarah A. and Steven S. Smith. 1996. *Politics or Principle?: Filibustering in the United States Senate*. Washington: Brookings Institution.

Black, Nathan. 1999. "Yes, I'm in a Clique," *New York Times* (April 29): A29 (Washington edition).

Boix, Carles and Daniel N. Posner. 1998. "Social Capital: Explaining Its Origins and Effects on Government Performance," *British Journal of Political Science* 28:666–74.

Bok, Sissela. 1978. *Lying*. New York: Pantheon.

Bollen, Kenneth. 1991. "Political Democracy: Conceptual and Measurement Traps." In Alex Inkeles, ed., *On Measuring Democracy*. New Brunswick, NJ: Transaction.

Bowles, Scott. 1996. "The Gains of Giving: For Area's Volunteers, Investing Time Pays a Rich Reward," *Washington Post* (October 21): B1, B4.

Boyle, Richard and Phillip Bonacich. 1970. "The Development of Trust and Mistrust in Mixed-Motive Games," *Sociometry* 33:123–39.

Bradburn, Norman M. with the assistance of C. Edward Noll. 1969. *The Structure of Psychological Well-Being*. Chicago: Aldine.

Brehm, John and Wendy Rahn. 1997. "Individual Level Evidence for the Causes and Consequences of Social Capital," *American Journal of Political Science* 41:888–1023.

Brewer, Marilynn B. 1979. "In-Group Bias in the Minimal Intergroup Situation: A Cognitive-Motivational Analysis," *Psychological Bulletin* 86: 307–24.

Bryce, James. 1916. *The American Commonwealth*. Volume 2. New York: Macmillan.

Butterfield, Fox. 1996. "Barrooms' Decline Underlies a Drop in Adult Killings," *New York Times* (August 19): A1, A11.

References 273

Caldeira, Gregory A. 1986. "Neither the Purse Nor the Sword: Dynamics of Public Confidence in the U.S. Supreme Court," *American Political Science Review* 80:1209–26.

Campbell, Angus. 1981. *The Sense of Well-Being in America*. New York: McGraw-Hill.

Campbell, Angus, Philip E. Converse, Warren E. Miller, and Donald E. Stokes. 1960. *The American Voter*. New York: John Wiley.

Campbell, Angus, Philip E. Converse, and Willard L. Rodgers. 1976. *The Quality of American Life*. New York: Russell Sage Foundation.

Carmines, Edward G., John P. McIver, and James A. Stimson. 1987. "Unrealized Partisanship: A Theory of Dealignment," *Journal of Politics* 49:376–400.

Carmines, Edward G. and James A. Stimson. 1989. *Issue Evolution*. Princeton: Princeton University Press.

Chong, Dennis. 1991. *Collective Action and the Civil Rights Movement*. Chicago: University of Chicago Press.

1994. "Values versus Interests in the Explanation of Social Conflict." Presented at the Annual Meeting of the American Political Science Association, New York, September.

Citrin, Jack. 1974. "Comment: The Political Relevance of Trust in Government," *American Political Science Review* 68:973–88.

Cloud, John. 1997. "Involuntary Volunteers," *Time* (December 1): 76.

Cnaan, Ram, Amy Kasternakis, and Robert J. Wineburg. 1993. "Religious People, Religious Congregations, and Volunteerism in Human Services: Is There a Link?" *Nonprofit and Voluntary Sector Quarterly* 22:33–51.

Cohen, Jean L. 1997. "American Civil Society Talk." College Park, MD: National Commission on Civic Renewal, Working Paper #6.

Cohen, Sheldon, William J. Doyle, David P. Skoner, Bruce S. Rabin, and Jack M. Gwaltney, Jr. 1997. "Social Ties and Susceptibility to the Common Cold," *Journal of the American Medical Association* (June 25): 1940–44.

Coleman, James S. 1990. *Foundations of Social Theory*. Cambridge, MA: Belknap.

Collie, Melissa P. 1988. "Universalism and the Parties in the U.S. House of Representatives," *American Journal of Political Science* 32:865–83.

Commager, Henry Steele. 1950. *The American Mind*. New Haven: Yale University Press.

Constable, Pamela. 1999. "India's Democracy In Uncertain Health," *Washington Post* (April 21): A17, A19.

Converse, Phillip E. 1964. "The Nature of Belief Systems in Mass Publics." In David E. Apter, ed., *Ideology and Discontent*. New York: Free Press.

Coppedge, Michael and Wolfgang H. Reinicke. 1991. "Measuring Polyarchy." In Alex Inkeles, ed., *On Measuring Democracy*. New Brunswick, NJ: Transaction.

Cox, Eva with Erica Lewis. 1998. "Measuring Social Capital As Part of Progress and Well-Being." In Richard Eckersley, ed., *Measuring Progress*. Collingswood, Australia: CSIRO.

Croly, Herbert. 1965. *The Promise of American Life*. Edited by Arthur M. Schlesinger, Jr. Cambridge, MA: Belknap.

Dahl, Robert A. 1961. *Who Governs?* New Haven: Yale University Press.

Damico, Alfonso J., M. Margaret Conway, and Sandra Bowman Damico. 2000. "Patterns of Political Trust and Mistrust: Three Moments in the Lives of Democratic Citizens," *Polity* 32:333–56.

Damon, William. 1988. *The Moral Child.* New York: Free Press.

Dasgupta, Partha. 1988. "Trust as a Commodity." In Diego Gambetta, ed., *Trust.* Oxford: Basil Blackwell.

Dawes, Robyn M., Alphons J. C. van de Kragt, and John Orbell. 1990. "Cooperation for the Benefit of Us – Not Me, or My Conscience." In Jane J. Mansbridge, ed., *Beyond Self-Interest.* Chicago: University of Chicago Press.

Deininger, Klaus and Lyn Squire. 1996. "A New Data Set: Measuring Economic Income Inequality," *World Bank Economic Review* 10:565–92.

Demerath, N. J. III, Gerald Marwell, and Michael T. Aiken. 1971. *Dynamics of Idealism: White Activists in a Black Movement.* San Francisco: Jossey-Bass.

Deutsch, Morton. 1958. "Trust and Suspicion," *Journal of Conflict Resolution* 2:265–79.

    1960. "The Effect of Motivational Orientation upon Trust and Suspicion," *Human Relations* 13:123–39.

Diener, Ed. 1984. "Subjective Well-Being," *Psychological Bulletin* 95:542–73.

    1995. "A Value Based Index for Measuring National Quality of Life," *Social Indicators Research,* 36:107–27.

Diener, Ed, Marissa Diener, and Carold Diener. 1995. "Factors Predicting the Subjective Well-Being of Nations," *Journal of Personality and Social Psychology* 69:851–64.

Diener, Ed, Eunkook Suh, and Shigehiro Oishi. 1997. "Recent Findings on Subjective Well-Being." University of Illinois manuscript, forthcoming in *Indian Journal of Clinical Psychology.*

Earle, Timothy C. and George T. Cvetkovich. 1995. *Social Trust.* Westport, CT: Praeger.

Easterly, William and Ross Levine. 1997. "Africa's Growth Tragedy: Policies and Ethnic Divisions," *Quarterly Journal of Economics* 112:1203–50.

Eckersley, Richard. 1998. "Perspectives on Progress: Economic Growth, Quality of Life, and Ecological Sustainability." In Richard Eckersley, ed., *Measuring Progress.* Collingswood, Australia: CSIRO.

Economist (The). 1990. *The Economist Book of Vital World Statistics.* New York: Times Books.

Eisenstadt, S. N. 2000. "Trust and Institutional Power in Japan: The Construction of Generalised Particularistic Trust," *Japanese Journal of Political Science* 1:53–72.

Erikson, Bonnie H. And T. A. Nosanchuk. 1990 "How an Apolitical Association Politicizes," *Canadian Review of Sociology and Anthropology* 27:206–19.

Erikson, Erik. 1963. *Childhood and Society.* Second ed. New York: W. W. Norton.

1968. *Identity: Youth and Crisis.* New York: W. W. Norton.

Esposito, John L. 1991. *Islam and Politics.* Third ed. Syracuse: Syracuse University Press.

Esposito, John L. and John O. Voll. 1996. *Islam and Democracy.* Oxford: Oxford University Press.

Etzioni, Amitai. 1996. *The New Golden Rule: Community and Morality in a Democratic Society.* New York: Basic Books.

Fedderke, Johannes and Robert Klitgaard. 1998. "Economic Growth and Social Indicators: An Exploratory Analysis," *Economic Development and Social Change* 46:455–90.

Feist, Gregory J., Todd E. Bodner, John F. Jacobs, Marilyn Miles, and Vickie Tan. 1995. "Integrating Top-Down and Bottom-Up Structural Models of Subjective Well-Being: A Longitudinal Investigation," *Journal of Personality and Social Psychology* 68:138–50.

Feldman, Stanley. 1983. "The Measurement and Meaning of Trust in Government," *Political Methodology* 9:341–54.

Fenno, Richard F., Jr. 1978. *Home Style.* Boston: Little, Brown.

Finkel, David. 1996. "In the Best Possible Light," *Washington Post Magazine* (May 12): 8–15, 27–8.

Forster, E. M. 1965. "Two Cheers for Democracy." In E. M. Forster, *Two Cheers for Democracy.* New York: Harcourt, Brace, and World.

Frank, Robert H. 1988. *Passions within Reason.* New York: W. W. Norton.

Fukayama, Francis. 1995. *Trust: The Social Virtues and the Creation of Prosperity.* New York: Free Press.

Gambetta, Diego. 1988. "Can We Trust Trust?" In Diego Gambetta, ed., *Trust.* Oxford: Basil Blackwell.

Gastil, Raymond Duncan. 1991. "The Comparative Survey of Freedom: Experience and Suggestions." In Alex Inkeles, ed., *On Measuring Democracy.* New Brunswick, NJ: Transaction.

Gerard, David. 1985. "What Makes a Volunteer?" *New Society,* November 8: 236–8.

Gerbner, George, Larry Gross, Michael Morgan, and Nancy Signorielli. 1980. "The 'Mainstreaming' of America: Violence Profile No. 11," *Journal of Communication* 30:10–29.

Gibson, James L. 2001. "Social Networks, Civil Society, and the Prospects for Consolidating Russia's Democratic Transition." *American Journal of Political Science* 45:51–69.

Giffin, Kim. 1967. "The Contribution of Studies of Source Credibility to a Theory of Interpersonal Trust in the Communication Process," *Psychological Bulletin* 68:104–20.

Granovetter, Mark S. 1973. "The Strength of Weak Ties." *American Journal of Sociology* 78:1360–80.

Greeley, Andrew. 1996. "Reading to Someone Else: The Strange Reappearance of Civic America." Unpublished manuscript, National Opinion Research Center, University of Chicago.

1997. "Coleman Revisited," *American Behavioral Scientist* 40:587–94.

Greenberg, Anna. 1999. "Doing God's Work? The Political Significance of Faith-Based Social Service Delivery." Presented at the Annual Meeting of the Midwest Political Science Association, April, Chicago.

Greif, Avner. 1993. "Contract Enforceability and Economic Institutions in Early Trade: The Maghribi Traders' Coalition," *American Economic Review* 83:525–48.

Gross, Jane. 2000. "As Volunteer Ranks Dwindle, Firehouse Tradition Gives Way," *New York Times* (June 22): A25.

Grunwald, Michael. 1999. "Volunteer Firefighters Fading Into the Past," *Washington Post* (January 10): A1, A6.

Gundelach, Peter and Lars Torpe. 1997. "Social Capital and the Democratic Role of Voluntary Associations." Presented at the European Consortium for Political Research Joint Sessions, February/March, Bern, Switzerland.

Gurr, Ted Robert, Keith Jaggers, and Will H. Moore. 1991. "The Transformation of the Western State: The Growth of Democracy, Autocracy, and State Power Since 1800." In Alex Inkeles, ed., *On Measuring Democracy*. New Brunswick, NJ: Transaction.

Hakim, Danny and Luke Mitchell. 1995. "Life in the Fez Lane," *Washington Post* (September 24): F1, F4.

Hall, Peter A. 1997. "Social Capital in Britain." Presented at the Bertelsmann Stiftung Workshop on Social Capital, Berlin, June.

Hamilton, W. D. 1964. "The Genetical Evolution of Social Behavior, II," *Journal of Theoretical Biology* 7:17–52.

Hansen, John Mark. 1985. "The Political Economy of Group Membership," *American Political Science Review* 79:79–96.

Hardin, Russell. 1991. "Trusting Persons, Trusting Institutions." In Richard J. Zeckhauser, ed., *Strategy and Choice*. Cambridge: MIT Press.

1992. "The Street-Level Epistemology of Trust," *Analyse & Kritik* 14:152–76.

1995. "Trust in Government." Prepared for presentation at the Pacific Division Meeting of the American Philosophical Association, April, San Francisco.

1998a. "Conceptions and Explanations of Trust." New York: Russell Sage Foundation Working Paper #129, April.

1998b. "Distrust." New York: Russell Sage Foundation Working Paper #130.

2000. *Trust and Trustworthiness*. Unpublished manuscript, New York University.

Harris, Frederick C. 1994. "Something Within: Religion as a Mobilizer of African-American Political Activism," *Journal of Politics* 56:42–68.

Hart, Keith. 1988. "Kinship, Contract, and Trust: The Economic Organization of Migrants in an African City Slum." In Diego Gambetta, ed., *Trust*. Oxford: Basil Blackwell.

Hartz, Louis. 1955. *The Liberal Tradition in America*. New York: Harcourt, Brace, and World.

Hayge, Howard V. 1991. "Volunteers in the U.S.: Who Donates the Time?" *Monthly Labor Review* 114:17–23.

Helliwell, John F. and Robert D. Putnam. 1996. "Correction," *PS: Political Science and Politics*, June: 138.

Hertzberg, Lars. 1988. "On the Attitude of Trust," *Inquiry* 31:307–22.

Hetherington, Marc J. 1998. "The Political Relevance of Trust in Government," *American Political Science Review* 92:791–808.

Hibbing, John and Elizabeth Thiess-Morse. 1995. *Congress as Public Enemy.* New York: Cambridge University Press.

Hodgkinson, Virginia A., Murray S. Weitzman, and Arthur D. Kirsch. 1990. "From Commitment to Action: How Religious Involvement Affects Giving and Volunteering." In Robert Wuthnow, Virginia Hodgkinson, and Associates, *Faith and Philanthropy in America.* San Francisco: Jossey-Bass.

Hodgkinson, Virginia A., Murray S. Weitzman, and Associates. 1992. *Giving and Volunteering in the United States: Findings from a National Survey.* Washington: INDEPENDENT SECTOR.

Hoffman, David. 1996. "Harsh History Stymies Civil Society: Russian Activists Strive to Be Heard as Democracy Takes Hold," *Washington Post,* December 26: A1, A40.

Hoffman, Martin L. 1975. "Development of Affect and Cognition and Its Implications for Altruistic Motivation," *Developmental Psychology* 11: 607–22.

Hofstede, Geert. 1980. *Culture's Consequences: International Differences in Work-Related Values.* Beverly Hills, CA: Sage.

Holton, Richard. 1994. "Deciding to Trust, Coming to Believe," *Australasian Journal of Philosophy* 72:63–76.

Horsburgh, H. J. N. 1960. "The Ethics of Trust," *Philosophical Quarterly* 10 (October):343–54.

Hume, David. 1960. *A Treatise on Human Nature.* Ed. L. A. Selby-Bigge. Oxford: Clarendon Press. Originally published in 1739.

Inglehart, Ronald. 1997. *Modernization and Postmodernization.* Princeton: Princeton University Press.

1999. "Trust, Well-Being and Democracy." In Mark Warren, ed., *Democracy and Trust.* Cambridge: Cambridge University Press.

Inglehart, Ronald, Miguel Basznez, and Alejandro Moreno. 1998. *Human Values and Beliefs: A Cross-Cultural Sourcebook.* Ann Arbor: University of Michigan Press.

Jackman, Robert W. and Ross A. Miller. 1996. "A Renaissance of Political Culture?" *American Journal of Political Science* 40:632–59.

Johnson, Simon, Daniel Kaufmann and Pablo Zoido-Lobatón. 1998. "Regulatory Discretion and the Unofficial Economy," *American Economic Review* 387–92.

Karter, Michael J., Jr. 1999. *U.S. Fire Department Profile Through 1998.* Quincy, MA: National Fire Protection Association.

Kimball, David C. and Samuel C. Patterson. 1997. "Living Up to Expectations: Public Attitudes Toward Congress," *Journal of Politics* 59:701–28.

Kinder, Donald R. and D. Roderick Kiewiet. 1979. "Economic Discontent and Political Behavior: The Role of Personal Grievances and Collective Economic Judgments in Congressional Voting," *American Journal of Political Science* 23:495–527.

Knack, Stephen. 1999. "Social Capital, Growth, and Poverty: A Survey of the Cross-Country Evidence." Center for Institutional Reform and the Informal Sector (IRIS), University of Maryland, College Park.

Knack, Stephen and Philip Keefer. 1997. "Does Social Capital Have An Economic Payoff? A Cross-Country Investigation," *Quarterly Journal of Economics* 112:1251–88.

Knight, Jack. 2000. "Social Norms and the Rule of Law: Fostering Trust in a Socially Diverse Society." In Karen S. Cook, ed., *Trust in Society*. New York: Russell Sage Foundation.

Koestner, Richard, Carol Franz, and Joel Weinberger. 1990. "The Family Origins of Empathetic Concern: A 26-Year Longitudinal Study," *Journal of Personality and Social Psychology* 58:709–17.

Kohut, Andrew. 1997. *Trust and Civic Engagement in Metropolitan Philadelphia: A Case Study*. Washington: Pew Center for the People and the Press.

Koren, Edward. 1997. "A Volunteer Spirit Asks, 'Where's the Fire?'" *New York Times*, December 9: C19.

Krehbiel, Keith. 1991. *Information and Legislative Organization*. Ann Arbor: University of Michigan Press.

Krygier, Martin. 1997. *Beyond Fear and Hope*. Sydney, Australia: ABC Books.

Ladd, Everett Carll and Karlyn H. Bowman. 1998. *What's Wrong?: A Survey of American Satisfaction and Complaint*. Washington: American Enterprise Institute.

Lafollette, Marcel C. 1990. *Making Science Our Own: Public Images of Science 1910–1955*. Chicago: University of Chicago Press.

Landau, Martin. 1965. "Objectivity, Neutrality, and Kuhn's Paradigm." In Martin Landau, *Political Theory and Political Science*. New York: Macmillan.

Lane, Robert E. 1959. *Political Life*. New York: Free Press.

LaPorta, Rafael, Florencio Lopez-Silanes, Andrei Schleifer, and Robert W. Vishney. 1997. "Trust in Large Organizations," *American Economic Review Papers and Proceedings* 87:333–38.

    1998. "The Quality of Government." Unpublished manuscript, Harvard University.

Larson, David, Dr., Mary Greenwold Milano, and Constance Barry. 1996. "Religion: The Forgotten Factor in Health Care," *The World and I* (February): 293–317.

Lawrence, Robert Z. 1997. "Is It Really the Economy, Stupid?" In Joseph S. Nye, Philip D. Zelikow, and David C. King, eds., *Why People Don't Trust Government*. Cambridge: Harvard University Press.

Lee, Shin-wa. 1993. *Minorities at Risk: Phase I Dataset User's Manual*. College Park: Minorities at Risk Project, Center for International Development and Conflict Management, University of Maryland.

Levi, Margaret. 1996. "Social and Unsocial Capital." *Politics and Society* 24:45–55.

    1997. "A State of Trust." Unpublished manuscript, University of Washington.

1998. "A State of Trust." In Margaret Levi and Valerie Braithwaite, eds., *Trust and Governance*. New York: Russell Sage Foundation.

1999. "When Good Defenses Make Good Neighbors: A Transaction Cost Approach to Trust and Distrust." New York: Russell Sage Foundation Working Paper #140.

Lewis, J. David and Andrew Weigert. 1985. "Trust as Social Reality," *Social Forces*, 63:967–85.

Liebling, A. J. 1970. *The Earl of Louisiana*. Baton Rouge: Louisiana State University Press.

Lipset, Seymour Martin. 1990. *Continental Divide*. New York: Routledge.

Lipset, Seymour Martin and William Schneider. 1983. *The Confidence Gap: Business, Labor, and Government in the Public Mind*. New York: Free Press.

Loomis, Burdett. 1988. *The New American Politician*. New York: Basic Books.

Loomis, James L. 1959. "Communication, the Development of Trust, and Cooperative Behavior," *Human Relations* 12:305–15.

Luhmann, Niklas. 1979. "Trust." In Niklas Luhmann, *Trust and Power*. New York: John Wiley and Sons.

1988. "Familiarity, Confidence, Trust: Problems and Alternatives." In Diego Gambetta, ed., *Trust*. Oxford: Basil Blackwell.

Luks, Samantha C. and Jack Citrin. 1997. "Revisiting Political Trust in an Angry Age." Presented at the Annual Meeting of the Midwest Political Science Association, April, Chicago.

Macaulay, Stewart. 1963. "Non-Contractual Relations in Business: A Preliminary Study," *American Sociological Review* 28:55–67.

Mahoney, John and Constance M. Pechura. 1980. "Values and Volunteers: Axiology of Altruism in a Crisis Center," *Psychological Reports* 47:1007–12.

Maimonedes, Moses ben. 1979. *The Code of Maimonedes, Book Seven: The Book of Agriculture* (Treatise Two, Chapter 10). Translated from the Hebrew by Isaac Klein. New Haven: Yale University Press.

Mansbridge, Jane. 1997. "Social and Cultural Causes of Dissatisfaction with U.S. Government." In Joseph S. Nye, Philip D. Zelikow, and David C. King, eds., *Why People Don't Trust Government*. Cambridge: Harvard University Press.

1999. "Altruistic Trust." In Mark Warren, ed., *Democracy and Trust*. New York: Cambridge University Press.

Masters, Roger D. 1989. *The Nature of Politics*. New Haven: Yale University Press.

Matthews, Donald R. 1960. *U.S. Senators and Their World*. Chapel Hill: University of North Carolina Press.

Mauro, Pablo. 1995. "Corruption and Growth," *Quarterly Journal of Economics* 110:681–712.

Mayer, William G. 1992. *The Changing American Mind*. Ann Arbor: University of Michigan Press.

Mayhew, David R. 1991. *Divided We Govern*. New Haven: Yale University Press.

280   *References*

Mcssick, David M. and Marilynn B. Brewer. 1983. "Solving Social Dilemmas: A Review." In Ladd Wheeler and Phillip Shaver, eds., *Review of Personality and Social Psychology*. Beverly Hills, CA: Sage Publications.

McKnight, Harrison, Larry L. Cummings, and Norman L. Chervany. In press. "Initial Trust Formation in New Organizational Relationships," *Academy of Management Review*.

Miller, Warren E. and J. Merrill Shanks. 1996. *The New American Voter*. Cambridge: Harvard University Press.

Milne, A. A. 1954. *Winnie-the-Pooh*. New York: Dell. Originally published in 1926.

Mishler, William and Richard Rose. 2001. "What Are the Origins of Political Trust? Testing Institutional and Cultural Theories in Post-Communist Societies," *Comparative Political Studies* 34:30–62.

Misztal, Barbara A. 1996. *Trust in Modern Societies*. Cambridge, U.K.: Polity Press.

Mondak, Jeffrey J. and Diana C. Mutz. 1997. "What's So Great About League Bowling?" Presented at the Annual Meeting of the Midwest Political Science Association, April, Chicago.

Mosle, Sara. 2000. "The Vanity of Volunteerism," *New York Times Magazine*, July 2: 22–7, 40–56.

Mueller, John. 1996. "Democracy, Capitalism, and the End of Transition." In Michael Mandlebaum, ed., *Post-Communism: Four Perspectives*. Washington: Council on Foreign Relations.

1999. *Democracy, Capitalism, and Ralph's Pretty Good Grocery*. Princeton: Princeton University Press.

Muller, Edward N. and Mitchell A. Seligson. 1994. "Civic Culture and Democracy: The Question of Causal Relationships." *American Political Science Review* 88:635–52.

Mutz. Diana C. and Jeffrey J. Mondak. 1997. "Dimensions of Sociotropic Behavior: Group-Based Judgements of Fairness and Well-Being," *American Journal of Political Science* 41:284–308.

Newton, Kenneth. 1997. "Social Capital and Democracy," *American Behavioral Scientist* 40:575–86.

1999. "Social and Political Trust." In Pippa Norris, ed., *Global Citizens: Global Support for Democratic Government*. New York: Oxford University Press.

Niemi, Richard G. 1980. "Reconstructing Past Partisanship," *American Journal of Political Science* 24:633–51.

Offe, Claus. 1996. "Social Capital: Concepts and Hypotheses." Unpublished manuscript, Humboldt University (Germany).

1997. "How Can We Trust Our Fellow Citizens?" Presented at the John F. Kennedy School of Government Conference on Confidence in Democratic Institutions, August, Washington.

1999. "Trust and Knowledge, Rules and Decisions: Exploring a Difficult Conceptual Terrain." In Mark Warren, ed., *Democracy and Trust*. Cambridge: Cambridge University Press.

Oliner, Pearl M. and Samuel P. Oliner. 1995. *Toward a Caring Society: Ideas into Action*. Westport, CT: Praeger.

O'Neill, William L. 1986. *American High: The Years of Confidence, 1945–1986.* New York: Free Press.

Onyx, Jenny and Paul Bullen. 1998. "Measuring Social Capital in Five Communities in NSW (New South Wales)." Unpublished manuscript, University of Technology, Sydney, Australia.

Orbell, John and Robyn M. Dawes. 1991. "A 'Cognitive Miser' Theory of Cooperators' Advantage," *American Political Science Review* 85:513–28.

Ornstein, Norman J., Thomas E. Mann, and Michael J. Malbin, comps. 1997. *Vital Statistics on Congress 1997–1998.* Washington: American Enterprise Institute.

Orren, Gary. 1997. "Fall From Grace: The Public's Loss of Faith in Government." In Joseph S. Nye, Philip D. Zelikow, and David C. King, eds., *Why People Don't Trust Government.* Cambridge: Harvard University Press.

Ostrom, Elinor. 1998. "A Behavioral Approach to the Rational Choice Theory of Collective Action," *American Political Science Review* 92 (March): 1–18.

Pagden, Anthony. 1988. "The Destruction of Trust and its Economic Consequences in the Case of Eighteenth-Century Naples." In Diego Gambetta, ed., *Trust.* Oxford: Basil Blackwell.

Parcel, Toby L. and Elizabeth G. Menaghan. 1993. "Family Social Capital and Children's Behavior Problems," *Social Psychology Quarterly* 56, 2:120–35.

Patterson, Orlando. 1999. "Trust and Democracy." In Mark Warren, ed., *Democracy and Trust.* Cambridge: Cambridge University Press.

Patterson, Samuel C. and Gregory A. Caldeira. 1990. "Standing Up for Congress: Variations in Public Esteem Since the 1960s," *Legislative Studies Quarterly* 15:25–48.

Perlez, Jane. 1996. "For Albanians, in Carts and BMW's, a Hard Road," *New York Times,* May 31: A3.

Piliavin, Jane Allyn and Peter L. Callero. 1991. *Giving Blood: The Development of an Altruistic Identity.* Baltimore: Johns Hopkins University Press.

Popenoe, David. 1994. "The Family Condition of America: Cultural Change and Public Policy." In Henry J. Aaron, Thomas E. Mann, and Timothy Taylor, eds., *Values and Public Policy.* Washington: Brookings Institution.

Potter, David M. 1954. *People of Plenty.* Chicago: University of Chicago Press.

Putnam, Robert D. 1993. *Making Democracy Work: Civic Traditions in Modern Italy.* Princeton: Princeton University Press.

1995a. "Bowling Alone: America's Declining Social Capital." *Journal of Democracy* 6:65–78.

1995b. "Tuning In, Tuning Out: The Strange Disappearance of Social Capital in America." *PS: Political Science and Politics,* December: 664–83.

1996. "The Strange Disappearance of Civic America," *The American Prospect,* Winter: 34–48.

2000. *Bowling Alone.* New York: Simon and Schuster.

Rahn, Wendy M., John Brehm, and Neil Carlson. 1997. "National Elections as Institutions for Generating Social Capital." Presented at the Annual Meeting of the American Political Science Association, August–September, Washington, D.C.

282

References

1999. "National Elections as Institutions for Generating Social Capital." In Morris P. Fioring and Theda Skocpol, eds., *Civic Engagement in American Democracy*. Washington: Brookings Institution.

Rahn, Wendy M. and John E. Transue. 1998. "Social Trust and Value Change: The Decline of Social Capital in American Youth, 1976–1995," *Political Psychology* 19:545–66.

Reddy, Richard. 1980. "Individual Philanthropy and Giving Behavior." In David Horton Smith, Jacqueline Macauley, and Associates, eds., *Participation in Social and Political Activities*. San Francisco: Jossey-Bass.

Reich, Robert B. 1999. "To Lift All Boats," *Washington Post*, May 16: B1, B4.

Rempel, John K., John G. Holmes, and Mark P. Zanna. 1985. "Trust in Close Relationships," *Journal of Personality and Social Psychology* 49:95–112.

Renshon, Stanley Allen. 1975. "Personality and Family Dynamics in the Political Socialization Process," *American Journal of Political Science* 19:63–80.

Rice, Tom W. and Jan Feldman. 1997. "Civic Culture and Democracy from Europe to America," *Journal of Politics* 59:1143–72.

Riker, William H. and Steven J. Brams. 1973. "The Paradox of Vote Trading," *American Political Science Review* 67:1235–47.

Rokeach, Milton. 1973. *The Nature of Human Values*. New York: Free Press.

Rosenberg, Morris. 1956. "Misanthropy and Political Ideology," *American Sociological Review* 21:690–5.

Rosenblum, Nancy L. 1998. *Membership and Morals*. Princeton: Princeton University Press.

Rosenhan, David. 1969. "Some Origins of Concern for Others." In David Rosenhan and Perry London, eds., *Theory and Research in Abnormal Psychology*. New York: Holt, Rinehart, and Winston.

Rosenstone, Steven J. and John Mark Hansen. 1993. *Mobilization, Participation, and Democracy in America*. New York: Macmillan.

Rosten, Leo. 1968. *The Joys of Yiddish*. New York: Washington Square Press.

Rotenberg, Ken J. and Carrie Cerda. 1994. "Racially Based Trust Expectancies of Native American and Caucasian Children," *Journal of Social Psychology* 134:621–32.

Rothstein, Bo. 2000. "Social Capital in the Social Democratic State: The Swedish Model and Civil Society." In Robert Putnam, ed., *The Decline of Social Capital? Political Culture as a Condition for Democracy*. Princeton: Princeton University Press.

In press. "Trust, Social Dilemmas, and Collective Memories: On the Rise and Decline of the Swedish Model," *Journal of Theoretical Politics*.

Rotter, Julian B. 1971. "Generalized Expectancies for Interpersonal Trust," *American Psychologist* 26:443–52.

1980. "Interpersonal Trust, Trustworthiness, and Gullibility," *American Psychologist*, January: 1–7.

Sachs, Jeffrey D. and Andrew M. Warner. 1997. "Natural Resource Abundance and Economic Growth." Center for International Development and Harvard Institute for International Development, Harvard University.

Safire, William. 1993. *William Safire's New Political Dictionary*. New York: Random House.

Samuelson, Robert J. 1995. *The Good Life and Its Discontents*. New York: Times Books.

Schattschneider, E. E. 1960. *The Semisovereign People*. New York: Holt, Rinehart, and Winston.

Schoenfeld, Eugen. 1978. "Image of Man: The Effect of Religion on Trust," *Review of Religious Research* 20:61–7.

Scholz, John T. and Neil Pinney. 1995. "Duty, Fear, and Tax Compliance: The Heuristic Basis of Citizenship Behavior," *American Journal of Political Science* 39:490–512.

Schuman, Howard and Stanley Presser. 1978. *Questions and Answers in Survey Research*. New York: Academic Press.

Scott, David and Geoffrey C. Godbey. 1992. "An Analysis of Adult Play Groups: Social Versus Serious Participation in Contract Bridge," *Leisure Sciences* 14:47–67.

Scott, James C. 1985. *Weapons of the Weak*. New Haven: Yale University Press.

Seligman, Adam B. 1997. *The Problem of Trust*. Princeton: Princeton University Press.

Seligman, Martin E. P. 1991. *Learned Optimism*. New York: Alfred A. Knopf.

Shah, Dhavan V. 1998. "Civic Engagement, Interpersonal Trust, and Television Use: An Individual-Level Assessment of Social Capital," *Political Psychology* 19:469–96.

Sheehan, William and Jerome Kroll. 1990. "Psychiatric Patients' Belief in General Health Factors and Sin as Causes of Illness," *American Journal of Psychiatry* 147:112–13.

Silver, Allan. 1989. "Friendship and Trust as Moral Ideals: An Historical Approach," *European Journal of Sociology* 30, 2:274–97.

Sitkin, Sim B. and Nancy L. Roth. 1993. "Explaining the Limited Effectiveness of Legalistic 'Remedies' for Trust/Distrust," *Organization Science* 4:367–92.

Smith, Elizabeth S. 1999a. "Youth Voluntary Association Participation and Political Attitudes: A Quasi-Experimental Analysis." Presented at the Annual Meeting of the American Political Science Association, September, Atlanta.

1999b. "The Effects of Investments in the Social Capital of Youth on Political and Civic Behavior in Young Adulthood: A Longitudinal Analysis." Presented at the Annual Meeting of the American Political Science Association, September, Atlanta.

Smith, Tom W. 1997. "Factors Relating to Misanthropy in Contemporary American Society," *Social Science Research* 26:170–96.

Sniderman, Paul M. and Thomas Piazza. 1993. *The Scar of Race*. Cambridge, U.K.: Belknap.

Sombart, Werner. 1976. *Why Is There No Socialism in the United States?* White Plains, NY: M. E. Sharpe. Originally published in 1906.

Staub, Erwin. 1979. *Positive Social Behavior and Morality: Socialization and Development*. New York: Academic Press.

Stimson, James A. 1998. *Public Opinion in America*. Second ed. Boulder, CO: Westview.

Stimson, James A., Michael B. MacKuen, and Robert S. Erikson. 1995. "Dynamic Representation," *American Political Science Review* 89:543–65.

Stolle, Dietlind. 1998a. "Getting to Trust: An Analysis of the Importance of Institutions, Families, Personal Experiences, and Group Membership." Presented at the Workshop on Social Capital and Political Capital, European Consortium for Political Research Joint Sessions, March.

1998b. "Bowling Together, Bowling Alone: The Development of Generalized Trust in Voluntary Associations," *Political Psychology* 19:497–526.

1999a. "Clubs and Congregations: The Benefits of Joining an Association." Presented at the Annual Meeting of the Midwest Political Science Association, April, Chicago.

1999b. "Communities, Citizens, and Local Government: Generalized Trust and the Impact of Regional Factors." Presented at the Annual Meeting of the American Political Science Association, September, Atlanta.

2000. "Clubs and Congregations: The Benefits of Joining an Association." In Karen S. Cook, ed., *Trust in Society*. New York: Russell Sage Foundation.

Sullivan, John H., James Piereson, and George E. Marcus. 1981. *Political Tolerance and American Democracy*. Chicago: University of Chicago Press.

Thernstrom, Stephan and Abigail Thernstrom. 1997. *America in Black and White*. New York: Simon and Schuster.

Thompson, Alexander M. III and Barbara Bono. 1993. "Work Without Wages: The Motivation for Volunteer Firefighters," *American Journal of Economics and Sociology* 52:323–43.

Tocqueville, Alexis de. 1945. *Democracy in America*. Volume 2. Translated by Henry Reeve. New York: Alfred A. Knopf. Originally published in 1840.

Torcal, Mariano and Jose Ramon Montero. 1999. "Facets of Social Capital in New Democracies: The Formation and Consequences of Social Capital in Spain." In Jan W. van Deth, Marco Maraffi, Kenneth Newton, and Paul F. Whiteley, eds., *Social Capital and European Democracy*. London: Routledge.

Toulmin, Stephen. 1950. *An Examination of the Place of Reason in Ethics*. Cambridge: Cambridge University Press.

Treisman, Daniel. 1999. "Decentralization and Corruption: Why Are Federal States Perceived to be More Corrupt?" Unpublished paper, University of California, Los Angeles.

Triandis, Harry C. 1989. "The Self and Social Behavior in Differing Cultural Contexts," *Psychological Review* 96:506–20.

1995. *Individualism and Collectivism*. Boulder, CO: Westview.

Triandis, Harry C., Robert Bontempo, Marcelo J. Villareal, Masaaki Asai, and Nydia Lucca. 1988. "Individualism and Collectivism: Cross-Cultural Perspectives on Self-Ingroup Relationships," *Journal of Personality and Social Psychology* 54:323–38.

Trivers, Robert L. 1971. "The Evolution of Reciprocal Altruism," *Quarterly Review of Biology* 46:35–57.

Tufte, Edward R. 1978. *Political Control of the Economy.* Princeton: Princeton University Press.

Tyler, Tom R. 1990. *Why People Obey the Law.* New Haven: Yale University Press.

United States Department of Commerce. 1998. *Measuring Fifty Years of Economic Change.* Washington: Economic and Statistics Administration, Bureau of the Census Current Population Reports P60-203.

Uslaner, Eric M. 1989. *Shale Barrel Politics.* Stanford: Stanford University Press.

——— 1993. *The Decline of Comity in Congress.* Ann Arbor: University of Michigan Press.

——— 1994. "Trends in Comity Over Time." Presented at the Wequassett Workshop on Social Capital and Democracy, July, Chatham, MA.

——— 1998a. "Faith, Hope, and Charity: Social Capital, Trust, and Collective Action." Unpublished manuscript. University of Maryland, College Park.

——— 1998b. "Social Capital, Television, and the 'Mean World': Trust, Optimism, and Civic Participation," *Political Psychology* 19:441–67.

——— 1999a. "Trust But Verify: Social Capital and Moral Behavior," *Social Science Information* 38:29–56.

——— 1999b. "Morality Plays: Social Capital and Moral Behavior in Anglo-American Democracies." In Jan W. van Deth, Marco Maraffi, Kenneth Newton, and Paul F. Whiteley, eds., *Social Capital and European Democracy.* London: Routledge.

——— 1999c. "Vrijwilligerswerk en Sociaal Kapitaal: Effecten van Vertrouwen Religie op Participatie in De Verenigde Staten" (Translated into Dutch from "Volunteering and Social Capital: How Trust and Religion Shape Civic Participation in the United States"). In Paul Dekker, ed., *Vrijwilligerswerk vergeleken.* The Hague, the Netherlands: Social and Cultural Planning Bureau.

——— 1999d. "Democracy and Social Capital." In Mark Warren, ed., *Democracy and Trust.* Cambridge: Cambridge University Press.

——— 2000. "Is the Senate More Civil Than the House?" In Burdett Loomis, ed., *Esteemed Colleagues: Civility and Deliberation in the Senate.* Washington: Brookings Institution.

Uslaner, Eric M. and Richard S. Conley. 1998. "Civic Engagement and Particularized Trust: The Ties that Bind People to Their Ethnic Communities." Presented at the Annual Meeting of the American Political Science Association, September, Boston.

Uslaner, Eric M. and M. Margaret Conway. 1985. "The Responsible Congressional Electorate: Watergate, the Economy, and Vote Choice in 1974," *American Political Science Review* 79:788–803.

Vanhanen, Tatu. 1997. *Prospects of Democracy.* New York: Routledge.

Verba, Sidney, Kay Lehman Schlozman, and Henry Brady. 1995. *Voice and Equality: Civic Voluntarism in American Politics.* Cambridge: Harvard University Press.

Warren, Mark E. 1996. "Deliberative Democracy and Authority," *American Political Science Review* 90:46–60.

Weber, Max. 1958. *The Protestant Ethic and the Spirit of Capitalism.* Translated by Talcott Parsons. New York: Charles Scribners' Sons. Originally published in 1930.

Whiteley, Paul F. 1999. "The Origins of Social Capital." In Jan W. van Deth, Marco Maraffi, Kenneth Newton, and Paul F. Whiteley, eds., *Social Capital and European Democracy.* London: Routledge.

Wijkstrom, Filip. 1998. "Hate Groups and Outlaw Bikers: Civil Society and Civic Virtues?" Unpublished manuscript, Stockholm School of Economics, Stockholm, Sweden.

Williams, Bernard. 1988. "Formal Structures and Social Reality." In Diego Gambetta, ed., *Trust.* Oxford: Basil Blackwell.

Williams, Robert F. 1986. "The Values of Volunteer Benefactors," *Mental Retardation* 24:163–8.

Wilson, James Q. 1993. *The Moral Sense.* New York: Free Press.

Wilson, John and Marc Musick. 1997. "Who Cares? Toward an Integrated Theory of Volunteer Work," *American Sociological Review* 62:694–713.

Wollebaek, Dag and Per Selle. 2000. "Voluntary Associations and Social Capital: The Case of Norway." Presented at the European Consortium for Political Research Joint Sessions, April, University of Copenhagen (Denmark).

Woolcock, Michael. 1998. "Social Capital and Economic Development: Toward a Theoretical Synthesis and Policy Framework," *Theory and Society* 27:151–208.

Wright, Louis B. 1957. *The Cultural Life of the American Colonies 1607–1763.* New York: Harper and Row.

Wrightsman, Lawrence S. 1991. "Interpersonal Trust and Attitudes Toward Human Nature." In John Robinson et al., *Measures of Personality and Psychological Attitudes.* San Diego: Academic Press.

Wuthnow, Robert. 1991. *Acts of Compassion.* Princeton: Princeton University Press.

   1997. "The Role of Trust in Civic Renewal." College Park, MD: National Commission on Civic Renewal, Working Paper #1.

   1998. *Loose Connections: Joining Together in America's Fragmented Communities.* Cambridge: Harvard University Press.

   1999. "Mobilizing Civic Engagement: The Changing Impact of Religious Involvement." In Morris Fiorina and Theda Skocpol, eds., *Civic Engagement in American Democracy.* Washington: Brookings Institution.

Yamigishi, Toshio. 1986. "The Provision of a Sanctioning System as a Public Good," *Journal of Personality and Social Psychology* 51 (July): 110–16.

   1988. "The Provision of a Sanctioning System in the United States and Japan," *Social Psychology Quarterly* 51:265–71.

Yamigishi, Toshio and Midori Yamigishi. 1994. "Trust and Commitment in the United States and Japan," *Motivation and Emotion* 18:129–66.

Author Index

Subject Index

abortion, 11, 60–2, 213
activists, 40, 82, 216, 274, 277
advocates, 115, 147
African Americans, 35–6, 47, 89,
    107, 112, 139, 153, 163, 167, 189,
    194–6, 211–12, 276
Albania, 19, 46, 82, 85, 253, 281
altruism, 192, 271, 279, 284
American National Election Study, 6,
    33, 42, 55–63, 66–7, 69–74, 77–8,
    90, 95–100, 102, 104–8, 114,
    122–6, 129–30, 133, 135, 137,
    144, 148–55, 157, 159, 164–7,
    170, 172–3, 178, 191, 196, 203,
    210, 252, 257–8, 261, 263, 274,
    278
American Creed, 84, 221
American Dream, 83, 179, 180
American High, 179, 189, 280
American Ideal, 83, 100
American Red Cross, 193, 203–7
Amish, 31
anti-authoritarianism, 78, 93, 100,
    104
anti-Semitism, 194–6
arts, 126, 130, 137–9, 207–8, 236,
    281
Asia, 232
Asians, 56, 91, 104, 107, 139
authoritarianism, 103, 106, 108

Baby Boomers, 6, 12, 37, 66–7, 91,
    132, 159–60, 170–3, 176; Early
    Boomers, 91, 160–1, 172–5, 178,
    180–2, 185, 189; Late Boomers,
    178; Pre-Boomers, 67, 172–3,
    177–81, 185
Bayesian decision-making, 24
Belgium, 225, 228, 232, 238, 254
benevolences, 206–9, 264
Bible, 63–4, 87, 105–6, 131–2, 154,
    156–7, 173, 258
bigotry, 84
bonding, 26, 121
Bosnia, 19, 37, 47, 85
Brazil, 225–6, 232, 237–8
bridging, 26, 116, 121
bureaucrats, 243, 269
business, 46, 81, 87, 126, 129–33,
    148, 168, 170, 195, 244, 253, 279

categorical imperative, 18
Catholic Church, 88, 116, 137, 231
Catholics, 33, 56, 88, 104, 131, 242,
    256, 261
Central Europe, 219, 226, 228–30
charitable giving, 125, 203, 216
charity, 5, 8, 10, 12, 19, 42–3, 56,
    94, 116–18, 121, 125, 129–32,
    134–9, 142, 192–3, 198, 203, 216,
    250, 264, 274, 285; arts and